Introduction to Modern Design

Introduction to Modern Design

Its History from the Eighteenth Century to the Present

GEORGE H. MARCUS

BLOOMSBURY VISUAL ARTS

LONDON · NEW YORK · OXFORD · NEW DELHI · SYDNEY

BLOOMSBURY VISUAL ARTS
Bloomsbury Publishing Plc
50 Bedford Square, London, WC1B 3DP, UK
1385 Broadway, New York, NY 10018, USA

BLOOMSBURY, BLOOMSBURY VISUAL ARTS and the Diana logo
are trademarks of Bloomsbury Publishing Plc

First published in Great Britain 2020

Cover design: Louise Dugdale
Cover image © Front Design

A catalogue record for this book is available from the British Library.

Library of Congress Cataloging-in-Publication Data
Names: Marcus, George H., author.
Title: Introduction to modern design : its history from the eighteenth century
to the present / George H. Marcus, University of Pennsylvania, USA.
Description: London ; New York, NY : Bloomsbury Visual Arts,
2020. | Includes bibliographical references and index.
Identifiers: LCCN 2019001494 | ISBN 9781474276658 (pbk. : alk. paper)
| ISBN 9781474277488 (ePDF) | ISBN 9781350032002 (eBook)
Subjects: LCSH: Design—History. | Decoration and ornament—History.
Classification: LCC NK1390 .M2716 2020 | DDC 745.4—dc23 LC
record available at https://lccn.loc.gov/2019001494

ISBN: PB: 978-1-4742-7665-8
        ePDF: 978-1-4742-7748-8
        eBook: 978-1-3500-3200-2

Typeset by Lachina Creative, Inc.
Printed and bound in India

To find out more about our authors and books visit
www.bloomsbury.com and sign up for our newsletters.

CONTENTS

List of Sidebar Excerpts

PREFACE
Defining Design

Look all around you! Just about everything you see has been designed: your clothing, your possessions, the room in which you find yourself, and all of its furnishings. The buildings before you, the urban space, and the vehicles that travel through it—all too have been designed. And, through the wisdom (or folly) of modern scientific and industrial exploits, much of our landscape, even the atmosphere itself, has also been altered by human design. "Design" may call up notions of cool electronics and cutting-edge furnishings, but even the nitty-gritty objects of our everyday lives are contributions to its rich narrative. The Crowd Sourced Wall at the Design Museum in London,

filled with examples of design suggested by people around the world, shows the wide range of objects that ordinary users considered indispensable: a Flying Pigeon bicycle made in China since about 1950, with some 500 million examples already having been produced; a recyclable shopping bag from the world's largest furniture manufacturer, Ikea, introduced in 1996; denim jeans first manufactured by Levi Strauss & Co. in 1873; a plastic chair designed by Charles and Ray Eames in 1951–52; a "mouse," or computer input device, released by Apple in 2005; the logo of the London Underground subway system, an anonymous graphic design created around 1908—all were

FIGURE 0.1.   Crowd Sourced Wall of examples of design suggested by the public, Design Museum, London, 2017.

selected as significant elements of our design milieu along with sports shoes, a mop, typewriter, and the American football (Figure 0.1).

In small ways, every one of us acts as a designer too, as all humans have done since the origin of our species. Every lifestyle choice we make, how we put together what we wear, how we organize our rooms, our desks, and our desktops, and how we adapt the design of others to our own needs is a type of design. In *Thoughtless Acts? Observations on Intuitive Design* (2005), Jane Fulton Suri (born 1950), a specialist in human behavior and member of the international design firm IDEO (founded in 1991), catalogued many of the impromptu ways in which we all modify (redesign) the world around us in order to take control of and personalize our own spaces. She showed how we rely on whatever is at hand to design something that will achieve our objectives, like putting together a makeshift doorstop as someone cleverly did by using the claws of a hammer to hold a door in place (Figure 0.2). Problem solving like this has often been cited as the definition of design, creating something that fills a particular need, but the needs are not always such practical ones and they can be extended into the realms of the emotional and psychological as well.

The type of design that is the subject of this book, and of other such books, magazines, television programs, exhibitions, and museums, has a precise definition, although it is not generally found in dictionaries in this way: objects singled out by our response to their aesthetic qualities in addition to their function and other attributes that might make them noteworthy. But it has been focused even further here, to the design that abruptly changed the world of objects and images around the beginning of the twentieth century, the design that we call "modern." What made design modern was the simplicity in which products were conceived, the outcome of a moment in history in which progressive designers gave up their reliance on decoration and on the styles of the past to bring forth serious, unadorned, and uncomplicated forms for the future. These comprised both handmade and industrial (or seemingly industrial) objects, for the way these works present themselves, not the process by which they were created, has become the determinant of what we consider modern in design.

Although in recent decades some academics, critics, and writers have downgraded their emphasis on artistic aspects of design in order to concentrate on theoretical, practical, and social issues, we would not be discussing objects as works of design if they did not have some aesthetic appeal; instead, we would be consigning them to such fields as engineering or invention. The common metal potato peeler is a good example (Figure 0.3). Clearly an invention, it was the work of an American, Ferdinand E. Fender, who patented it in 1941 and claimed that its novelty was "a pivoted blade adapted to follow the uneven surface of the fruit or vegetable during the peeling stroke" (Figure 0.4).

FIGURE 0.2. Makeshift Doorstop, from Jane Fulton Suri, *Thoughtless Acts? Observations on Intuitive Design*, 2005.

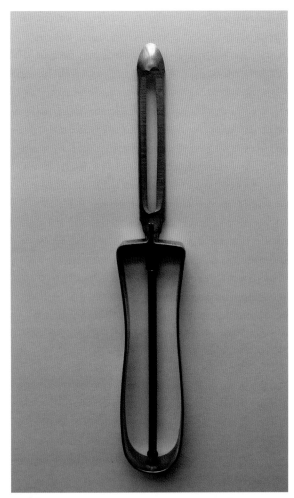

FIGURE 0.3. Ferdinand E. Fender, Potato Peeler, 1940. Metal.

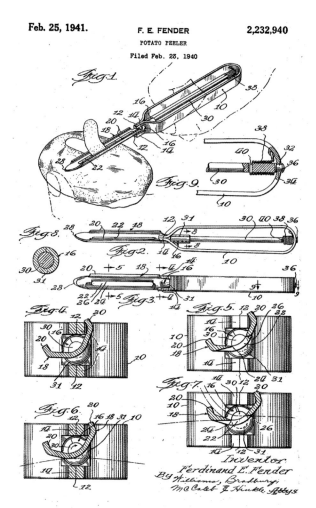

FIGURE 0.4. Ferdinand E. Fender, United States Utility Patent for Potato Peeler, 1941.

This new method must have been a considerable breakthrough for the functionality of such a common utensil, for today, after three quarters of a century, the peeler is still on the market and still filling a culinary need in its original, if somewhat awkward, shape.

Fender's potato peeler does not seem to have been noticed in histories of design, however, but when the international product-design firm Smart Design (established in 1980) redesigned the handle of the peeler in 1990 to accommodate those with diminished grasping ability, its new OXO brand Good Grips vegetable peeler quickly became one of the most pictured products of its time (Figure 0.5). This flurry of interest was aroused not just by the much discussed functionality of its thick handle and improved grip, which Smart Design had arrived at after considerable research, but by its looks as well. On the one hand, the peeler had a universal handle, one that was newly engineered for comfort, for which its Smart Design inventors CEO Davin Stowell (born 1953) and designer and model builder Michael Callahan (born 1960) received a United States utility patent for the way it works in 1990; on the other hand, the peeler had a new form, for which its Smart Design designer Tucker Viemeister (born 1948) received a United States ornamental-design patent for the way it looks in 1992 (Figure 0.6). Its sensuous black handle made of nonslip Santoprene (a type of plastic that combines the qualities of both rubber and plastic) with flexible fins to enhance the grip made it an early example of the then emerging field of universal, or inclusive, design, which may be defined as design for everyone, including those with disabilities. Universal design mandates that designers consider aesthetics along with functionality to avoid ungainly forms that could stigmatize users with special needs, once again underscoring the importance of visual appeal in design today.

As we have seen, the Good Grips vegetable peeler was not the work of an individual designer who had a clear and definitive epiphany about how the object would look and function and then went on to produce it. A design is almost never the work of a single person. Most craftspeople have assistants to help them, and most industrial firms rely on an entire corps of workers who collaborate to bring an original idea into being, among them industrial designers, engineers, materials specialists, 3-D modelers, management professionals, and marketing experts. Historically, this group effort has often not been recognized, and products have generally been attributed solely to the person whose name is on the door of the design office, architectural firm, or corporation that produced it. Today, design practice has become more transparent than it was in the past and design associates are now more likely to get (or at least share) credit for their work.

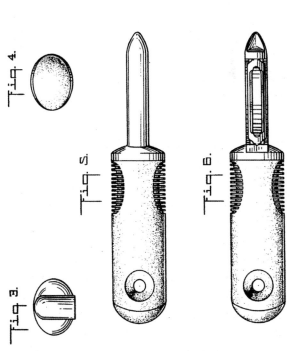

FIGURE 0.5.   Michael Callahan, Davin Stowell, and Tucker Viemeister for Smart Design, Good Grips Vegetable Peeler, 1990. Made by OXO. Santoprene and metal.

FIGURE 0.6.   Tucker Viemeister for Smart Design, United States Design Patent for Good Grips Vegetable Peeler, 1992.

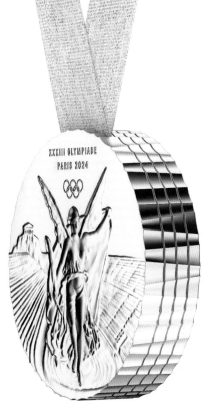

FIGURE 0.7. Philippe Starck, Proposal for the Medal for the 2024 Paris Olympics (entire and in its four parts), 2016.

How we talk about objects, how we categorize them so we can comprehend their meanings, is an ongoing issue for design discussion. In 2004, when the French National Fund for Contemporary Art (Fonds national d'art contemporain) wanted to exhibit its entire design collection of some two thousand objects, they could do little more than lay them out in a large exhibition space in Paris. In trying to make sense of it all, the staff rejected the temptation to organize them by grand themes and decided instead to arrange the objects according to the most basic facts about their creation. They showed clusters of works by individual designers; grouped objects by the nationalities of their designers; arranged them by types, decades of creation, materials and techniques, and colors; joined those that could change dimensions, for example, by folding or inflating; presented those that were created as ensembles or systems; and organized them by the stages of their production, scale of production, places of manufacture, and the manufacturers themselves. These topics have always been points of departure for the discussion of objects, but we also recognize the importance of the circumstances surrounding an object's creation, consumption, meaning, and use in its own time. Thus, in a series of sidebars, we have called upon a selection of writings by designers and cultural thinkers to illuminate further our understanding of the past, and the present, of design.

In facing the evolution of design in our own day, we have expanded our definition to embrace issues and disciplines that are new, and to admit that many of the concerns that were central to design history in the past have now become irrelevant. These have been challenged by a more fluid understanding of what design is, what it can do, and how, with an interdisciplinary approach, the process of design might be applied to innovation in other fields. While we need to recognize that the range of the design profession is growing wider, within the context of this introduction to modern design,

objects, whether two- or three-dimensional, remain its focus.

They might be a limited series like the component medal that the French designer Philippe Starck (born 1949) proposed in 2016 for the 2024 Paris Olympics (Figure 0.7). Composed of four elements, it would allow medalists to take apart their medal and share the glory of their achievement with trainers, mentors, family members, and others who contributed to their success.

Or design might have global resonance, used by millions, like the Nike + Fuelband fitness tracker, which came onto the market in 2012 to keep users abreast of the details of their daily exercise (Figure 0.8). This new minimalist device measured the number of steps taken and the amount of calories burned. Users could preset their activity targets, and the stylish LED (light emitting diodes) display changed colors to mark their advancement toward their goals, awarding aspirational NikeFuel "points" to motivate these twenty-first-century consumers toward their anticipated success.

FIGURE 0.8.   Nike, Nike + Fuelband, 2012. Thermoplastic elastomers, polypropylene, magnesium, and stainless steel.

DESIGN AND DECORATION

1750 to 1860

CHAPTER 1

Design and Industry

For the nineteenth century, design meant decoration, as the Scottish designer and botanist Christopher Dresser (1834–1904) explained in his *Art of Decorative Design* in 1862: "Ornament is that which, superadded to utility, renders the object more acceptable through bestowing upon it an amount of beauty that it would not otherwise possess." Objects that were ornamented and received this added beauty, such as furniture and fabrics, tableware and toiletry sets, had historically been the province of gentlefolk, and those who aspired to their lifestyle. But as wealth and education became more widespread during the eighteenth century, the emerging middle classes started to acquire them, and eventually, in soaring amounts. By the nineteenth century, when factory-produced decorated objects, known as "art manufactures," made objects of design less expensive, those in the working classes gained access to them as well.

Beauty is not the only element that ornament adds to objects, however; it adds meaning as well. Even a simple motif or overall pattern, no less an allegorical figure or a recognizable image, can reveal much about the outlook of those who made an object, and offer clues about what kind of person might have owned it. The sophisticated decoration on this dessert plate, with its painted and gilded bands, its picturesque landscape, and its motifs drawn from the arts of ancient Greece and Rome, suggests that it was intended for someone of great means and cultivated taste whose lifestyle would be imbued with luxury and display (Figure 1.1). Records at the Sèvres Porcelain Factory, the former royal workshop located just outside of Paris, where the plate was produced, confirm this. They show that it was part of a costly, one-of-a-kind, seventy-two-piece dessert service bought in 1811 by Prince Eugène de Beauharnais (1781–1824), son of the French Empress Josephine (1763–1814) and adoptive son of her second husband, Napoleon I (1769–1821). The service was made of porcelain, a much-sought-after hard, white, translucent ceramic, which was developed in China about the ninth century but not manufactured in Europe until the early eighteenth, and at Sèvres, until the 1770s. At the center of each plate in the service is a different Swiss landscape, this one depicting a church at the edge of Lake Lugano in the southern part of the country, which was the kind of view that wealthy young travelers might have brought back as souvenirs from their Grand Tour of Europe. The narrow inner band that surrounds it shows a repeating pattern of gilded palmettes, a classical fan-shaped ornament resembling palm leaves; the wider outer one is gilded and painted in rose pink (one of the brilliant colors for which the Sèvres factory was famous) with medallions

FIGURE 1.1.   Sèvres Porcelain Factory, Plate with View of the Lake Lugano, Switzerland, 1811. Enameled and gilded porcelain.

resembling sculptural reliefs and hexagons enclosing ancient emblems: armor, crown, helmet, lyre, and shield. These ornaments are distinctive expressions of the Neoclassical style, which had been sparked by the discovery of the remains of antique civilizations in the early part of the eighteenth century and had become the universal Western artistic style by its end.

The emphasis on decoration in the nineteenth century does not mean that plain, undecorated objects were not also produced during the period; they were and in great quantities, but lacking decoration, they did not then fall under the banner of design (and would not until the twentieth century). A clear distinction was made at that time between decorative art manufactures and practical, undecorated (or minimally decorated) everyday goods, common objects that were associated with work, modest lifestyles, and little stature. These useful items included a multitude of household wares, furniture, tools, and equipment. They could be found in both ordinary homes and the hidden areas of well-off houses, in conservatories, kitchens, and pantries and the quarters reserved for servants and children, as well as in commercial locations such as factories, workshops, hotels, and cafes.

The absence of ornament does not imply that such objects lacked meaning: it was to be found in their intrinsic elements, their forms, materials, colors, textures, and workmanship, and in the way they were designed for use, not in anything added to them. The simple unadorned form of this wooden chair suggests that it was intended as a purely functional object without the expectation of any added beauty (Figure 1.2). The chair was designed

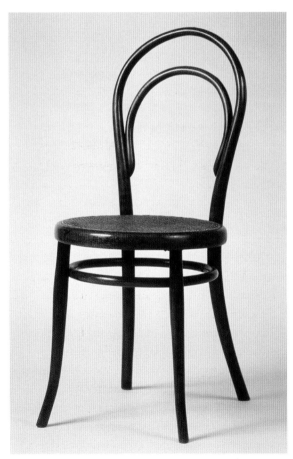

FIGURE 1.2.   Michael Thonet, Chair, c. 1859. Stained beech.

about 1859 by Michael Thonet (1796–1871), a Viennese craftsman who had invented and patented a process for softening solid wood with steam so it could be bent into furniture components. It was made by the firm he founded in 1853, which within several decades became a huge, multinational business producing a wide range of inexpensive furniture with this technique. Its beechwood furniture was mass-produced in large numbers in Austria and Eastern Europe; light in weight, easily taken down into their few parts, and packed flat in large crates, these chairs could be shipped economically, ready for assembly at their final destination. When Thonet furniture was exhibited in 1862 at the London International Exhibition, the awards jury noted that "the excellent application of a happy thought, the elegant simplicity of the forms, and the cheapness of these productions have aided to render the use of this furniture almost universal." This cheap and strong Model 14 chair, reduced to a few structural bentwood components, became the most successful of all Thonet products. Hundreds of millions of this chair (including those made by other manufacturers after its patent expired) have been sold in the century and a half since it was first introduced, and it continues to be manufactured today.

Industrialization

It can be hard for us to grasp in our era of extreme mass consumption just how much manufacturing and commerce was also carried out during the eighteenth and nineteenth centuries. This large scale could not have been achieved without the introduction of new methods of manufacture that came with the Industrial Revolution, which began around the second half of the eighteenth century in Great Britain. It brought great societal changes, including technical innovations in many sectors of the economy; improved transportation; new forms of power; concentration of labor in urban centers, with workers often living in substandard conditions;

and an economy that favored investment and growth. By the later eighteenth century, cotton factories using newly invented and improved machines for carding, spinning, and weaving with relatively few unskilled, often child, laborers to run them, were opened in rural Britain. Operated first by water power, and then steam by applying the rotary engine patented in 1769 by the Scottish inventor James Watt (1736–1819), these large mills were able to produce huge quantities of cotton cloth economically, creating Britain's largest export by the early nineteenth century.

But most manufacturing continued on a smaller scale, even with the introduction of advanced methods of production. Before the Industrial Revolution most goods had been made at home or in small craft-based workshops that might have employed several artisans, who completed entire objects themselves, perhaps assisted by apprentices. But in larger factories, a system of industrial manufacture known as the "division of labor" had been instituted in which workers who were taught specialized skills each completed but one, or a few, of the many sequential steps in production, whether using hand tools or simple machinery. The division of labor was not new, for its impact had been felt in such ancient industries as pottery and coinage, but it was now applied to the manufacture of cheap ordinary objects on a large scale in a rationalized, or logical and efficient, way.

Such an arrangement is pictured in a pottery in Staffordshire, the center of England's ceramic production, in which many workers, both men and women, take part in the operation (Figure 1.3). The process of making common dinnerware is shown, from the throwing of a vessel on a potter's wheel (upper left) and the refining of its form as it turns on a pottery lathe (upper right) to readying the wares to be fired in a large kiln, or pottery oven (center), to be hardened. This pottery used an economical method of decoration, known as transfer printing, which had been developed in England around the 1750s. Transfer printing was cheap because it avoided the expense of hand

decoration. Instead, it used designs on paper pulled from a printing press (bottom left), which with the prints turned face-side down while the ink was still wet, were pressed onto the surface of the pottery (bottom right).

The division of labor was held up as the basis of Great Britain's economic growth by the Scottish philosopher and economist Adam Smith (1723–1790) in *The Wealth of Nations*, published in 1776. Smith showed that even by the latter part of the eighteenth century, factory output had been fully industrialized in certain industries, employing from just a handful to hundreds of workers to manufacture large numbers of articles in a sequence of mostly hand operations. Taking the example of a pin maker, Smith explained that an ordinary worker alone could perhaps make just a few pins in a day but when each worker completed only one or several specialized steps in the process, many thousands of pins could be produced (see Sidebar 1).

Among the eighteenth-century firms that introduced such industrial methods of production and met the challenges of expanding markets were two remarkable factories in the Midlands of England, the Soho metal works of Matthew Boulton (1728–1809) and the Etruria pottery of Josiah Wedgwood (1730–1795). They each employed hundreds of workers, with Wedgwood strictly rationalizing the work (and regulating the lifestyle) of his employees as he sought to achieve perfection by making "such *Machines* of the *Men* as cannot Err." Through their ingenuity, their energy, their passion for research and experimentation, and their understanding of new marketing possibilities, these entrepreneurs built up large, profitable businesses, producing quality products to be sold at home and throughout Europe and sending seconds or out-of-fashion products for sale to the colonies abroad. They broadened the market for their wares by publishing sales catalogues, among the first manufacturers to do so, and by selling directly to the public, with Wedgwood opening a much-frequented showroom in London and Boulton's

FIGURE 1.3. *Various Processes in a Factory in the Potteries, Staffordshire, England*, c. 1880. Engraving.

SIDEBAR 1   Adam Smith, "The Division of Labour," 1776

To take an example, therefore, from a very trifling manufacture; but one in which the division of labour has been very often taken notice of, the trade of the pin-maker; a workman not educated to this business (which the division of labour has rendered a distinct trade), nor acquainted with the use of the machinery employed in it (to the invention of which the same division of labour has probably given occasion), could scarce, perhaps, with his utmost industry, make one pin in a day, and certainly could not make twenty. But in the way in which this business is now carried on, not only the whole work is a peculiar trade, but it is divided into a number of branches, of which the greater part are likewise peculiar trades. One man draws out the wire, another straights it, a third cuts it, a fourth points it, a fifth grinds it at the top for receiving the head; to make the head requires two or three distinct operations; to put it on, is a peculiar business, to whiten the pins is another; it is even a trade by itself to put them into the paper; and the important business of making a pin is, in this manner, divided into about eighteen distinct operations, which, in some manufactories, are all performed by distinct hands, though in others the same man will sometimes perform two or three of them. I have seen a small manufactory of this kind where ten men only were employed, and where some of them consequently performed two or three distinct operations. But though they were very poor, and therefore but indifferently accommodated with the necessary machinery, they could, when they exerted themselves, make among them about twelve pounds of pins in a day. There are in a pound upwards of four thousand pins of middling size. Those ten persons, therefore, could make among them upwards of forty-eight thousand pins in a day. Each person, therefore, making a tenth part of forty-eight thousand pins, might be considered as making four thousand eight hundred pins in a day. But if they had all wrought separately and independently, and without any of them having been educated to this peculiar business, they certainly could not each of them have made twenty, perhaps not one pin in a day; that is, certainly, not the two hundred and fortieth, perhaps not the four thousand eight hundredth part of what they are at present capable of performing, in consequence of a proper division and combination of their different operations.

metalware factory having its own sales shop and teahouse with which to draw shoppers and tourists, as many factories do today.

Wedgwood's breakthrough at the pottery he opened in Burslem, Staffordshire, in 1759 came with his creation of creamware, a highly refined pottery like that used for this household platter, which was transfer printed with a pastoral scene in the center and floral sprays around it (Figure 1.4). Creamware was made of a whitish clay mixture with a cream-colored glaze, an economical stand-in for the white of porcelain. Wedgwood derived it from secret nightly experiments with the chemistry of ceramics, wary of any competition that might impinge on his market. His work came to notice when the luxurious hand-painted creamware table service that he made in 1765 for Queen Charlotte (1744–1818), wife of George III (1738–1820), brought him the right to call this pottery "Queens Ware." With this royal patronage, his inexpensive pottery drew a broad middle-class market, which typically imitated the aristocracy in its stylistic choices. In 1769, anticipating the Neoclassical mania of the late eighteenth century, he expanded his production into expensive ornamental wares imitating classical pottery, made at his new factory,

FIGURE 1.4. Josiah Wedgwood, Platter, c. 1780. Creamware with transfer-printed decoration.

Etruria, named after the Etruscans of ancient Italy. Always trying to keep ahead of his competitors, Wedgwood, like Boulton, hired fine artists to supply up-to-date designs, most notable of whom was the young English Neoclassical sculptor John Flaxman (1755–1826). Flaxman's scene of the Greek poet Homer (active about 750 BCE) being raised into the realm of the immortals appears as a white, low-relief design against a pale blue ground on Wedgwood's Pegasus vase of 1786 (Figure 1.5). The vase was made of a dense translucent pottery body that he invented, called "Jasper," which with such molded relief decoration became Wedgwood's signature product and a branding legacy that distinguishes even now the popular ceramics that bear his name.

Industrialization advanced along a different path in the United States, where mechanization was introduced much earlier than in England. With fewer skilled craftsmen at hand because of readily available farmland and the lure of westward expansion, American manufacturers replaced them with unskilled workers, machinery, and progressive production methods. These were welcomed by the workers, not fought as they were by the Luddites in England, who between 1811 and 1816 rebelled against textile manufacturers and smashed the

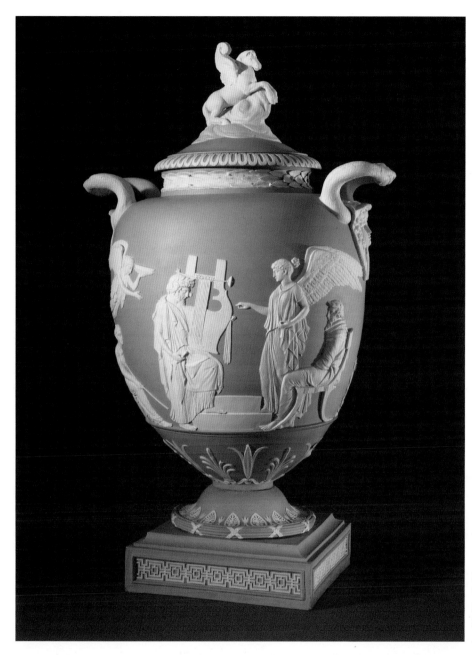

FIGURE 1.5. Josiah Wedgwood, after design by John Flaxman, Pegasus Vase, 1786. Jasperware.

machinery that threatened their jobs. Most particularly, American industry used specialized machines geared to very specific tasks, which sped up the manufacture of individual components and made the assembly of products much more efficient. With this method, which became known as the "American System" of manufacture, factory owners could hire inexperienced labor to produce goods at considerably lower prices, opening up new markets for products formerly thought to be out of reach for many.

In Connecticut, one of the early centers of nineteenth-century industrial production, the clock-making firm of Eli Terry (1772–1852) produced the first successful line of mass-produced consumer products in the United States, using standardized parts and machinery run by water power. In the late eighteenth century, Terry began to make tall-case, or grandfather, clocks with movements of wood, which could be completed by unskilled workers using specialized machines, instead of movements of brass, which required skilled craftsmen. Using similar economical methods, he later introduced inexpensive box clocks made to fit on a shelf. His simplest clock, introduced in 1816, had a plain wooden case with a dial that was simply painted in reverse on the inside of the glass door, which revealed the compact arrangement of wooden gears, shortened pendulum, and lead weights (Figure 1.6). This basic model brought him a new market niche, rural populations who had never felt the need for clocks before but were turned into consumers when itinerant merchants brought them these cheap, utilitarian products.

FIGURE 1.6. Eli Terry, Box Clock, c. 1816. Wood, metal, and glass.

The American System was fine-tuned in other industries, among them, a group of armories that were centered in the Connecticut River Valley. Samuel Colt (1814–1862) led the field, basing the success of his Colt's Patent Fire Arms Manufacturing Company (established 1845) on the revolver he patented in 1836, a pistol that could be fired multiple times without reloading. But much of the company's productivity was due to Elisha K. Root (1808–1865), whom Colt hired as factory superintendent in 1849. An exceedingly skilled and experienced mechanic, inventor, and technical innovator, Root perfected the manufacturing system and created the means to fill the ever-increasing orders that Colt's remarkable salesmanship abilities stimulated. Root invented, and patented, scores of machines for specialized roles in the manufacturing process and organized the machines and manpower into a logical production system, thus overhauling, and bringing a high degree of efficiency to, the way Colt's arms were made. Removing chance from production with its hundreds of machines

ensured that every gun that was mass-produced, like this 1850 navy model (or .36 caliber) revolver, was exactly the same (Figure 1.7). Although these early revolvers were usually made of steel without ornament of any kind, the revolver could also be special-ordered in silver as this one was, with added engraved decoration, which in Colt's factory was also done by purpose-designed machines. Colt, in an address to the Institute of Civil Engineers in London in 1851, proudly touted the advantages of the American System for the production of his revolvers, which by that time had reached tens of thousands annually: "A large number of machines is necessarily required for these operations; as it has been found advantageous to confine each one to its peculiar province, rather than to employ any more comprehensive machine, for several operations. By this system the machines become almost automatons, performing certain labour under the guidance of women, or children, and thus the economy and precision of the manufacture are insured."

FIGURE 1.7.   Samuel Colt, Navy Percussion Revolver, Serial No. 2, 1850. Made by Colt's Patent Fire Arms Manufacturing Company. Steel, brass, silver, and walnut.

Style and Ornament

Although the conventional image we have of a machine is a utilitarian object free of decoration, many machines in the nineteenth century were embellished with ornamental patterning to bring them into the realm of design, especially when they were made for use at home. Sewing machines were first produced commercially in Great Britain and the United States in the 1850s, and typewriters, in the 1860s. They were often decorated with colorful flowers, or with gilding like that on this domestic cast-iron sewing machine (Figure 1.8). Labeled as an arm and platform machine, it was patented in 1873 by Edward Ward (1829–1896), a London inventor known best for this advance in design, which raised up the platform for the fabric to make sewing easier. While objects decorated like this one with classical motifs continued to be made throughout the century, the Neoclassical style had lost its universal application and other styles were being advanced at the same time. In the past, artisans and architects did not have to consider what style they should use. Greek architects did not question whether to design with columns, Romans with round arches and domes, and Gothic masons with pointed arches, for they all worked within a vocabulary of harmonious forms that were common to their times. But in the nineteenth century, without any one style driving design, many options were open and the historic styles were there for the taking. Designers transformed them into original redesigns, what has become known as "revival styles."

Borrowing styles from earlier periods, described as "historicism," meant reusing characteristic forms found in those past styles, but it did not necessarily mean reproducing them in their entirety

FIGURE 1.8. Edward Ward, Sewing Machine, 1873. Cast iron, japanned and gilded.

or imitating them directly. "It will ever be known," the brothers Henry and Aaron Arrowsmith acknowledged in 1840 in their *House Decorator & Painter's Guide*, "that the talent of the age was not confined to the bare imitation of any one style, but that all were used and improved. If, indeed, there be one circumstance which distinguishes the history of the arts in our own day, it is the appropriation of them to all the domestic comforts of life." Designers also created "exotic" styles, those adapted from the architecture and design of the far-off lands that were then being visited by increasing numbers of European travelers, particularly China, Turkey, and North Africa (and later in the century, Japan). Often several styles were used at the same time, which is called "eclecticism," a term that has as its derivation the idea of choosing, and designers at that time readily chose from among the many styles that were available and combined them freely.

While eclecticism proliferated in the nineteenth century, it had its roots in the eighteenth. Buildings in historic and exotic styles had made a tentative appearance as the small ornamental structures known as follies that were built on the grounds of great houses in Great Britain and Europe, which served to magnify the grandeur of these estates and the reputation of their owners. Such assemblies of architectural forms from across the globe might include classical temples, medieval ruins, Gothic churches, Chinese buildings, and the like, as in the group of follies erected at the royal residence at Kew (situated to the west of London) by the Scottish architect Sir William Chambers (1723–1796). There, in 1763, he built an imposing Chinese pagoda decorated with golden dragons, as seen in a watercolor view by William Marlow (1740–1813) (Figure 1.9). Chambers, who had traveled in China in the 1740s, was one of the few Western architects

FIGURE 1.9.   William Marlow, *View of the Wilderness at Kew*, 1763. Watercolor.

to have done so, bringing new interest in Europe for things Chinese with the publication of his *Designs for Chinese Buildings* in 1757. The pagoda towered above the other follies, two of which are also shown in the watercolor: at left is the Alhambra, a pavilion inspired by the renowned thirteenth-century palace in Granada, Spain, built by the Moors, the North African Muslims who ruled Spain in that era, and in the distance at right is a Turkish mosque. With his charming designs, Chambers, who was tutor to the future George III and later his architect, brought to this piece of English countryside a virtual history of world architectural styles as they were then known, considering his structures educational tools for the young prince.

At the same time, adventuresome landowners were building houses in the revived Gothic style; one of the earliest, and the most influential, was Strawberry Hill, situated on a hillside near the river Thames, southwest of London. The house was the expressive creation of Horace Walpole (1717–1779), famed letter writer, politician, and author of the novel *The Castle of Otranto* (1764), an early Gothic horror story. Beginning in 1753, he transformed an existing house into a castle-like structure with whimsical Gothic details that served as settings for his eclectic collection of art treasures and memorabilia. Gothic was also advanced along with other styles by the noted cabinetmaker Thomas Chippendale (1718–1779) in his 1754 pattern book, *The Gentleman and Cabinet-Maker's Director*, which was subtitled *Being a Large Collection of the Most Elegant and Useful Designs of Household Furniture in the Gothic, Chinese and Modern* ["French"] *Taste*. His reinvention of the style included a "Gothick" four-poster bed with a canopy of carved pointed arches and cloth hangings offering a counterpoint to this motif (Figure 1.10).

FIGURE 1.10.   Thomas Chippendale, "Gothick Bed," from *The Gentleman and Cabinet-Maker's Director*, 1754. Engraving.

As eclecticism increased, the abundance of styles ready for the choosing became a dilemma for serious thinkers in the nineteenth century who had hoped to create a single universal style for their own time, but this never happened. They found it hard to accept the obvious, that the nineteenth century did have its own style, and by default it was eclecticism. "From this *manufacture of ornament*," the artist and design reformer Richard Redgrave (1804–1888) wrote disparagingly in 1852, "arises all that mixture of styles, and that incongruity of parts, which, perhaps, is itself 'the style' of this characterless age."

Ornament of all types was celebrated at the Great Exhibition of the Works of Industry of All Nations in London in 1851, the first of a series of extravagant international exhibitions that in the nineteenth century would include those in New York (1853), Paris (1855, 1867, 1878, 1889, 1900), London (1862), Vienna (1873), Philadelphia (1876), and Chicago (1893), and which continue in the world's fairs of today. It was held in a vast structure of cast iron and plate glass designed like a massive greenhouse by Sir Joseph Paxton (1803–1865) and built in London's Hyde Park (Figure 1.11). Paxton, architect and botanist, had stepped in just in time to save the exhibition with his design for the enormous pavilion, basing it on that of his glass Lily House at Chatsworth in Derbyshire (1850), the home of the Duke of Devonshire, where he was head gardener. Immediately dubbed the "Crystal Palace," it was made of interchangeable elements and modular sections precut off-site and assembled in military fashion. Completed in only nine months by employing the division of labor on a grand scale, it paralleled the new industrial methods introduced by American industry. The structure was so radical that many questioned whether it had any architectural merit or whether it could even be considered architecture at all, considering that it displayed so few of the familiar stylistic features and conventional materials then recognized as the substance of architectural beauty.

The exhibition can be seen as a prime, and for its time, glorious, triumph of early globalization even as it reinforced the colonial aspirations of

FIGURE 1.11.   Sir Joseph Paxton, Crystal Palace, London, 1851, from *Dickinson's Comprehensive Pictures of the Great Exhibition of 1851*, 1854. Chromolithograph.

Great Britain and Europe. The significance of the exhibition as a great step in the progress of nineteenth-century industry had been anticipated by its royal sponsor, Prince Albert (1819–1861), consort of Queen Victoria (1819–1901), when he spoke in 1849: "Gentlemen, the Exhibition of 1851 is to give us a true test and a living picture of the point of development at which the whole of mankind has arrived in this great task, and a new starting point from which all nations will be able to direct their own further exertions." First proposed by Sir Henry Cole (1808–1882), a multitalented, dedicated, Victorian public servant, it had been conceived as a presentation of the products of British manufacture inspired by a series of national industrial expositions held in France during the first half of the century. Later Cole convinced Prince

Albert of the economic advantages of turning it into an international undertaking. The exhibition achieved one of Britain's greatest economic aims, to open up new international markets for its goods, but failed with another, to challenge the dominant position of its major competitor in the decorative arts, France, which continued to enjoy a long-standing reputation for superior products with a higher quality of design and craftsmanship.

The Great Exhibition turned out to be an overwhelming financial and public success. It was published in great detail in the press and in guides, catalogues, official reports, and commemorative albums, among them *Dickinson's Comprehensive Pictures of the Great Exhibition of 1851*. Its two volumes included fifty-three lush color plates taken from watercolors commissioned by Prince

FIGURE 1.12.   Hardware, 1851, from *Dickinson's Comprehensive Pictures of the Great Exhibition of 1851*, 1854. Chromolithograph.

Albert from three painters, Louis Haghe (1806–1885), Joseph Nash (1808–1878), and David Roberts (1796–1864), accompanied by detailed commentaries on the exhibits. These fine early examples of chromolithography, or color printing from a design drawn on polished stones, showed the brilliant Crystal Palace building and its lofty interior, with its ironwork painted in primary colors according to a decorative scheme proposed by the architect and color theorist Owen Jones (1809–1874). They magnificently captured its grandeur and the startling variety of objects among the British and foreign exhibits, with the products on display divided into four categories: raw materials, machinery, manufactures, and the fine arts.

The color plate entitled "Hardware" displayed works by Birmingham manufacturers, an array of metal chandeliers and other ornamental lighting devices, stove grates, and bronze sculptures viewed by a group of genteel visitors showing off the bright contrasting colors of their 1851 fashions (Figure 1.12). At right is the stand of Jennens & Bentridge, a firm also from Birmingham that specialized in papier-mâché, a newly improved and popular material made of glued paper that was exceedingly strong and could be sawn, steam molded, and easily worked. Papier-mâché goods were usually japanned (covered with a hard black varnish imitating Japanese lacquer work), inlaid with mother-of-pearl and decorated with floral motifs, antique patterns, and pictorial imagery. It achieved a broad popularity and even influenced designs in other materials, such as the metal sewing machine made by Edward Ward in the later part of the century (see Figure 1.8). Like the new electroplating process patented by George Richards Elkington (1801–1865) in 1840, which used an electric current to deposit a skin of silver on a base-metal object, papier-mâché was valued for its economy of material and manufacture. It was fashionably employed for such objects as tea trays and writing and toiletry boxes, and in combination with wood, for pieces of furniture, like this ornate chair (Figure 1.13). With its molded

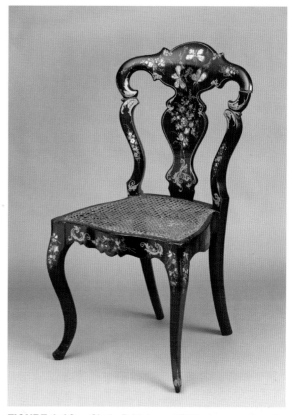

FIGURE 1.13. Chair, British, c. 1850. Japanned and painted wood, papier-mâché, and mother-of-pearl.

papier-mâché back, its painted and mother-of-pearl floral decoration and gilding, and its doubly curved wooden legs inspired by the elegant, florid mode of eighteenth-century France, it is an example of the Rococo Revival, the historic style that was most popular at the exhibition.

Renaissance Revival, taking inspiration from fifteenth- and sixteenth-century styles in Italy, France, Germany, and England, was a second favorite. The London decorator and cabinetmaker Jackson and Graham presented this sideboard in the English Elizabethan style as one of its many exhibits (Figure 1.14). Instead of simply bemoaning the superiority of French design over English, the firm had chosen to take the second best route and hire a prolific French architect and draftsman, Alexandre-Eugène Prignot (1822–after 1876), to supply designs for furniture and interiors in a

FIGURE 1.14. Alexandre-Eugène Prignot, for Jackson and Graham, Sideboard, 1851, from M. Digby Wyatt, *The Industrial Arts of the Nineteenth Century at the Great Exhibition*, 1851–53.

variety of ornamental styles. His conception for this elaborate oak sideboard drew together romanticized elements from the Renaissance style, among them rounded arches, broken pediments, and strapwork (ornamental motifs imitating interlaced leather bands). The relief panels between the cherubic figures on the bottom at front represent hunting and fishing (and on the side, agriculture and winemaking), emblems that symbolized food for the table and announced the purpose of the sideboard.

The Gothic Revival style was considerably less present at the exhibition as it had yet to become widely used for art manufactures. For English exhibitors, such works were concentrated in the Medieval Court, which was conceived and organized by Augustus Welby Northmore Pugin (1812–1852), the architect who is credited with bringing the Gothic style fully back into fashion in England. Among the designs Pugin himself exhibited there was this bread plate, made by Minton, the leading English manufacturer of ceramics during this period (Figure 1.15). To decorate it, he followed the medieval encaustic technique, creating the design by inlaying blue and reddish-brown clays into hollows made in the buff-colored earthenware of the plate before it was fired in the kiln. Like Prignot's sideboard, the bread plate is an example of the nineteenth-century fondness for ornament that communicates the use of an object, with the ears of wheat and the motto "Waste Not Want Not" alluding to bread on different levels, to its agricultural source and its association with thrift and charity.

FIGURE 1.15.
A. W. N. Pugin, Bread Plate, c. 1849. Made by Minton. Inlaid earthenware.

Design Reform

A. W. N. Pugin was an early exponent of design reform based on his conception of medieval architectural principles. After he converted to Catholicism in the mid-1830s, Gothic became for him an essential expression of spirituality, representative of the values of the church in England before the Anglican Reformation of the sixteenth century. In his compelling book *Contrasts: or, a Parallel between the Noble Edifices of the Fourteenth and Fifteenth Centuries, and Similar Buildings of the Present Day; Shewing the Present Decay of Taste* (1836), Pugin made his case for the superiority of medieval architecture and society over those of his own time, and for the return to the Gothic style for church building. This led to commissions for religious buildings throughout Great Britain, which he designed and also fitted out with his own objects in a medieval style.

Pugin's French contemporary medievalist Eugène-Emmanuel Viollet-le Duc (1814–1879) was also devoted to reviving the appreciation of the styles of the Middle Ages, but his interest as an architect was structural, not spiritual, and his theories leaned to finding the rational basis of these historic structures. Much of his career was spent restoring historic buildings, many that had been damaged during the French Revolution, and supplying furnishings and decorations for them. Viollet-le Duc's restoration work was not always historically accurate, although he took an archaeological approach to his understanding of each building. His contribution was often more a re-creation than a return to the basics of the original design, like much of his work on the twelfth- to thirteenth-century Cathedral of Notre-Dame in Paris. His design for the renovation of one of its side chapels shows a total scheme, introducing a suite of wall paintings and "painted windows,"

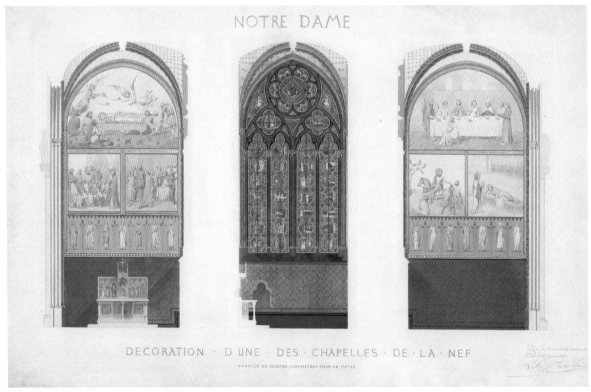

FIGURE 1.16. Eugène-Emmanuel Viollet-le-Duc, Plan for the Renovation of a Chapel in the Nave of the Cathedral of Notre-Dame, Paris, 1843. Watercolor, shell gold, pen and ink.

which he said "was one of the most splendid means of interior decoration. Nothing equals the richness of these transparent pictures, which are an indispensable complement to the monuments of this epoch" (Figure 1.16).

Pugin was also instrumental in establishing the legitimacy of the Gothic style for public buildings in England, calling on its historic and patriotic associations to supplant what was then a preference for styles with imposing columnar facades of classical inspiration. In a collaboration with its architect, Sir Charles Barry (1795–1860), he supplied most of the Gothic ornament for the British Houses of Parliament in London, which had to be rebuilt after a fire destroyed its earlier building in 1834. Constructing England's most visible example of the revived Gothic style was a mammoth

undertaking, lasting from 1840 to about 1860. Noted craftsmen and manufacturers employing hundreds of workers produced the interior woodwork and furnishings that Pugin designed— wood carving, brasswork, furniture, floor tiles, ceiling paintings, wallpaper, and textiles—much of it realized with the help of machines (Figure 1.17). The machines that had been gradually introduced in England to aid craftsmen in art manufactures were principally used for roughing out the forms, which would be finished by the craftsman's hand. "The Sculptor, relieved of his former drudgery," the catalogue of the Patent Wood Carving Company in London from 1844 reassured its clients, "is enabled to take his place as an Artist, with fresh hand and unjaded powers, to add those finishing touches which mind and taste only can impart."

FIGURE 1.17.   A. W. N. Pugin, Prince's Chamber, Houses of Parliament, London, 1840–60.

Among the principles of design put forth in Pugin's writings, his assertion in *Contrasts* that "the great test of Architectural beauty is the fitness of the design to the purpose for which it is intended, and that the style of a building should so correspond with its use that the spectator may at once perceive the purpose for which it was erected" became an enduring touchstone for architects and designers and those who discussed their work. Fitness for purpose was the central point of Richard Redgrave's critique of the Great Exhibition published in his "Supplementary Report on Design" in 1852, in which he objected to the inescapable demotion of function in favor of ornamentation. "It is impossible," he wrote, "to examine the works of the Great Exhibition, without seeing how often utility and construction are made secondary to decoration . . . This, on the slightest examination, will be found to be the leading error in the Exhibition, an error more or less apparent in every department of manufacture connected with ornament, which is apt to sicken us of decoration, and leads us to admire those objects of absolute utility (the machines and utensils of various kinds), where use is so paramount that ornament is repudiated, and, fitness of purpose being the end sought, a noble simplicity is the result." Redgrave's criticism, following Pugin, was an all-out attack on the art manufactures themselves; he was hopeful of imposing the standards of his own elite coterie for simplified and uplifting decoration on the millions of profusely ornamented objects then being manufactured, which were highly admired and eagerly bought by growing numbers of consumers.

A second debate about design at the exhibition focused on the nature of ornament itself. One viewpoint favored conventionalized ornament, ornament or pattern created according to formalized rules such as symmetry or two-dimensionality, like the woven silk Chandos textile designed by Owen Jones, in which the tight pattern of abstracted flowers, leaves, birds, and scrolling ornament is flattened against the surface (Figure 1.18). The opposing side of the debate,

FIGURE 1.18.   Owen Jones, Chandos Textile, c. 1868. Made by Warner, Sillet & Ramm. Woven wool, silk, and cotton.

favoring a truthful representation of nature, had as its advocate John Ruskin (1819–1900), England's most influential art critic and an artist devoted to depicting nature in all its specificity himself. Ruskin objected to conventionalized ornament, notably in his *Seven Lamps of Architecture* (1849), propounding from a religious viewpoint that beautiful ornament could only arise from the direct imitation of natural form. Ornament, he wrote, "must consist of such studious arrangements of forms as are imitative or suggestive of those which are commonest among natural existences, that being of course the noblest ornament which represents the highest orders of existence. Imitated flowers are nobler than imitated stones, imitated animals than flowers; imitated human forms of all animal forms the noblest."

Conventionalized decoration had been supported by Redgrave in his report as he lambasted a recent development in vogue at the exhibition: "There has arisen a new species of ornament of the most objectionable kind, which it is desirable at once to deprecate on account of its complete departure from just taste and true principles. This may be called the *natural* or merely imitative style . . . Thus we have metal *imitations* of plants and flowers, with an attempt to make them a strict resemblance, forgetting that natural objects are rendered into ornament by subordinating the details to the general idea, and that the endeavour ought to be to seize the simplest expression of a thing rather than to imitate it." A curtain-rod holder with a glass convolvulus flower and gilded-brass stem and leaves, attributed to R. W. Winfield & Co., one of the major brass founders of Birmingham, is a fine example of this type of direct imitation of nature (Figure 1.19). Such exactly realistic objects were exhibited in 1851 to public admiration, contrary to Redgrave's take on them as a transgression of the principles of tasteful design.

Redgrave and other outspoken critics of the exhibition were following a strain of design absolutism that had developed in Great Britain over the previous decades, beginning significantly

FIGURE 1.19. Attributed to R. W. Winfield & Co., Curtain Rod Holder, 1845. Gilded brass and glass.

with the writings of Pugin, whose ideas of fitness, truth to the nature of materials, and honesty of construction underlined a movement for reform. Pugin's furniture, like this softly curving prayer bench made for his own use, followed his principle of revealing how objects were constructed (Figure 1.20). Its exaggerated tenon-and-key joints, in which a separate piece of wood (the key) fits tightly into a hole in the tenon (the protruding part of the joint) to hold it in place, expresses how the top was attached to the sides. For Pugin, design was a moral and spiritual undertaking, outweighing the imaginative and expressive decoration that had beautified buildings and furnishings in the past.

FIGURE 1.20. A. W. N. Pugin, Prayer Bench, c. 1844. Oak.

FIGURE 1.21. "Gothic" Textile, British, 1830–35. Printed cotton.

His attitude to design was serious, introducing logic and rationality into its creation. In his book *The True Principles of Pointed or Christian Architecture* (1841), he dictated, for example, that the decoration of walls should remain flat, with no perspective or shading added to it. Among other "absurdities," he condemned certain "Gothic-pattern papers . . . where a wretched caricature of a pointed [Gothic] building is repeated from the skirting to the cornice in glorious confusion,—door over pinnacle, and pinnacle over door," designs that also appeared on textiles (Figure 1.21).

Henry Cole had set an example for the reform of design for industrial production when he entered a competition for the creation of an ordinary tea service organized in 1846 by the Royal Society of Arts. His entry was an attempt to combine utility, decoration, and economy in a service that was inexpensive enough for those with lesser means to buy (Figure 1.22). Submitting his design under the pseudonym Felix Summerly, a name he had used

for a series of children's books that he published, he explained that his goal was practical: "to obtain as much beauty and ornament as is commensurate with cheapness. A higher standard in the ornamental parts would have led to much greater cost. The forms in principle are new combinations of those of the best Etruscan Pottery, with ornaments at the handles, &c., super-added and designed so as not to interfere with the simplicity of the outlines." The superadded ornament on the

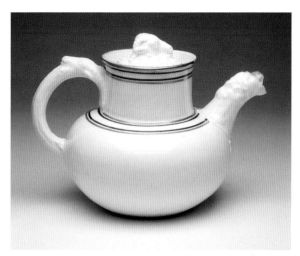

FIGURE 1.22.   Sir Henry Cole, Teapot, 1846. Made by Minton. Earthenware.

teapot, including vines on the spout, a goat's head on the handle, and a ram's head on the lid, was softly modeled with no exacting detail, making it easier and cheaper to produce. Having won a silver medal for the service, he felt confident enough the next year to put together an association of manufacturers, designers, and artists that he called Summerly's Art Manufactures to create products in which these ideas would be followed. The association, which included such artists as Redgrave and the sculptor John Bell (1811–1895), aimed "to produce in each article superior utility, which is not to be sacrificed to ornament; to select pure forms; to decorate each article with appropriate details relating to its use, and to obtain these details as directly as possible from nature."

These principles, following Pugin's, were also the mainstay of *The Journal of Design and Manufactures*, which Cole and Redgrave founded in 1848. The *Journal* put forth design for serious examination with a universal scope that was breathtaking for its time. It investigated and evaluated newly manufactured foreign and domestic products on an object-by-object basis, taking a strict position on the centrality of function and fitness in design yet also supporting naturalism as long as it did not interfere with utility. The

Journal looked closely at individual objects in different mediums and criticized them frankly, both some of the finest pieces created for wealthy clients as well as some of the cheapest that were meant for the mass of new consumers. Engravings of new products were shown and assessed, and where possible, actual samples of fabrics and wallpapers were included in its volumes. The *Journal* also had more pressing goals; it spoke out on issues of design and manufacture that were important in its day, especially the need for effective copyright laws, reform of the government-sponsored schools of design to make them more attuned to designing for industry, and efforts to combat pirating by competing manufacturers.

Cole's involvement with debates about the future of design, his work on the *Journal*, and his advisory role on the executive committee for the 1851 exhibition put him in line for major positions after the exhibition closed. In 1852 he was given the leadership of the government schools of design, and with it, the Museum of Ornamental Art, the predecessor of the South Kensington (now Victoria and Albert) Museum in London, which he directed until 1873. In 1852, eager to educate the public about taste in design, he installed a group of objects in the museum made with what he called "false principles of decoration," such as illusionism, or the "direct imitation of nature," which was quickly dubbed the "Chamber of Horrors" by the public and soon removed in the face of outspoken criticism from their manufacturers.

His desire to provide students at the design schools with images of fine examples of ornament led to the publication of Owen Jones's *Grammar of Ornament* in 1856. This large chromolithographic volume was filled with 100 color plates, dense compositions of a thousand examples of ornament from disparate cultures around the world. These encompassed historic ornament from the Western tradition as well as exotic designs from countries of North Africa and the Near and Far East, some of which are seen in a plate based on the mosaic decoration from the Alhambra palace in Spain

MAURISCH   MORESQUE N° 5   MAURESQUES

TAFEL XLIII   PL XLII

FIGURE 1.23. Owen Jones, Moresque No. 5, from *The Grammar of Ornament*, 1856. Chromolithograph.

(Figure 1.23). The *Grammar* also included three plates devoted to the "Ornament of Savage Tribes," the first publication to present the art and design of tribal cultures as serious, aesthetically valid, expressions, and he showed how in many ways they were superior to those of Europe. Ten final plates were devoted to examples of "Leaves and Flowers from Nature," including one created by Christopher Dresser (1834–1904), then a young botanist who was directed more to the study of plants than to design. Dresser used his scientific knowledge to propose a path to ornament not through geometry,

FIGURE 1.24.
Christopher Dresser, Leaves & Flowers from Nature, No. 8, from Owen Jones, *The Grammar of Ornament*, 1856. Chromolithograph.

as Jones had proposed in the thirty-seven principles of conventionalized ornament and color theory that he set forth in his introduction, but through a regularized imitation of natural growth, what he called "artistic botany." He exaggerated the way various plants and flowers were formed to promote a flattened, symmetrical ornament based on the structures of nature (Figure 1.24). With these illustrations, and Jones's design principles, the *Grammar* would be a major influence on design into the early twentieth century, when interest in decoration began to wane.

CHAPTER 2
Life, Art, and Design

During the 1860s two new and overlapping circles addressed themselves to issues of design other than the proper form of ornament: those associated with John Ruskin and William Morris (1834–1896), who questioned the morality of industrialization, and those of the Aesthetic Movement, who eschewed strictures of morality for an all-encompassing lifestyle that was meant to be an art form in itself. Both looked to the past for artistic inspiration, Ruskin and Morris finding it in the art of medieval times, and the Aesthetes in the simple styles of late seventeenth- and early eighteenth-century England and in the artifacts of exotic cultures. Toward the end of the century, a highly original style known as Art Nouveau, or the New Art, overtook these and other ornamental styles, finding inspiration in contemporary creativity rather than in the past. From about 1890 to 1910, it spread across Europe and abroad, a movement with many variants dedicated explicitly to creating a modern decorative style.

Arts and Crafts Movement

The critic John Ruskin looked back with great longing to what he understood as the simple and morally elevated life of medieval times, when handcraftsmanship gave proper dignity to the worker. He contrasted it with the cold, industrial lifestyle of his own age, when the factory system dehumanized the life of the workers, making them like machines, as Josiah Wedgwood had desired. In one of the most fervent passages about the evils of industrialization to be found in English literature, Ruskin cried out against the harmful effects of the division of labor on the human psyche. Interrupting a chapter in his three-volume work *The Stones of Venice* (1851–53) in which he was discussing Italian Gothic architecture, he turned to the realities of his own time, and in a trenchant response to Smith's *Wealth of Nations* (see Sidebar 1), lamented:

We have much studied and much perfected, of late, the great civilized invention of the division of labour; only we give it a false name. It is not, truly speaking, the labour that is divided; but the men:—Divided into mere segments of men—broken into small fragments and crumbs of life; so that all the little piece of intelligence that is left in a man is not enough to make a pin, or a nail, but exhausts itself in making the point of a pin, or the head of a nail. Now it is a good and desirable thing to make many pins in a day; but if we could only see with what crystal sand their points were polished,—sand of human soul, much to be magnified before it can be discerned for what it is,—we should think there might be some loss in it also. And the great cry that rises from all our manufacturing cities, louder than their furnace blast, is all in very deed for this,—that we manufacture everything there except men; we blanch cotton, and strengthen steel, and refine sugar, and shape pottery; but to brighten, to strengthen, to refine, or to form a single living spirit, never enters in to our estimate of advantages.

In advocating the return to a craft-based society that referenced Gothic times, Ruskin championed individual expression and the signs of handwork that came with craftsmanship—roughness,

inaccuracy, asymmetry, irregularity—valuing an aesthetic that not surprisingly was completely at odds with what could best be achieved by machines, which could provide a high finish and precision from one object to the next.

William Morris, Ruskin's disciple, and designer, craftsman, entrepreneur, poet, translator, conservationist, and socialist, likewise favored the romantic ideal of the simple, satisfied life of the medieval craftsman, deploring the harm that the machine had done to English culture and working hard to save what was left of it. Like Ruskin, he sought the return of design to a craft-based production, relying on ornament to give pleasure both to those who used the products and to those who made them (see Sidebar 2). His insistence on

SIDEBAR 2   William Morris, "The Lesser Arts," 1877

I have not undertaken to talk to you of Architecture, Sculpture, and Painting, in the narrower sense of those words, since, most unhappily as I think, these master-arts, these arts more specially of the intellect, are at the present day divorced from decoration in its narrower sense. Our subject is that great body of art, by means of which men have at all times more or less striven to beautify the familiar matters of everyday life: a wide subject, a great industry; both a great part of the history of the world, and a most helpful instrument to the study of that history.

A very great industry indeed, comprising the crafts of house-building, painting, joinery and carpentry, smiths' work, pottery and glass-making, weaving, and many others: a body of art most important to the public in general, but still more so to us handicraftsmen; since there is scarce anything that they use, and that we fashion, but it has always thought to be unfinished till it has had some touch or other of decoration about it. True it is that in many or most cases we have got so used to this ornament, that we look upon it as if it had grown of itself, and note it no more than the mosses on the dry sticks with which we light our fires. So much the worse! For

there *is* the decoration, or some pretence of it, and it has, or ought to have, a use and a meaning. For, and this is at the root of the whole matter, everything made by man's hands has a form, which must be either beautiful or ugly; beautiful if it is accord with Nature, and helps her; ugly if it is discordant with Nature, and thwarts her; it cannot be indifferent: we, for our parts, are busy or sluggish, eager or unhappy, and our eyes are apt to get dulled to this eventfulness of form in those things which we are always looking at. Now it is one of the chief uses of decoration, the chief part of its alliance with nature, that it has to sharpen our dulled senses in this matter: for this end are those wonders of intricate patterns interwoven, those strange forms invented, which men have so delighted in: forms and intricacies that do not necessarily imitate nature, but in which the hand of the craftsman is guided to work in the way that she does, till the web, the cup, or the knife, look as natural, nay as lovely, as the green field, the river bank, or the mountain flint.

To give people pleasure in the things they must perforce *use*, that is one great office of decoration; to give people pleasure in the things they must perforce *make*, that is the other use of it.

staying true to his materials and maintaining the quality of fine workmanship in the face of mass production, his determination (albeit unsuccessful) to make well-designed goods economically accessible, and his faith that eventually everyone would find pleasure in their work have inspired makers in their choice of occupation and their quest for excellence ever since.

Morris, who had come under the influence of Ruskin while attending Oxford, apprenticed himself to one of England's most individualistic Gothic Revival architects, George Edmund Street (1824–1881), in 1856. But he soon abandoned architecture for art, and then turned to design, if only by chance. Dissatisfaction with the decorated machine-made products of his day, many sold at the large shops that had emerged after the 1851

exhibition inspired a great burst of consumerism, led him to create his own simple furnishings for his new home, Red House. This was a picturesque brick dwelling just outside of London, which he commissioned in 1859 from his friend the architect Philip Webb (1831–1915) (Figure 2.1). Webb, following Morris's vision, built him a charming house of red-orange brick using vernacular, or local and traditional, techniques and adding such medieval elements as turrets, pointed arches, and windows of different sizes and shapes placed asymmetrically, which captured the sense of a simpler past. Furnishing the house was both a challenge and an adventure, and Morris invited his artist friends to join him and his wife, Jane Morris (1839–1914), in this enterprise. Together they painted murals and patterned ceilings, designed

FIGURE 2.1.   Philip Webb and William Morris, Red House, Bexleyheath, Kent, England, 1859–60.

stained glass and furniture, and embroidered textiles to fit out its interior following reform principles of fitness, honesty, and simplicity.

In 1861, testing the commercial possibilities of introducing their vision of simplicity to design, he teamed up with Webb and five other friends—Ford Maddox Brown (1821–1893), Sir Edward Burne-Jones (1833–1898), and Dante Gabriel Rossetti (1828–1882), painters and members of the Pre-Raphaelite Brotherhood, who took extreme realism as the essentials of their art; and two Oxford associates, Peter Paul Marshall (1830–1900) and Charles Faulkner (1833–1892)—to set up a decorating firm, Morris, Marshall, Faulkner & Company (years later reorganized as Morris & Company). In their shop in London they sold everything needed to furnish an entire house in a simple style—furniture, glasswares, pottery, tiles, metalwork, textiles, stained glass, and other household objects—much of which was designed by the partners and produced in their own workshops.

The line of utilitarian Sussex chairs, pieces designed by several of the partners and introduced about 1861, was the most successful of all the firm's products and the closest they ever came to the affordable furnishings that Morris had hoped to produce. These were made of lathe-turned, ebonized (blackened) or stained wood (Figure 2.2), simplified versions of what was known as "fancy back" chairs, extra chairs brought out for parties and dances or used for furnishing the less-important areas of fine houses. As much as Morris tried, he could not bring any other examples of such well-designed and well-crafted objects to those with modest means, prevented by the economics of handcraftsmanship and the small production runs that this fledgling firm could afford. But he encouraged those who came to hear him lecture all over England to follow his ideals, admonishing them to "have nothing in your houses that you do not know to be useful or believe to be beautiful."

One of the firm's early commissions was the decoration of the Green Dining Room in the

FIGURE 2.2.   Attributed to Philip Webb, Sussex Chair, c. 1861. Made by Morris, Marshall, Faulkner & Company. Ebonized beech and rush seat.

new South Kensington Museum in London in 1865–67, where Henry Cole had become its first director (Figure 2.3). Designed by Webb and Morris, with painted panels and stained glass by Burne-Jones, the densely patterned room with its horizontal bands of eclectic ornamentation stood as a public advertisement for the complete decorating services that Morris's firm could perform. Theirs was a layered ensemble of contrasting patterns: the bottom part of the wall, or dado, is paneled in blue-green; above are painted figures of the months alternating with fruit-tree branches and foliage against a golden ground by Burne-Jones; then an allover pattern of olive branches and above, a gilded classical frieze with hounds chasing hares by Webb;

FIGURE 2.3.   Philip Webb, William Morris, and Sir Edward Burne-Jones, Green Dining Room, South Kensington (now Victoria and Albert) Museum, London, 1865–67.

and culminating in a white plaster ceiling with conventionalized floral designs.

Morris himself obsessively practiced many traditional crafts, most of which he taught himself. A gifted pattern maker, he created designs for textiles, wallpapers, carpets, tapestries, tiles, and stained glass. His preferred subjects were flowers, fruit, and animals, and his attachment to natural forms can be seen in his Trellis wallpaper from 1864 with its lively arrangement of red roses and green leaves, blue birds (which were added by Webb), and a variety of insects against the orderly green grid of the trellis (Figure 2.4). This wallpaper, the first he designed, was inspired by the trellises

of roses in the medieval-style garden he planted at Red House. His last great achievement was the Kelmscott Press, the printing office he established in 1891, where he designed books and type faces, set type, and in its six years of existence, published fifty-two titles. These included his own poems and stories, literary works of his own era, and legends and writings from the past, culminating in an edition of the works of Geoffrey Chaucer (1342/43–1400). With eighty-five woodcut illustrations by Burne-Jones, his own dense floral decorations in the margins, and type and layout that he designed himself, it was completed in 1896, just before Morris's death (Figure 2.5).

FIGURE 2.4.   William Morris, Trellis Wallpaper, 1864.
Printed by Jeffrey & Co. Block-printed paper.

the ideal of honest handwork was honored and the status of craft was elevated. The most important among them were, in England, the Century Guild, established by the architect A. H. Mackmurdo (1851–1942) and the designer Selwyn Image (1849–1930) in 1882, and the School and Guild of Handicraft, established by C. R. Ashbee (1863–1942) in 1887 and 1888, respectively. Mackmurdo and Image summed up the perspective of many of these associations in their journal, *The Hobby Horse*, first published in 1886: "The aim of the Century Guild is to render all branches of Art the sphere, no longer of the tradesman, but of the artist . . . to emphasize the *Unity of Art*; and by thus dignifying Art in all its forms, it hopes to make it living, a thing of our own century, and of the people." In the United States, the Roycroft community, established in 1895, was an early such association, while in Austria, the Vienna Workshop (Wiener Werkstätte) was established in 1903.

The story of the Guild of Handicraft underscores some of the difficulties surrounding these associations and their faith in handcraftsmanship. Ashbee was an adherent of both the social and aesthetic ideas of Morris, building the school and guild into a successful craft workshop in the impoverished East End of London at the end of the nineteenth century. It was best known for its decorative metalwork, especially that of Ashbee himself, often luxury items like this bowl with elongated curved handles made of silver, colored enamel, and mother-of-pearl (Figure 2.6). In 1902, as a utopian experiment, Ashbee moved the guild to Chipping Camden in the English countryside; he conceived it as home to those who wanted to live the ideal communal life of the craftsman, where the joy of work and the art of life were conjoined without the intrusion of any trace of modern machinery or often even modern conveniences. The move was initially successful, but within just a few years the guild ran into financial troubles and had to be restructured in an attempt to survive with its principle of handcraftsmanship intact. But by 1907, the guild had closed its doors.

It was not so much Morris's work, however admirable it was, as his ideology that made his lasting reputation. Although he is closely associated with the Arts and Crafts Movement, which he inspired, he himself remained independent of it, and he did not participate in the exhibitions of the Arts and Crafts Exhibition Society (founded in 1888), which gave the movement its name. Many organizations took up Morris's (and Ruskin's) lead, however, creating schools and workshops in which

FIGURE 2.5.   William Morris and Sir Edward Burne-Jones, *The Works of Geoffrey Chaucer*, 1896. Printed at the Kelmscott Press.

Over the next years as he worked as a teacher and met with the architect Frank Lloyd Wright during his travels in the United States, Ashbee reversed his views on the machine and its social benefits, and by 1911 in his book *Should We Stop Teaching Art*, he could write: "Modern civilization rests on machinery, and no system for the endowment, or the encouragement, or the teaching of art can be sound that does not recognize this."

The line between the retrogressive, anti-machine attitudes of the Arts and Crafts Movement in England and the forward-looking attitude to design that would take hold in the United States at the turn of the century was definitively drawn by Frank Lloyd Wright (1867–1959). In his lecture "The Art and Craft of the Machine," which he presented in Chicago in 1901, Wright expressed a "deepening conviction that in the Machine lies the only future of art and craft—as I believe, a glorious future; that the Machine is, in fact, the metamorphosis of ancient art and craft; that we are at last face to face with the machine—the Modern Sphinx—whose riddle the artist must solve if he would that art live." While he extoled in futuristic terms a world

FIGURE 2.6.
C. R. Ashbee, Bowl and Spoon, 1903. Made by the Guild of Handicraft. Silver, enamel, and mother of pearl.

run by machines, his answer to the riddle for the artist of his day was more practical, acclaiming the possibilities of the machine as "the normal tool of our civilization." For him, the tool belonged to the artist-craftsman more than the factory worker, and only rarely were Wright's own designs industrially produced.

Aesthetic Movement

The Aesthetic Movement brought design into a personal sphere; it was free of any dogma, promoting art as an end in itself based on individual feeling and a refined lifestyle to which all the arts— painting, decorative arts, interior design, literature, music—would contribute harmoniously. It shared much with William Morris, particularly his credo of simplicity and his striving for "artistic" harmony, and Morris & Company products were frequently found in Aesthetic homes. But the goal of social improvement and the disdain for the machine

that Ruskin, Morris, and their followers exhibited had little interest for those who found themselves among the Aesthetes.

Aestheticism took the unified interior as its artistic domain, mirrored in the decorating advice given by the writer and museum curator Charles Locke Eastlake (1836–1906) in his popular guide *Hints on Household Taste in Furniture, Upholstery and Other Details* (1868), which went through many editions in Great Britain and the United States. Eastlake's book was directed to women, whose role it now was to be the designer and guardian of the home, urging them to follow the reform principles of good taste and restraint in design that had been promoted over the past years. The frontispiece of *The House Beautiful* (1878), written by Clarence Cook (1828–1900), an American art critic following in Eastlake's mold, stood as a model for the values of the upper-middle-class Aesthetic home (Figure 2.7). Drawn by Walter Crane (1845–1915), an English designer and book illustrator and friend and collaborator of

"MY LADY'S CHAMBER"

FIGURE 2.7. Walter Crane, "My Lady's Chamber," from Clarence Cook, *The House Beautiful*, 1878.

William Morris, it is an image of ideal domesticity with an elegant, simply attired woman pouring tea from a silver urn accompanied by a satisfied cat licking milk in the foreground. She is surrounded by tasteful objects drawn from different periods: an eighteenth-century armchair and tea urn, a Morris & Company Sussex armchair (see Figure 2.2), patterned wallpaper, blue and white tiles, Chinese blue and white porcelain, and Japanese fans. Its harmony of simple eclecticism fitted out with objects removed from their symbolic and cultural associations was meant to be serendipitous, a chance arrangement of comfortable pieces that seemed to work together without regard for their origins or their designers.

Aestheticism was a loose movement created by a small group who considered themselves "enlightened" members of the artistic class responsive to art for its own sake, with aesthetic and intellectual aspirations and outward manifestations of elite refinement that easily opened them up to satire and parody. The Gilbert and Sullivan spoof *Patience*, an operetta from 1881 that had long runs in London and in the United States, lampooned the young Irish playwright and dandy Oscar Wilde (1854–1900) as the personification of the movement, who the following year toured the United States to promote it. The satires did not stop with operettas, but included cartoons, popular songs, calling cards, and advertisements, which often made fun of the Aesthetic attachment to the sunflower, peacock feather, and lily, its symbols of constancy, beauty, and purity. In his timely book *The Aesthetic Movement in England*, published in 1882, Walter Hamilton provided an insight into what Aestheticism was really all about. "The essence of the movement," he wrote, "is the union of persons of cultivated tastes to define, and to decide upon, what is to be admired, and their followers must aspire to that standard in their works and lives. Vulgarity, however, wealthy it may be, can never be admitted into this exclusive brotherhood, for riches without taste are of no avail, whilst taste without money, or with very little, can always effect much."

The later nineteenth century witnessed a mania for Japanese art and design in the West, and Japanese objects were particularly to be found in Aesthetic homes. Artifacts from Japan began to arrive in England soon after the country was forcedly opened to foreign trade in 1853–54 by the American Commodore Matthew Perry (1794–1858) and drew great interest after an unofficial showing of some thousand lacquers, bronzes, silks, china, and other objects at the Japanese Court at the International Exhibition of 1862 in London. By the time of the official entry of Japan at the Universal Exposition in Paris in 1867, things Japanese had become almost a cliché, and they could be readily found in such specialty shops as Liberty in London, which opened in 1875. Japanese objects and prints greatly influenced

Western art and design from Impressionist painting to graphics and furniture. These included the works of the English architect and journalist E. W. Godwin (1835–1886), who furnished his own house in 1867 and other architectural commissions with his interpretation of it, which he conceived in a blended style that he dubbed "Anglo-Japanese." His spare, ebonized sideboard with inset panels of embossed Japanese leather paper from 1867–70 is reduced to a simple openwork structural grid that would, however, have been softened by the many Aesthetic objects displayed on its surfaces (Figure 2.8). This is an early example of his exploration of the Anglo-Japanese style, which he said borrowed Japanese principles, not Japanese forms, describing

his concept for this severe furniture as having "no mouldings, no ornamental metal work, no carving. Such effect as I wanted I endeavoured to gain, as in economical building, by the mere grouping of solid and void and by a more or less broken outline."

Christopher Dresser was also devoted to Japanese design, and the travel records that he published in 1882 after returning from a trip there, *Japan: Its Architecture, Art, and Art Manufactures*, gave an unprecedented picture of the country's achievements. He immediately designed a series of metal objects, among them electroplated silver tureens, whose understated forms were derived from treasures he saw in the Japanese imperial collections (Figure 2.9). By this time, Dresser had already published *The Art*

FIGURE 2.8.   E. W. Godwin, Sideboard, 1867–70. Made by William Watt & Co. Ebonized mahogany, silver-plated metal, and embossed Japanese leather paper.

FIGURE 2.9.   Christopher Dresser, Tureen, 1880. Made by Hukin & Heath. Electroplated silver and ebonized wood.

FIGURE 2.10.   Christopher Dresser, U-Shaped Vase, 1886 or 1889. Made by Minton. Glazed and gilded porcelain.

of Decorative Design (1862) and become a full-time designer, moving beyond botany to draw on many other sources for the forms and ornamentation of his work. Because some of his metal works lacked surface ornamentation and their manufacture was economical, Dresser has been seen as a precursor of modern design, although the forms of these objects were clearly derived from historic precedents, those of ancient Greece as well as Japan. Dresser was a great eclectic, able to move easily from culture to culture and medium to medium, drawing ideas from each and easily combining them into unified designs. An industrially molded U-shaped porcelain vase, made by Minton, combines the form of a pre-Colombian vessel with an intense blue glaze imitative of that of the Sèvres Porcelain Factory and a gilded band of chrysanthemums designed in a Japanese style, which was applied by transfer printing (Figure 2.10). Because of his extensive output of pottery, textiles, glass, metalware, furniture, and textiles and his collaboration with some fifty different manufacturers, Dresser has gained the reputation of being the first true industrial designer.

With the display of both Japanese and "aesthetic" objects at the Centennial Exhibition in Philadelphia in 1876, held to celebrate the one hundredth anniversary of the signing of the Declaration of

Independence, the Aesthetic Movement gained a significant following in the United States. Women especially responded to the decorative arts that were shown there, arts that were allied to those that many had already learned at home and at school. The exhibition gave birth to the American art pottery movement, spurred by the enthusiasm of many visitors for the artistic ceramics seen there. One of the visitors, Maria Longworth Nichols (1849–1932), was an amateur china painter whose work was on view in the Women's Pavilion at the exhibition and who was particularly attracted to the displays of Japanese pottery. She returned to her home in Cincinnati hoping to bring a Japanese pottery to the United States, but she then decided to establish her own ceramic works, naming it Rookwood after her family's estate. Opened in 1880, Rookwood was one of the earliest American art potteries, which like many others began as an amateur undertaking, but it soon turned into a highly successful commercial venture, taking many prizes at international exhibitions and remaining in business until 1967. Nichols designed many of the first pieces herself, but the following year she began to hire other designers, with the first full-time painter being the American Albert Valentien (1862–1925), who would become Rookwood's head decorator. One of the early pieces that Nichols herself created was her Aladdin vase, painted with sea creatures caught in a golden net. This belonged to a group of works greatly influenced by Japanese pottery that was described in *Harper's* magazine in 1881 as depicting "the inevitable dragon coiled about the neck of the vase, or at its base varied with gods, wise men, the sacred mountain, storks, owls, monsters of the air and water, bamboo, etc., decorated in high relief, underglaze color, incised design, and an overglaze enrichment of gold" (Figure 2.11). In spite of its industrial organization with a true division of labor, Rookwood was quick to position itself as different from commercial potteries, announcing in its literature that it was "an artist's studio, not a factory," and its ceramics, which were produced in many different styles, were cited as "fine arts."

Among other potteries and associations that emerged in the wake of the Centennial was the Cincinnati Pottery Club, founded in 1879 by an innovative ceramist and rival of Nichols from Cincinnati, Marie Louise McLaughlin (1847–1939). This was the first American pottery association, which gathered its members from a large number of local women who had become dedicated to decorating ceramics. It served as inspiration for many other American social and educational groups, from the pottery opened in 1895 at Newcomb College in New Orleans (now part of Tulane University) to the Saturday Evening Girls Club in Boston, which from 1906 to 1908 taught the craft to immigrant women.

Candace Wheeler (1827–1924), an amateur American artist and needleworker, was inspired by the artistic English embroideries exhibited at the Centennial by the Royal School of Art Needlework.

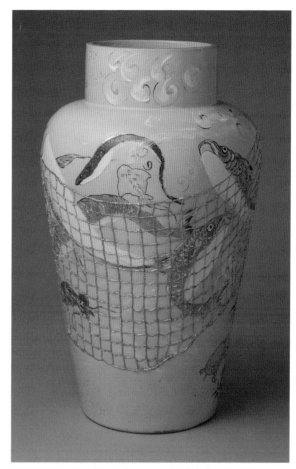

FIGURE 2.11.   Maria Longworth Nichols, Aladdin Vase, c. 1881. Made by Rookwood. Glazed and gilded earthenware.

The school had been founded in London in 1872 to revive the art of embroidery and to help women prepare for employment, and Wheeler went on to establish similar organizations in New York. Soon she found herself in the design profession, in 1879 joining the well-connected painter and designer Louis Comfort Tiffany (1848–1933) in a decorating firm, Tiffany and Wheeler (which in 1880 expanded into Louis C. Tiffany and Company, Associated Artists). The firm was renowned for its eclectic interiors, like the one they designed for the American humorist author Mark Twain (1835–1910) in Hartford in 1881. As partner and textile specialist Wheeler quickly became influential as an interior decorator, and like Eastlake, gave aesthetic

SIDEBAR 3   Candace Wheeler, "The Philosophy of Beauty Applied to House Interiors," 1893

The instinct of the house-maker may do much, but it cannot, without study of appropriateness in every direction, make even the simplest summer cottage a true expression of beauty.

The instinct of home-making which abides in the minds of women at the present period in America is greatly stimulated by a very general artistic impulse—a drift of the popular mind towards art. The enjoyment of perfected methods of manufacture, of beautiful lines and surfaces, of exquisite harmonies of color—in short, of the material creations of the true artist-artisan—is an almost universal feminine experience.

It follows that those who are possessed of this artistic insight and love of beauty not only find the keenest enjoyment in the natural exercise of those gifts in house-furnishing, but often produce most charming and original effects by the clever choice and happy arrangement of things which go to make up the home.

It is true that they sometimes fail in compassing the fitness or appropriateness which makes the full perfection of this beautiful art, and shirk the preliminary study which is necessary to thorough completeness. They are apt to follow fancy and taste not based upon the requirements of circumstances, and as a consequence the result is a lack of the restfulness and calm which are given by careful fitting of beauty upon use.

A perfectly furnished house is a crystallization of the culture, the habits, and the tastes of the family, and not only expresses but makes character.

and practical decorating advice with a moral overtone to housewives in her popular articles and books (see Sidebar 3). After her partnership with Tiffany was dissolved in 1883, she borrowed "Associated Artists" from its name and started her own textile firm, where wall hangings, tapestries, and curtains were made by both hand and factory production, all done exclusively by women employees. Wheeler herself was inspired by the Japanese aesthetic of nature when she depicted the languid, interlaced tulips for a wall hanging made of pieces of velvet fabric appliquéd, or stitched, to a golden metallic-silk background (but which she never finished) (Figure 2.12).

While English Aesthetes were typically defined by their refined, understated taste, the Aesthetic Movement in the United States had different tendencies, making inroads with the very wealthy. Industrial magnates built great mansions and

FIGURE 2.12. Candace Wheeler, Tulips Panel, 1883–87. Made by Associated Artists. Appliquéd silk and metallic cloth.

furnished them with an abundance of eclectic objects as a way to show off their riches, what the American economist Thorstein Veblen (1857–1929) famously called "conspicuous consumption." These wondrous ensembles depended on large decorating establishments such as Tiffany and Wheeler's Associated Artists and on the art dealers who sold the paintings, sculptures, and decorative objects that these millionaires collected. One of the leading American decorating firms was Herter Brothers in New York, which was founded in 1865 and could supply every aspect of decorative design that was required. Their workers produced entire ensembles in a variety of revival and exotic styles, most importantly, in the Anglo-Japanese mode

that was a hallmark of the American Aesthetic Movement. The Fifth Avenue mansion of William Henry Vanderbilt (1821–1885), heir to his family's enormous shipping and railroad fortune, was their most lavish interior commission (Figure 2.13). *Artistic Houses*, two volumes published in 1883 and 1884 that illustrated the dwellings of America's elite, could scarcely find enough superlatives to praise the house and its eclectic interiors, which Herter furnished between 1879 and 1882. "The effect is gorgeous in the extreme," *Artistic Houses* gushed. "Everything sparkles and flashes with gold and color—with mother-of-pearl, with marbles, with jewel-effects in glass—and almost every surface is covered, one might say weighted, with ornament."

FIGURE 2.13. Herter Brothers, Drawing Room, William H. Vanderbilt House, New York, 1879–82, from *Artistic Houses*, 1883–84.

Art Nouveau

The two decades from 1890 to 1910 witnessed a turning point in the history of design, when the decoration of the past was first renounced and a sequence of distinct new artistic expressions appeared, each asserting itself as the ornament of modernity. Known generally as Art Nouveau, or the New Art, this was an experimental movement that saw an outpouring of new forms in many stylistic variations, some sinuous and organic, others naturalistic, and others geometric. Still others called on folk designs in a revival of nationalistic spirit, seen, for example, in the interlaced linear patterns of the metalwork of Archibald Knox (1864–1933), chief designer for the London department store Liberty, that were sparked by the renewal of interest in the Celtic traditions of Scotland and Ireland (Figure 2.14). While international Art Nouveau drew on many and diverse artistic sources, it was initially inspired by British design, images of which were featured in such journals as *The Studio*, launched in 1893, the first art magazine to spread news of this new style emanating from the United Kingdom.

The French term "Art Nouveau," which was also taken as the movement's name in English, was borrowed from that of the gallery that the German-born art critic and entrepreneur Siegfried Bing (1838–1905) opened in 1895 in Paris, where he showed radical developments in international design. In Germany the style was known as Jugendstil (Style of Youth, after the name of an avant-garde magazine, *Jugend*, or *Youth*, founded in 1896), and in Austria it was called Sezessionstil (after the Secession, a radical group founded by revolutionary artists and students who in 1896 seceded from the official Viennese art academy). In Italy, it was called Stile Liberty after the decorative fabrics that Liberty's sold abroad, while their curving floral motifs suggested the alternate Italian name, Stile Floreale. In other centers of the international movement, like Prague, Moscow, and Barcelona, the names for the style were adapted from their terms for "modern."

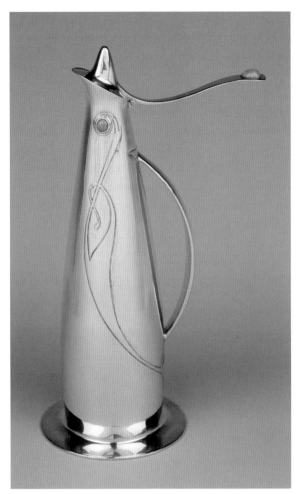

FIGURE 2.14.   Archibald Knox, Claret Jug, 1900–1901. Made by W. H. Haseler. Silver and chrysoprase.

Art Nouveau immediately embraced the widest range of mediums, from painting and interior furnishings to graphics and advertising, with the goal of creating total, harmonious designs through an all-encompassing vision of the unification of the arts. It could not have made its mark without the loosening of the distinctions that had been set up centuries earlier, during the Renaissance, between the intellectual fine arts and the manual decorative arts. Beginning in 1890 with the first exhibition of the dissident National Society of Fine Arts (Société Nationale des Beaux-Arts) in Paris, the annual art salons and international exhibitions opened their galleries to both, showing decorative arts alongside painting and sculpture.

Among the foreign designers whose work Siegfried Bing represented was Louis Comfort Tiffany, who had moved on from his decorating business to producing art glass, opening a glass studio in New York in 1893. He employed highly skilled craftsmen to execute his spectacular designs for what he trademarked as Favrile (hand-blown) glass, looking to nature for inspiration and borrowing techniques of glassmaking from those of ancient civilizations. Bing himself stood in awe of Tiffany's achievement and in 1898 marveled at the difficulty of "rendering Nature in her most seductive aspects" as Tiffany had done so well in creating his Peacock vase (Figure 2.15): "This power which the artist possesses of assigning in advance to each morsel of glass, whatever its colour or chemical composition, the exact place which it is to occupy when the article leaves the glassblower's hands—this truly unique art is combined in these peacocks' feathers with the charm of iridescence which bathes the subtle and velvety ornamentation with an almost supernatural light."

Belgium was one of the first centers to witness the large-scale emergence of a sinuous Art Nouveau style, where the architects and designers Paul Hankar (1859–1901), Victor Horta (1861–1947), Gustave Serrurier-Bovy (1858–1910), and Henry van de Velde (1863–1957) introduced it in the early 1890s. From 1893 to 1903, Horta defined and refined the elements of the style in Brussels, principally for private houses in which the architecture and furnishings were stylistically unified and conceived as total works of art. His architecture explored the structural and decorative use of cast iron, and his light-filled buildings were profusely decorated with organic motifs, extreme curvilinear forms inspired by nature. Horta's Tassel house in Brussels, built in 1892–93, perhaps best exemplifies this new style (Figure 2.16). Taking the vitality of the whiplash, which would become one of the quintessential motifs of organic Art Nouveau, he insistently repeated in paint, tile, and ironwork interlacing tendrils turning back on themselves,

FIGURE 2.15. Louis Comfort Tiffany, Peacock Vase, 1893–96. Favrile glass.

FIGURE 2.16. Victor Horta, Staircase, Hôtel Tassel, Brussels, 1892–93.

SIDEBAR 4   Henry van de Velde, "A Chapter on the Design and Construction of Modern Furniture," 1897

We can succeed in modernising the appearances of things by carrying out the simple intention to be strictly rational, by following the principle of rejecting without exception all forms and ornamentation which a modern factory could not easily manufacture and reproduce, by plainly stating the essential structure of every piece of furniture and object and by constantly bearing in mind that they must be easy to use. Is there anything which has been the object of keener striving for new forms than a hall-stand, a folding-table, or an armchair? And yet these articles simply show that new results can be obtained by using means and materials which are as old as the

hills. And I must confess that my own means are the same as those which were used in the very early stages of popular arts and crafts. It is only because I understand and marvel at how simply, coherently and beautifully a ship, weapon, car, or wheelbarrow is built that my work is able to please the few remaining rationalists who realise that what has seemed odd to others has in fact been produced by following unassailable traditional principles, in other words unconditionally and resolutely following the functional logic of an article and being unreservedly honest about the materials employed, which naturally vary with the means of each.

which could be seen on the walls, ceiling, floor, and railing of its resplendent hall.

Van de Velde, originally a painter, interpreted Art Nouveau differently, as a rational, structural style with a freedom from representation that was entirely new (see Sidebar 4). Following the example of William Morris, to whom he was devoted, van de Velde found little artistic choice but to design his own house, Bloemenwerf, which he built outside of Brussels in 1895 and furnished with functional, unified forms and patterns of taut Art Nouveau curves. The chairs he originally conceived for the dining room followed his rational principle of "plainly stating the essential structure of every piece of furniture," giving the structural members a tense, outwardly curving linearity (Figure 2.17). Although French critics decried his furnishings when they appeared in the opening exhibition of Bing's gallery L'Art Nouveau in 1895, the reaction was just the opposite when they were shown in an exhibition in Germany in 1897. This encouraged him to open a workshop in Brussels the next year, where he produced these chairs and many other designs in quantity, with his trade card announcing that he could supply "complete interior furnishings,

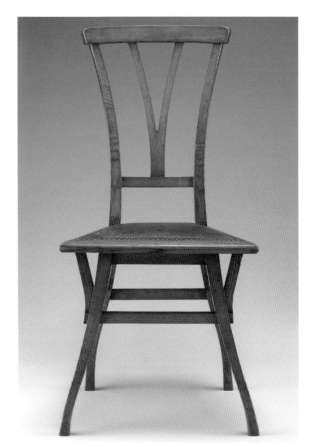

FIGURE 2.17.   Henry van de Velde, Chair, c. 1898. Made by Societé Van de Velde. Elm, leather, and brass.

FIGURE 2.18. Hector Guimard, Entrance to Métro on the Boulevard Pasteur, Paris, c. 1900.

wallpaper, carpets, embroideries, stained glass, fixtures for both gas and electric lighting, jewelry, useful and ornamental objects."

France saw its own flourishing of Art Nouveau, with both an abstract and a naturalistic vocabulary. The architect Hector Guimard (1867–1942) was its most visible designer; he created a personal expression using curvilinear forms that became known in France as the "Style Guimard." His were some of the most recognizable structures of Paris: the cast-iron stations of the Métro, the underground rail system built in Paris in conjunction with the Universal Exposition, which opened there in 1900. One of Guimard's designs for the entrances of the Métro is signaled by its large floral-inspired lamps framing a great metal arch and the intertwined vegetal ornament on its stairway plaques, with the urbane typography he developed for the transportation system summing up the lyricism of his style (Figure 2.18).

The designer, botanist, and horticulturist Emile Gallé (1846–1904) looked to nature as

the single source of modern ornament. For him, it was to be represented truthfully, although he often gave it symbolic meaning by inscribing his works with quotations that added suggestion and association to his images. Gallé was an adherent of Symbolism, a literary and artistic movement founded in the 1880s that included such figures as the French writer Charles Baudelaire (1821–1867) and painter Paul Gauguin (1848–1903) and the Austrian artist Gustav Klimt (1862–1918). It emphasized subjectivity, drawing on dreams and new developments in psychology to give insights into artistic expression. Gallé's tall bottle-shaped vase ornamented with flying swallows is an example of what he called "talking glasswares," artistic forms annotated with evocative lines from literature (Figure 2.19). On the base of the vase he painted the opening lines from the poem "What the Swallows Say" by the French writer Theophile Gautier (1811–1872), which speak sorrowfully of the annual migration of the birds and the impending return of winter: "The rain splashes in

FIGURE 2.19.   Emile Gallé, Bottle with Swallows (La Pluie au Bassin Fait des Bulles), 1889. Enameled glass.

the basin; The swallows on the roof hold secret gatherings: Winter is here, cold is here."

In Glasgow between 1896 and 1910, the architect Charles Rennie Mackintosh (1868–1928) introduced a new artistic style with an abstracted geometric and Symbolist vocabulary, clearly seen in the graphic works he did in tandem with the Group of Four. Formed in the early 1890s with three fellow students at the Glasgow School of Art, Herbert MacNair (1868–1955), Frances Macdonald (1873–1921), and her sister and Mackintosh's future wife Margaret Macdonald (1864–1933), the group designed gravely symbolic posters and paintings that earned them the name "Spook School." The meaning of his symmetrical, stylized design of an elongated haloed woman accompanied by song birds and overprinted with a symbolic flowering tree of life remains enigmatic, even if it appeared on the streets of Glasgow as an eight-foot-high billboard poster in 1896 advertising the *Scottish Musical Review*, a magazine published between 1894 and 1897 (Figure 2.20).

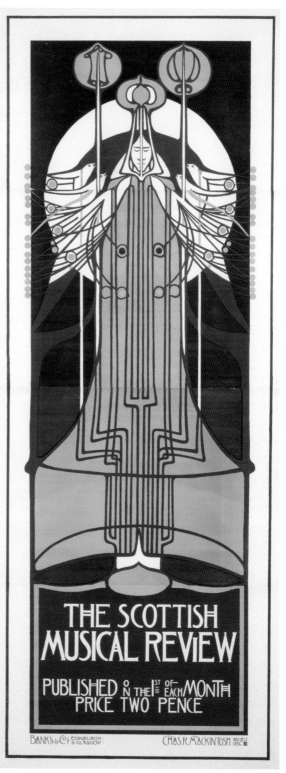

FIGURE 2.20.   Charles Rennie Mackintosh, Poster for the *Scottish Musical Review*, 1896. Printed by Banks & Co. Lithograph.

In his buildings, notably the Glasgow School of Art (erected between 1897 and 1909), as well as Hill House (a private home built in Helensburgh, north of Glasgow, in 1902–3), Mackintosh introduced a geometric expression to Art Nouveau architecture. But at Hill House he left room for symbolic organic form, also. The stenciled decoration on the walls of the bright drawing-room alcove has both a black-and-white checkerboard motif and abstracted, pink roses, a romantic motif suggesting art, love, and beauty, which recurs throughout the house (Figure 2.21). But its blackened furniture and built-in white settee and shelves are purely geometric, probably influenced by the forms of Japanese design and inspired by the rectilinear work of E. W. Godwin as well (see Figure 2.8).

Mackintosh's geometric furnishings were shown in Vienna at the Secession exhibition in 1900, where the architect Josef Hoffmann (1870–1956) drew inspiration from them for his own ornamental, geometrical language. This was an essential element in the new Secession style, giving a unique identity to the crafts of the Vienna Workshop (Wiener Werkstätte), which he established in 1903 with the painter and designer Koloman Moser (1868–1918) and the industrialist and art patron Fritz Wärndorfer (1867–1939). The Vienna Workshop was a commercial venture pledged to Morris's ideals of simplicity, honesty, and integrity, although most of the decorative designs that the workshop produced, like Hoffmann's spectacular silver and ebony coffee service with its rounded vessels and strictly angular handles (Figure 2.22), were luxury items, not objects in the reach of workers that Morris had championed. Calling on the craftspeople who produced its furniture,

FIGURE 2.21.   Charles Rennie Mackintosh, Living Room, Hill House, Helensburgh, Scotland, 1902–3.

FIGURE 2.22. Josef Hoffmann, Tea Service, c. 1910. Made by Wiener Werkstätte. Silver, amethyst, carnelian, and ebony.

metalwork, glass, ceramics, and textiles made either in its own craft shops or by their industrial manufacturers, the Vienna Workshop could completely fulfill commissions for harmonious architectural interiors, which were often executed with geometric, mainly black and white, forms. Yet, while the Workshop had been founded with decoration as its intent, some of its earliest products were simple, unornamented, and ruthlessly rigorous designs made of perforated and painted industrial sheet iron, like Moser's geometric flower basket from 1904–6 (Figure 2.23). "We will seek to decorate," Moser and Hoffmann stated in the Workshop's founding program in 1905, but then they added, "without any compulsion to do so, and certainly not at any cost."

With the affirmation of Art Nouveau in a host of artistic centers from Russia to Spain and beyond, the call for a modern decorative style that began in the early nineteenth century had finally paid off. This was a totally original and broadly adopted style with an ornamental vocabulary free from any reference to the historic past. But it was short-lived and too late: short-lived because Art Nouveau was the victim of its own success, its

FIGURE 2.23. Koloman Moser, Flower Basket, 1904–6. Made by Wiener Werkstätte. Painted zinc-plated sheet iron.

wide and immediate popularity soon leading to the plummeting of its prestige, and too late because its ornamental undertakings overlapped with a new idea of design that was not about style and decoration but about form, a vision of modernity that was emerging as the twentieth century began.

DESIGN
AND FORM

1900 to 1940

CHAPTER 3

Birth of Modern Design

If design for the nineteenth century meant decoration, design for the twentieth century meant form (Figure 3.1). Even as Art Nouveau designers were searching for a modern style through decoration, others were rejecting the impulse to decorate, a legacy of eons and eons of human history (and prehistory), to discover modernity in simple, unadorned form. Beauty was no longer dependent upon adding ornament to an object, as Christopher Dresser had described, but something intrinsic to it in the simplicity of its shape, structure, material, texture, and color and in its function. Turning to form meant more than just the absence of decoration, however; it signified a new understanding of what modern design might be. Form brought universality to design, eliminating the distinctions of taste in ornament that came with education and privilege and offering the possibility of a design that could be grasped equally by the entire population even if it was not always to their liking.

How simple form came to define modern design can be attributed to a number of causes, but why and how it happened so quickly at the beginning of the twentieth century has still not been resolved. One of the factors behind the abandonment of ornament was the continuing authority of Arts and Crafts values, with their emphasis on simplicity. A second was the growing emphasis on efficiency in manufacture in which rationalized, standardized, undecorated forms were thought to be easier than decorated ones to fabricate by machine. A third was the influence of modern art movements and the advent of abstraction as a primary mode of twentieth-century artistic expression.

From Ornament to Form

The shift from ornament to form did not necessarily mean that a whole new class of objects had to be created; in a complete reversal of prestige, the countless utilitarian objects that had been omitted from design in the nineteenth century, like Thonet's 1859 bentwood chair (see Figure 1.2), were suddenly reassessed for their elegance of functional form. Form goes hand in hand with function, the two having been forever linked by the familiar expression "form follows function," which was appropriated from the writings of the Chicago architect Louis Sullivan (1856–1924). While the lack of decoration meant that the function of an object might now be more apparent, this phrase was misunderstood and misapplied to suggest that

FIGURE 3.1.   Richard Herre, Poster for Die Form (Form), 1924. Published by Deutsche Werkbund. Lithograph.

function alone should determine the form of an object, and if the form satisfied its function, the object would by its very nature be beautiful. By the 1930s it had become a rallying cry for legions of modern designers and architects, who adopted it as a notion that was central to their practice. But this belief, which dates back at least to classical Greece, had already been dispelled many times, as it was in 1913 by Hermann Muthesius (1861–1927), architect, civil servant, and spokesperson for progressive design in Germany. In his article "The Problem of Form in Engineering," he protested: "The idea that it is quite sufficient for the engineer designing a building, an appliance, a machine, merely to fulfill a purpose, is erroneous, and the recent oft-repeated suggestion that if the object fulfills its purpose then it is beautiful as well is even more erroneous. Usefulness has basically nothing to do with beauty. Beauty is a problem of form, and nothing else."

The centrality of form was underscored as the term took its place in the discourse of design during the first quarter of the century. *Form* was the name of a number of twentieth-century craft and design journals, among the first those of the Swedish Society of Industrial Design (Svenska Slöjdföreningen, founded in 1905) and of the German Werkbund, or Work Association (Deutscher Werkbund, founded in 1907), which renamed its journal *Form* in 1922. But modern form, at least in its early years, did not call for a single look or style, as was demonstrated when in 1924, the Werkbund mounted its exhibition Die Form with a catalogue entitled *Form without Ornament*. The Werkbund had been founded by Muthesius as an association of artists, industrialists, manufacturers, and merchants with the mission of upgrading the quality of German design by bringing artists to work in industry and creating a modern national style for the sake of Germany's economy and international reputation. The exhibition poster by Richard Herre (1885–1959), an architect, designer, and graphic artist whose furniture was

also included in the exhibition, depicts a large advertising kiosk drawn in extreme perspective with the text raised upon it in crisp, three-dimensional lettering. Its clean lines and modern sans-serif typeface (type that does not have small projections at the ends of the characters) would seem to suggest that the exhibition had a single premise, to display objects with an austere geometry like this, an industrial aesthetic that was then moving to the forefront of progressive design. But to respect the work of its designers of all aesthetic persuasions, the Werkbund showed a range of products that embodied the complex tensions and tendencies that modern design was experiencing in Europe as it was first being defined. While such products as stainless-steel cutlery, ovenproof-glass kitchenware, and metal door handles brought the industrial aesthetic into the exhibition, other objects that were displayed there revealed quite different attitudes. These included pieces that although simplified continued to draw inspiration from the historic styles of the past, from the energy of the Art Nouveau experience, and from the handwork of the Arts and Crafts movement, as well as geometric designs showing the influence of new developments in modern art. With such a diversity of artistic approaches, it was clear that a universal, full-blown aesthetic of modern form had not yet been achieved.

The emphasis on form in the twentieth century does not mean that decorated objects were not also produced during the period; they were and in great quantities, affirming the persistence of the basic human desire for decoration that would not be obliterated by the sudden emergence of new ideas from an avant-garde elite. Much of the continuing decorative design at this time seemed to retreat to the past, however. The historic ornament produced during the early twentieth century was generally less innovative than the revival designs of the nineteenth, when the past had been dramatically reconfigured as a new style for the present, but reproductive, where the past was recreated in the

FIGURE 3.2.   Advertisement for Victrola Record Player, 1922.

false guise of authenticity, as in much of American Colonial Revival design. New appliances for the home, such as radios, record players, and later televisions, typically relied on the comfort of historic styles for their form and their cabinetry. Although the dancers in a Victrola advertisement from 1922 are decked out in the latest fashions, their console record player uneasily recalls French furniture from the eighteenth century, with its concave panels, curvilinear moldings, and ball feet on casters, but tepid reminders of the elegance of French Rococo design (Figure 3.2).

At the same time, Emile-Jacques Ruhlmann (1879–1933), the most respected of French twentieth-century furniture makers, was updating traditional cabinetry, leading the field with his elegant works of the highest level of craftsmanship

and most luxurious of materials. His designs, which were executed by a large staff of architects and craftsmen, demonstrated how simplification and stylization could take traditional precedents and make them seem modern. His beautifully crafted decorative objects, like this lady's writing desk with its gently curving legs, exotic ebony wood, ivory inlays and drawer pulls, and silken tassels, revived the long tradition of fine design that had defined a national style (Figure 3.3). André Mare (1887–1932), a painter and decorator, gave his own prescription for reconstituting the national past for the modern day. "First of all," he wrote in a letter to the French glassmaker Maurice Marinot (1882–1960), "make something very *French*, stay within the tradition . . . Return to simple, pure, logical and even slightly harsh lines . . . return to

FIGURE 3.3.   Emile-Jacques Ruhlmann, Lady's Writing Desk, c. 1923. Macassar ebony, ivory, silver, and silk.

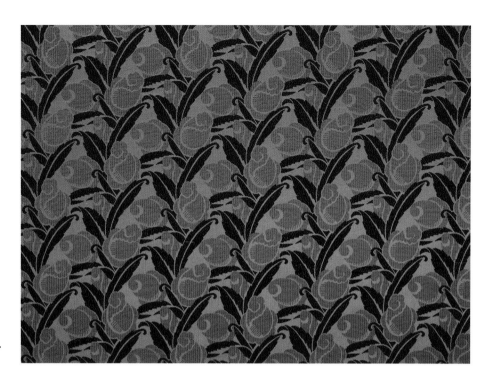

FIGURE 3.4. André Mare, Textile, c. 1923. Silk and cotton.

bold, very pure, very daring colors"—descriptive of the dense, bold pink and black floral pattern of one of his own silk textiles in which the stylized forms of the flowers and leaves are defined in swirling linear detail and flattened against the fabric's silken surface (Figure 3.4).

Many had hoped that the Art Nouveau explorations of new styles would save decoration, but its time was brief and had only a limited impact on the future development of modern design. Josef Hoffmann's attempt to create an ornament appropriate for the twentieth century through geometry was discredited, for example, by the Viennese architect and journalist Adolf Loos (1870–1933). Loos took aim at him, along with several Jugendstil masters, in his 1908 essay "Ornament and Crime," where he scoffed at Hoffmann's efforts as an unnecessary and pointless pursuit for the modern era. Loos adopted an aesthetic of simple form that was suggested by the industrial architecture and standardized commonplace products he had come across during the several years he spent in the United States. He was also taken by the subtlety of the English craft tradition, particularly its immaculate tailoring,

which he deeply admired and often praised in his journalistic writings. "Ornament and Crime," which is now read as an embarrassingly colonialist and racist diatribe, portrayed the history of design as a great Darwinian march of progress from the "urge to ornament" of tribal cultures to contemporary industrial society with its "lack of ornament," which he regarded as "a sign of intellectual power." This led to his claim that "the evolution of culture is synonymous with the removal of ornament from objects of daily use," adding "we have out-grown ornament, we have struggled through to a state without ornament." While his account of the march toward unadorned form was seemingly historic, his underlying argument was economic: ornament, he asserted, "represents a crime against the national economy, and, as a result of it, human labour, money and material are ruined." Why waste time, money, and manpower producing decorated goods, he essentially said, when simple and honest objects in standardized forms free from an ever-changing nod to style are already available to us. "Ornament and Crime" remained relatively unknown after the text was composed as a lecture in 1908 and then published obscurely in France a few years later, and it could have had little direct influence on the early international abandonment of decoration. Only after the essay was reprinted in 1920 in *L'Esprit Nouveau* (The New Spirit), the art journal that the Swiss-born French architect and painter Le Corbusier (originally Charles Edouard Jeanneret, 1887–1965) founded with several friends that year, did it get a wider readership and enter a larger discourse on the role of ornament in modern design.

The admiration for standardized objects that Loos described and his attack on what he saw as the decadence of decoration were assimilated by Le Corbusier in his own work. He had already been familiar with the strides taken in Germany toward the simplification and standardization of design, having published his *Study of the Decorative Arts Movement in Germany* in 1912 after an extended

study trip there. At the International Exposition of Modern Decorative and Industrial Arts in Paris in 1925, he and his Swiss architect-cousin Pierre Jeanneret (1896–1967) proposed a standardized way of building with their Esprit Nouveau pavilion, which was submitted under the patronage of Le Corbusier's journal. Jeanneret had joined him in a partnership in Paris in 1922 (which dissolved at the beginning of the Second World War and resumed in 1951) to which he brought the necessary architectural credentials for the new firm.

The Esprit Nouveau pavilion was not a conventional exhibition structure but a prototype two-story apartment unit, which Le Corbusier planned to join together with many other such reinforced-concrete building blocks to make up the large buildings that he called "apartment homes" (*immeubles villas*) (Figure 3.5). To furnish

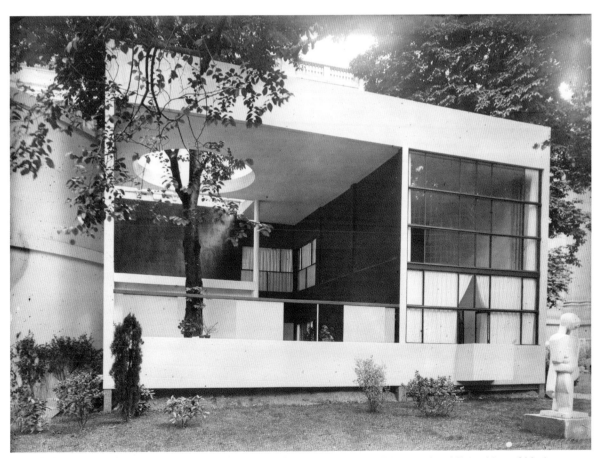

FIGURE 3.5.   Le Corbusier and Pierre Jeanneret, Esprit Nouveau Pavilion, International Exposition of Modern Decorative and Industrial Arts, Paris, 1925.

the Esprit Nouveau unit, he selected a group of utilitarian objects that he described as universal objects not subject to changing styles, what he called "types" because they responded to basic human needs: "chairs to sit on, tables to work at, devices to give light, machines to write with" (Figure 3.6). He cited in particular two Thonet bentwood chairs, the famous nineteenth-century side chair (see Figure 1.2) and an early twentieth-century armchair, as anonymous "machines for sitting in," a variant of his infamous maxim, "a house is a machine for living in."

Even though the rules of the Paris exhibition demanded that everything shown there should be modern (that is, designed in a new style), Le Corbusier interpreted this differently, defining "modern" in his own way by including a number of type objects that had come into use considerably earlier. Along with the Thonet chairs, these comprised plain leather club chairs that had first appeared a half century before in England's gentlemen's clubs, functional ceramics and glassware that had been designed for laboratory use in the previous century or even earlier, and exotic tribal carpets made in simple age-old designs. In this way Le Corbusier demonstrated that design did not have to be new to be considered modern, it just had to be simple. By claiming modernity for simplicity, as he boldly did in furnishing the pavilion, Le Corbusier made modernity timeless. This is why the Museum of Modern Art in New York can have a plain black teacup and saucer designed by Josiah Wedgwood in 1768 in its collection of modern design, and why the museum could as easily have chosen from a multitude of other examples of earlier undecorated everyday objects for the same

FIGURE 3.6. Le Corbusier and Pierre Jeanneret, Interior of the Esprit Nouveau Pavilion, International Exposition of Modern Decorative and Industrial Arts, Paris, 1925.

FIGURE 3.7. Josiah Wedgwood, Teacup and Saucer, 1768. Black basalt. Collection of the Museum of Modern Art, New York.

reason (Figure 3.7). Le Corbusier's equation of simple forms with modernity was unprecedented, but it stuck; when he published photographs of the pavilion after it was razed at the close of the exhibition, they were studied closely by architects and designers of his day as they have been ever since, and the Esprit Nouveau pavilion remains the archetype of how simplicity alone can make an interior modern.

Simplicity

Although inspired by William Morris and the design of Great Britain, the initial leap to modern form mostly took place outside of it, in Europe and the Americas, and industrial manufacture was often a major component. The example of Morris extended both to those who espoused his social aims along with his teachings about craftsmanship as well as those who adopted his precepts of truth, honesty, and simplicity regardless of how and with what means their work was to be carried out. Frank Lloyd Wright honored William Morris's principle of simplicity but followed it through the artistic use of the machine, as he explained in his article "In the Cause of Architecture" in 1908:

"The present industrial condition is constantly studied and the treatment simplified and arranged to fit modern processes and to utilize to the best advantage the work of the machine," adding that "the furniture takes the clean-cut, straight-line forms that the machine can render far better than would be possible by hand." This pointed directly to the clean straight lines of his own work, like the oak chair he designed in 1904 for his studio in Oak Park, Illinois, and the machine tools that had made it (Figure 3.8). He reduced the chair to a few rectilinear components, holding the angled back in place with pegs that were left exposed, a nod to Pugin and Morris in its truth to materials and structure. The rectangular wooden plank alone conveys Wright's message of simplicity, where nothing more than the natural color of the wood, its texture, and its distinct graining were needed to bring beauty to its undisguised form. This was but

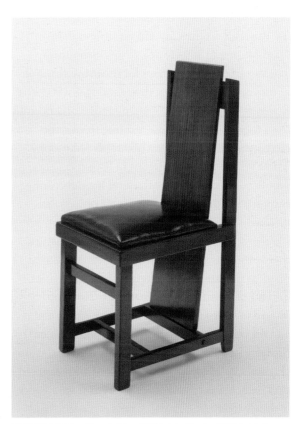

FIGURE 3.8. Frank Lloyd Wright, Chair, 1904. Oak with leather upholstery.

one of the thousands of furnishings of all types, including built-in and free-standing wooden and metal furniture, metalwork, stained glass, and textiles, that Wright created for his interiors, which he, like Morris, conceived as complete works of art.

The first significant endeavor to market objects based on Morris's principles in the United States was that of the Roycroft community, a commercial but communal venture established in 1895 by Elbert Hubbard (1865–1915) as a printing firm and publishing house in East Aurora, New York (not far from Buffalo). A successful businessman with a background in advertising, Hubbard had visited Morris's Kelmscott Press in London the previous year and intended to bring the revived art of fine printing back home. He supported his community by publishing inspirational books, many of which he wrote, including the best-selling *Message to Garcia* (1899). He soon expanded into making furniture, metalwork, and lighting, relying on a succession of designers, most notably the Roycroft art director and versatile craftsman Dard Hunter (1883–1966), to give them form. These started out as fittings for the many Roycroft houses and workshops, and, beginning in 1903, the Roycroft Inn, which Hubbard had his workers build from native stone for those wanting to visit the extensive campus and learn about his philosophy. These visits awakened interest in Roycroft products, which led to a successful manufacturing enterprise with catalogues and mail-order sales directed to the rising American middle class. Hubbard added more workshops to manufacture these products and eventually Roycroft employed as many as five hundred workers for all its activities.

This plain massive oak chair with "Roycroft" incised in large Gothic-style letters on its top rail and the community's trademark orb and cross on the front of its seat rail was probably used at the inn (Figure 3.9). Made of solid oak joined with exposed pegs, which was typical of early Roycroft woodwork, it closely followed Arts and Crafts precedents and principles. Much of Roycroft's copper work also

FIGURE 3.9. Roycroft Shops, Chair, 1900–1905. American White Oak.

showed an Arts and Crafts adherence to revealing its hand techniques, with the marks of the craftsman's work deliberately left visible. The tall, hammered-copper American Beauty vase designed by Victor Toothaker (1882–1932), an eclectic designer who arrived at Roycroft in 1912 after Hunter's departure, was made in large numbers, part of a substantial order for lighting, hardware, and decorative objects to furnish a large resort hotel in Asheville, North Carolina (Figure 3.10).

FIGURE 3.10. Roycroft Shops, American Beauty Vase, c. 1912. Hammered copper.

Movement (the first issue was devoted to William Morris and the second to John Ruskin) and a wide range of other topics, including medieval objects, manual training, socialism, Art Nouveau, pottery, gardens, and Japanese craftsmanship (Figure 3.11).

After returning from travels in England and Europe during the 1890s, where he had seen firsthand the new furnishings he knew from international design magazines such as *The Studio*, Stickley began to manufacture solid oak furniture in simple, sturdy Arts and Crafts forms. His hexagonal, leather-top library table made of oak about 1901 clearly follows the principles of emphasizing structure, with the key-and-tenon joints, like those of Pugin's prayer bench (see

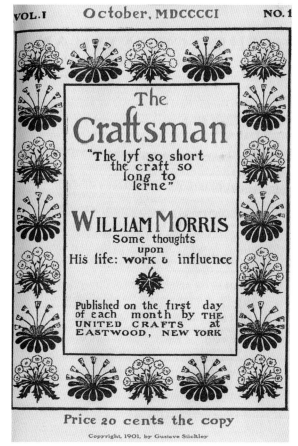

FIGURE 3.11. Gustav Stickley, Cover of *The Craftsman*, vol. 1, no. 1, 1901.

It was the American entrepreneur Gustav Stickley (1857–1942), however, who truly popularized the Arts and Crafts Movement in the United States, where he endeavored "to promote and to extend the principles established by Morris, in both the artistic and socialistic sense." The furniture made in his United Crafts Workshops, founded in Syracuse, New York, in 1901 (later called the Craftsman Workshops), and his idealistic monthly review *The Craftsman*, which he published between 1901 and 1916, brought national attention to the firm. *The Craftsman* was an educational and promotional tool, with discrete images of Stickley furnishings populating its pages each month alongside articles about the Arts and Crafts

FIGURE 3.12.   Gustav Stickley, Library Table, c. 1901. Oak and leather.

Figure 1.20), conspicuous elements of the design (Figure 3.12). Stickley promoted his company as a collective of master craftsmen and their associates, but when popularity led to the expansion of his business, he simplified and standardized his products and began to use factory methods and some machine processes to produce them in larger numbers. The cost of expansion and the increasing competition from many imitators, along with the return to popularity of the Colonial Revival style, eventually led him into bankruptcy, however, and he closed the Craftsman Workshops by 1916.

Craft too was the focus of the early years at the Bauhaus design school, which opened in Weimar, Germany, in 1919 with the architect Walter Gropius (1883–1969) as its director (and continued until 1933, when the politics of National Socialism forced its closure). While the Bauhaus maintains an undeniable reputation for its many key monuments of modern machine-style design, the school began as a craft-based academy and was a direct descendant of the Arts and Crafts Movement. Gropius had founded the Bauhaus by restructuring and amalgamating two existing schools, the Weimar Academy of Fine Arts

(Hochschule für Bildende Kunst) and the School of Handicraft (Kunstgewerbeschule), the latter having previously been headed by Henry van de Velde, who on his departure on the eve of the First World War (1914–18) recommended Gropius as a possible successor. The name "Bauhaus" had no exact meaning in German but implied that the school would be a center where the crafts of building (*Bauen*) were taught. Turning his back on his earlier industrial buildings boldly built of glass and steel, Gropius returned to traditional materials and techniques and to a collective utopianism that brought him back to the world of William Morris. The emphasis on craft would have been a realistic move at that time for the German economy following the devastating war had not yet seen a substantial revival of its industrial production.

Gropius took as his model the ideal of the medieval craftsman and the unity of design that Morris had celebrated, outlining his ideals for the school in its founding manifesto (see Sidebar 5). In establishing the school, Gropius envisioned a united craft community focused on the "complete building" as the goal of design, where no distinctions would be made between artists and craftspeople. This was made very clear in the words of his manifesto: "Architects, sculptors, painters, we all must return to the crafts!" At first, the Bauhaus faculty comprised artists under the sway of Expressionism, an early twentieth-century movement that emphasized subjectivity, expressing the artists' emotional concerns at a time of political uncertainty rather than simply depicting aspects of the visual world around them. Students began their studies in the school's legendary preliminary course (*Vorkurs*) initiated by the Swiss artist Johannes Itten (1888–1967), a specialist in color theory and a spiritualist, and one of the first teachers to be hired under Gropius's early vision for the school. He brought to his course an intense introduction to the basics of form and materials, which students were told to explore by delving into their own inner creativity, reflecting Itten's leanings to self-education and self-expression. Afterward, they chose a specialty

SIDEBAR 5   Walter Gropius, Program of the State Bauhaus in Weimar, 1919

The ultimate aim of all visual arts is the complete building! To embellish buildings was once the noblest function of the fine arts; they were the indispensable components of great architecture. Today the arts exist in isolation, from which they can be rescued only through the conscious, cooperative effort of all craftsmen. Architects, painters, and sculptors must recognize anew and learn to grasp the composite character of a building both as an entity and in its separate parts. Only then will their work be imbued with the architectonic spirit which it has lost as "salon art."

The old schools of art were unable to produce this unity; how could they, since art cannot be taught. They must be merged once more with the workshop. The mere drawing and painting world of the pattern designer and the applied artist must become a world that builds again. When young people who take a joy in artistic creation once more begin their life's work by learning a trade, then the unproductive "artist" will no longer be condemned to deficient artistry, for their skill will now be preserved for the crafts, in which they will be able to achieve excellence.

Architects, sculptors, painters, we all must return to the crafts! For art is not a "profession." There is no essential difference between the artist and the craftsman. The artist is an exalted craftsman. In rare moments of inspiration, transcending the consciousness of his will, the grace of heaven may cause his work to blossom into art. But proficiency in a craft is essential to every artist. Therein lies the prime source of creative imagination. Let us then create a new guild of craftsmen without the class distinctions that raise an arrogant barrier between craftsman and artist! Together let us desire, conceive, and create the new structure of the future, which will embrace architecture and sculpture and painting in one unity and which will one day rise toward heaven from the hands of a million workers like the crystal symbol of a new faith.

and entered one of the workshops for their training, following the stages of the traditional German guild system by serving as apprentices and then journeymen on their way to becoming masters in their chosen fields. The workshops (which over the years were redefined and renamed) each had two masters to guide the students, an artist, or master of form, and a craftsperson, or master of craft. They initially included cabinetmaking, pottery, printing, stagecraft, stained glass, stone sculpture, wall painting, bookbinding, weaving, and metalwork. It was in the metal workshop that as an assistant, the Ukrainian Naum Slutzky (1894–1965) made his spherical copper box, an example of the early Bauhaus adherence to decorative craft techniques that revealed the hand of the workers as they formed their objects (Figure 3.13).

FIGURE 3.13.   Naum Slutzky, Covered Box, 1920. Made by the Bauhaus Metal Workshop. Copper.

Standardization and Rationalization

The achievements of the American System of manufacture continued to influence design and manufacture into the twentieth century, and the German Werkbund weighed in heavily on this. Many of its members adopted the aesthetic ideals of the Arts and Crafts Movement to a program of standardization and efficient production in an effort to raise the quality of Germany's industrial output. The two best-known German programs for furniture standardization were the *Maschinenmöbel* (machine-made furniture) series that Richard Riemerschmid (1868–1957), the leading figure in German design in the first decades of the twentieth century, created for the Dresden Workshops for Handicraft Art (Dresdener Werkstätten für Handwerkskunst) in 1906 and the *Typenmöbel* (type furniture) line that the architect Bruno Paul (1874–1968) designed for the United Workshops for Art in Handicraft (Vereinigte Werkstätten für Kunst im Handwerk) in Munich in 1907. The programs were well publicized and financially successful and had a great impact on later mass-produced furniture in Germany. That these manufacturing programs could be openly advertised as having been made with the aid of machinery suggests that by the first decade of the century, a significant number of German consumers were comfortable with machine-made objects (Figure 3.14).

Maschinenmöbel was produced in three lines and sold at three different price points, from one that would fit the pocketbook of ordinary citizens to that of the upper-middle-class consumer. Although it was industrially made, the furniture came in different styles and did not look very different from those in period styles or handmade arts and crafts furnishings, like that in Riemerschmid's Gentleman's Study, with its plainly crafted, angular and unornamented smoked oak cabinets (Figure 3.15). The furniture was assembled by hand

FIGURE 3.14.   Advertisement for Bruno Paul's *Typenmöbel* (Type Furniture) Exhibition, Vereinigte Werkstätten für Kunst im Handwerk, Munich, 1907.

from elements made by machine and the cabinets could be stacked or joined at the side to construct larger pieces. *Typenmöbel* products were aimed at an even broader market and a more varied audience with vastly different levels of taste. While some of the furniture was simple and made of plain solid wood, others were veneered and ornamented and related to historic decorative styles. *Typenmöbel* production was fully rationalized, and therefore more efficient, and the success of the program drew such other designers as Josef Hoffmann and Adelbert Niemeyer (1867–1932) to create furniture for it as well. In 1914, the British *"Studio" Yearbook of Decorative Art* described the concept of the *Typenmöbel* series in an article on the state of the German furniture industry:

> Their constituent parts are made in many different but definitely standardised sizes, shapes, and proportions, and admit of manifold combinations and varieties of shape ... [with] practically no restraint on the exercise of artistic fantasy and formative skill. The great economic advantage of this mode of production arises from the fact that all these single parts, of which there are something like 800 different kinds, can be made in large

RICHARD RIEMERSCHMID

MASCHINENMÖBEL ● AUSGEFÜHRT VON DEN „DRESDENER WERKSTÄTTEN FÜR HANDWERKSKUNST", DRESDEN

HERRENZIMMER AUS GERÄUCHERTEM EICHENHOLZ

FIGURE 3.15.
Richard Riemerschmid, *Maschinenmöbel*: Gentleman's Study, 1907. Made by Dresdener Werkstätten für Handwerkskunst. Smoked oak. From *Die Kunst*, 1907.

quantities and with the most advantageous employment of machine labour; while the extensive range of combinations ensures to the complete article an individuality and a character of its own, without betraying the use of machinery in its production.

This suggests that British consumers, unlike those in Germany, would not have been knowingly receptive to machine-made furniture regardless of the styles in which it was made.

In 1907, the year the Werkbund was founded, the German electric company AEG (Allgemeine Electrizitäts Gesellschaft) took a major step in line with the association's goal of bridging the gap between art and industry by hiring the artist Peter Behrens (1868–1940) as an advisor. Behrens moved well beyond the area of graphic design for which he had been hired to create one of the first rationalized corporate-identity systems, with everything from the company's beehive logo and somewhat eccentric typeface (which he designed) to its products and its

buildings (which, although self-taught as architect and designer, he also designed) falling into line. To underscore the authority of the company, Behrens relied on traditional associative forms for the design of his colossal turbine factory in Berlin in 1909–10, but built the great uninterrupted interior space with modern iron, concrete, and glass for efficiency of function (Figure 3.16). The huge alternating glass windows and the steel supports along the sides suggest the rhythmic placement of classical columns while the pediment at front is emblazoned with the company's logo cut into the stone, a symbolic gesture usurping the place traditionally reserved for a sculptural narrative. Behrens's reputation drew many young architects to his firm, and his office was a training ground for three of the twentieth century's most important architects and designers, Le Corbusier, Walter Gropius, and the German Ludwig Mies van der Rohe (1886–1969).

Behrens standardized and rationalized the design and production of a number of AEG's products, notably its arc lamps, clocks, fans,

FIGURE 3.16.   Peter Behrens, AEG Turbine Factory, Berlin, 1909–10.

and kettles, subtly simplifying their forms so that they were, as he said in a statement on his arrival, "appropriate to machine production" (see Sidebar 6). His series of electrical kettles shared heating components and had interchangeable parts: lids, handles, and bases (Figure 3.17). The kettles came in three shapes, round, octagonal, and oval; three finishes, smooth, grooved, and hammered; and three materials, nickel-plated brass, matte brass, and copper. Contrary to Behrens's goals, those with grooved and hammered finishes, which were introduced to meet the tastes of the company's broad market, were blatant imitations of handcraftsmanship. Not all the possible variations were made, but one could buy the kettles in some thirty different formats.

In a number of his graphics for the company, including his cover image for an AEG lighting catalog from 1910, Behrens borrowed a new approach to advertising that had recently come into fashion (Figure 3.18). His design simply shows the company's signature product, a lightbulb, against a flat blue ground, linked to the large-scale initials, AEG, by which the company was known. This new strategy had been introduced in 1907 by the graphic designer Lucian Bernhard (1883–1972), whose poster featuring a large, boldly drawn pack of matches on a flat background with no typography other than the company's name had then won a design competition. In these works, which became known as "Object Posters," Bernhard packed power through strong, simplified images, placing the products front and center with only the manufacturer's name beside them; often they promoted standardized objects such as matches, cigarettes, lightbulbs, and spark plugs, products that

SIDEBAR 6 Peter Behrens, "Art in Technology," 1907

I have been commissioned by the Allgemeine Electricitätsgesellschaft, Berlin, to produce new designs for the products manufactured by the company. The company probably proceeded from the following considerations: In the manufacturing process until now, the emphasis had been laid simply on the technical aspects. The determining factor in the matter of the external form has been the taste of the Werkmeister [foreman], and this was true of all firms concerned with the production of technical goods. From now on, however, the tendency of our age should be followed and a manner of design established appropriate to machine production. This will not be achieved through the imitation of handcraftsmanship, of other materials and of historical styles, but will be achieved through the most intimate union possible between art and industry. This could be done by concentrating on and implementing exactly the technique of mechanical production in order to arrive by artistic means at those forms that derive directly from and correspond to the machine and machine production.

It is well known that the Allgemeine Electricitätsgesellschaft manufactures the most diverse products related to electricity, such as arc lamps for direct and indirect lighting, electric fans, switchgear, heaters, and all manner of small articles like circuit breakers, contacts, etc. For these products, the attempt should now be made, using standard types, to achieve a graceful beauty that is cleanly constructed and appropriate to the materials used. On no account, however, should an individualistic style be established. As all products of society have a more or less close relationship to architecture, this design aim is of general significance. For the new approach will make it possible for the three-dimensional artist and the architect to reintegrate those objects whose technical character previously upset the artistic layout of a room into the all-embracing artistic order.

There is no longer any doubt that the future of industry also has an artistic dimension, and that our age calls for the type of product that is most responsive to this dimension. In the realm of the applied arts, our age calls for *Industriekunst* [industrial art].

FIGURE 3.17. Peter Behrens, Kettles, c. 1909. Made by AEG. Metal and wicker.

FIGURE 3.18.   Peter Behrens. Cover of AEG Lighting Catalogue, 1910. Lithograph.

FIGURE 3.19.   Lucian Bernhard, Poster for Bosch Spark Plugs, 1914. Lithograph.

had no recognizable features that would distinguish one brand's offerings from another's (Figure 3.19).

The question of how objects that were standardized could at the same time have an "artistic dimension" and yet not be individualized was at the center of a controversy that rocked the membership of the Werkbund at its annual conference in Cologne in 1914. As the conference began, Hermann Muthesius distributed a list of ten propositions that he said would lead to the future health of German exports and industry. Only standardization, he wrote, drawing on Behrens's earlier viewpoint, would "make possible the development of universally valid, unfailing good taste," and if that were not achieved, one could not "count on German arts and crafts making their influence effectively felt abroad" (see Sidebar 7). Henry van de Velde, who had closed his Art Nouveau workshop in Belgium and moved to Germany in 1902 to design and head the new School of Handicraft in Weimar, protested. He spoke out for the values of individual creativity and rejected any attempt to impose a single standard on the artist for commercial aims. "By his innermost essence," he countered successfully at that time, "the artist is a burning idealist, a free spontaneous creator. Of his own free will, he will never subordinate himself to a discipline that

imposes upon him a type, a canon." Here again the argument set the craftsman ideal against the industrial imperative, and with the Werkbund members not being able to agree even on a single definition of "standardization," no resolution about the future goals of the Werkbund or German industry came out of the conference. In 1918, however, the German Institute for Standardization (Deutsches Institut für Normung), which was founded the previous year, introduced an ongoing set of standards for the design of everyday products and processes that eventually would cover everything from paper sizes and hardware to data-entry technology.

If in 1914 van de Velde could successfully scuttle the case for standardization among the members of the Werkbund, Le Corbusier would make it central to his ideas on modern architecture and industrial design. These appeared in a series of articles in *L'Esprit Nouveau* beginning in 1920, many of which were reprinted in his seminal book *Towards a New Architecture* in 1923. He denied the notion that standards could be chosen superficially and explained how rigorous their selection should be: "The establishment of a standard involves exhausting every practical and reasonable possibility, and extracting from them a recognized type conformable to its functions, with a maximum

SIDEBAR 7   Hermann Muthesius, Proposals at the Congress of the Deutscher Werkbund, 1914

1. Architecture, and with it the whole area of the Werkbund's activities, is striving towards standardization and only through standardization can it recover that universal significance which was a characteristic of architecture in times of harmonious culture.

2. Standardization, which is the result of a beneficial concentration, will alone make possible the development of universally valid, unfailing good taste.

3. As long as a universal high level of taste has not been achieved, we cannot count on German arts and crafts making their influence felt abroad.

4. The world will demand our products only when they are the vehicles of a convincing stylistic expression. The foundations for this have now been laid by the German movement.

5. The most urgent task is to develop creatively what has already been achieved. Upon it, the movement's ultimate success will depend. Any relapse and deterioration into imitation would today mean the squandering of a valuable possession.

6. Starting from the conviction that it is a matter of life and death for Germany constantly to improve its production, the Deutscher Werkbund, as an association of artists, industrialists, and merchants, must concentrate its attention upon creating the preconditions for the export of its industrial arts.

7. Germany's advances in applied art and architecture must be brought to the attention of foreign countries by effective publicity. Next to exhibitions the most obvious means of doing this is by illustrated periodical publications.

8. Exhibitions by the Deutscher Werkbund are only meaningful when they are restricted radically to the best and most exemplary. Exhibitions of arts and crafts abroad must be looked upon as a national matter and hence require public subsidy.

9. The existence of efficient large-scale business concerns with reliable good taste is a prerequisite of any export. It would be impossible to meet even internal demands with an object designed by the artist for individual requirements.

10. For national reasons, large distributive and transport undertakings whose activities are directed abroad ought to link up with the new movement, now that it has shown what it can do, and consciously represent German art in the world.

---

output and minimum use of means, workmanship and material, words, forms, colours, sounds" (see Sidebar 8). He had been fascinated with the way that offices were furnished with systematized equipment, which allowed such essentials as paper in standard sizes to be filed efficiently, and he drew on that idea for his own concepts of modern furnishings. Standardized, industrially produced office equipment had followed the model of the bookcases made by the Globe-Wernicke Company, an American manufacturer whose office products had been distributed widely across Europe since the end of the previous century. These bookcases were composed of modular rectangular shelving units with glass doors that could be stacked and were held together by patented interlocking hardware.

Le Corbusier introduced standardized type objects as domestic furnishings in the Esprit Nouveau pavilion at the Paris exhibition in 1925—Thonet bentwood chairs, club chairs, laboratory glassware and ceramics, tribal carpets—but he had to design his own modular storage pieces for it because no suitable standardized cabinets were yet on the market. Turning away from traditional

SIDEBAR 8   Le Corbusier, "Eyes Which Do Not See: Automobiles," 1923

It is necessary to press on towards the establishment of *standards* in order to face the problem of *perfection*.

The Parthenon [in Athens, 447–432 BCE] is a product of selection applied to an established standard. Already for a century the Greek temple had been standardized in all its parts.

When once a standard is established competition comes at once and violently into play. It is a fight; in order to win you must do better that your rival *in every minute point*, in the run of the whole thing and in all the details. Thus we get the study of minute points pushed to its limits. Progress.

A standard is necessary for order in human effort.

A standard is established on sure bases, not capriciously but with the surety of something intentional and of a logic controlled by analysis and experiment.

All men have the same organism, the same functions.

All men have the same needs.

The social contract which has evolved through the ages fixes standardized classes, functions and needs producing standardized products . . .

The establishment of a standard involves exhausting every practical and reasonable possibility, and extracting from them a recognized type conformable to its functions, with a maximum output and a minimum use of means, workmanship and material, words, forms, colours, sounds.

The motor-car is an object with a simple function (to travel) and complicated aims (comfort, resistance, appearance), which has forced on big industry the absolute necessity of standardization. All motor-cars have the same essential arrangements. But, by reason of the unceasing competition between the innumerable firms who make them, every maker has found himself obliged to get to the top of this competition and, over and above the standards of practical realization, to prosecute the search for a perfection and harmony beyond the mere practical side, a manifestation not only of perfection and harmony, but of beauty.

Here we have the birth of style, that is to say the attainment, universally recognized, of a state of perfection universally felt.

cabinets and storage pieces designed for specific functions, he opted for a universal format that could be used throughout the unit (see Figure 3.6). But because the forms of these pieces were generalized, he had to design the interiors to fit their contents. He did this by studying the sizes, shapes, and storage needs of common objects and partitioning the interiors of his cabinetry so that, as he wrote, they were "meticulously fixed with the strictest economy of dimensions (arrangements for wardrobes, for underwear, for bedding, for shoes, hats, etc., for glassware, for different types of dishes, for kitchen equipment, for writing materials, for filing, etc., for bookcases, for gramophone records, for the wireless, etc., etc.)."

While Le Corbusier and others during the 1920s studied type objects to organize them meticulously into storage of various kinds, a much more far-reaching system of rationalization of the home took place later in the decade, a mass-produced kitchen that the Austrian architect Margarete Schütte-Lihotzky (1897–2000) designed in 1926–27 for the city of Frankfurt in Germany (Figure 3.20). This drew on the concept of time-study work systems elaborated by the American management specialist Frederick Winslow Taylor

FIGURE 3.20.   Margarete Schütte-Lihotzky, Frankfurt Kitchen, from the Ginnheim-Höhenblick Housing Estate, Frankfurt, Germany, 1926–27.

(1856–1915) and published in his book *The Principles of Scientific Management* (1911), which greatly influenced manufacturing systems in the United States, especially in heavy industries, and abroad. His systems had a significant impact on the development of the moving assembly line, introduced by the automobile magnate Henry Ford (1863–1947) in 1913, where everything in the production of his Model T Ford (see Figure 6.1) was systematized and standardized so that maximum efficiency could be achieved. Each step in the production of the automobile was analyzed and rationalized into discrete tasks so that a worker completed only one or two actions repeatedly throughout the workday as the automobile bodies moved to them along the line. Taylor's principles were further applied to the efficient design of the home by Christine Frederick (1883–1970), consulting household editor of the American magazine *Ladies' Home Journal*. Her book *The*

New Housekeeping: Efficiency Studies in Home Management, published in 1913, analyzed and rationalized household tasks, offering homemakers the hope that "the beginnings made in the application of efficiency science to the household (however modest and inadequate) may yet assist in cutting from women the most dreary shackles of which they have ever complained." This was an attempt to professionalize the role of the housewife, to provide her with a status that could rival that of her husband. Frederick's closest analysis was directed to the kitchen, where she examined the sequences in completing ordinary tasks, from washing dishes to making an omelet, and then diagrammed the most efficient layout of utilities, equipment, and storage for productive workflow in a compact space (Figure 3.21).

Lihotzky took Frederick's book (which was published in a German translation in 1922) as her bible, following her principles of workflow

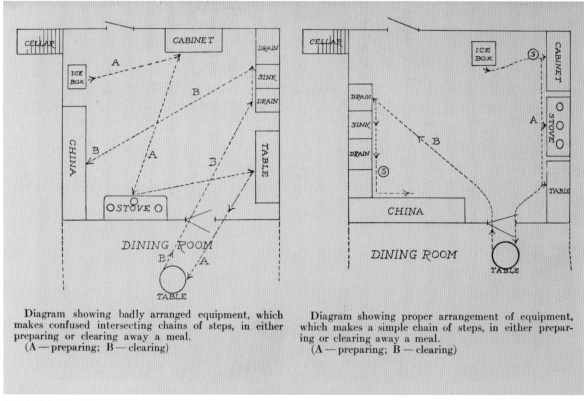

Diagram showing badly arranged equipment, which makes confused intersecting chains of steps, in either preparing or clearing away a meal.
(A — preparing; B — clearing)

Diagram showing proper arrangement of equipment, which makes a simple chain of steps, in either preparing or clearing away a meal.
(A — preparing; B — clearing)

FIGURE 3.21.   Christine Frederick, Diagrams of Kitchen Layouts, from *The New Housekeeping*, 1913.

and efficiency in her kitchen design. Some ten thousand examples of what became known as the Frankfurt Kitchen were industrially fabricated and transported to the many affordable concrete housing projects that were being built as part of a massive post First World War initiative undertaken by the municipality. She laid out the kitchen with efficiency of labor in mind, following the American studies and the results of her own additional research derived from interviewing women and analyzing workflow. The kitchen attempted to meet the standard needs of the homemaker with adjustable lighting; adequate storage; labeled bins for flour, sugar, and other staples; a drawer for garbage; a fold-down ironing board; and a swivel stool. Efficient kitchens such as this were heralds of the standardized kitchens of the 1930s and 1940s and became universal type forms by the 1950s in the United States.

German designers continued to explore modular furnishings during the 1920s. Among these was a rationalized system of strictly rectilinear

Typenmöbel created in 1927 by Erich Dieckmann (1896–1944) as an example of inexpensive furnishings that would be suitable for the compact living and dining rooms in these new housing estates. From 1925 to 1930, Dieckmann was head of the furniture workshop at the State Academy of Craft and Architecture (Staatliche Bauhochschule) in Weimar, the successor of the Bauhaus there, where he designed this standardized wooden furniture for machine manufacture. The pieces in this system, which included cabinets, tables, and chairs made of oak or cherry, were designed on a module that reflected Dieckmann's formulation of an ideal human measurement (Figure 3.22).

Rationalized furnishing systems for domestic use were introduced into the United States by the Herman Miller Furniture Company following designs by Gilbert Rohde (1894–1944), who had been trained as an artist and began to work as a consultant for the company in 1932. A trip to Europe in 1927 had brought Rohde in touch with the logic of advanced design in Germany, where

88
Büffet von Erich Dieckmann, Weimar

FIGURE 3.22.   Erich Dieckmann, Cabinet, c. 1926. Made by Staatliche Bauhochschule, from *Die Wohnung*, 1927.

FIGURE 3.23. Gilbert Rohde, Mahogany Group, from *Catalogue and Sales Guide*, Herman Miller Furniture Company, 1939.

(1900–1990), a former Bauhaus student, designed his Kubus pressed-glass refrigerator system in 1939. Its seven differently sized, modular cubic pieces, which fit together tightly for spatial economy, demanded a complete rethinking of kitchen storage to allow for a product that was highly efficient and reasonably priced for Germany's consumers (Figure 3.24). At the Lausitzer glassworks, where he served as artistic director, Wagenfeld continued to bring modern ideas of modularity and standardization to market during the 1930s even though the country's products had become more conservative under Nazi rule, with a preference for historic and nationalistic styles.

FIGURE 3.24. Wilhelm Wagenfeld, Kubus Stacking Storage Containers, 1939. Made by Lausitzer Glaswerke. Glass.

he was one of the only professional American designers known to have spent time assessing the work and methodology at the Bauhaus itself. His modular systems and sectional seating for Herman Miller drew on ideas that he had brought back from Germany. His storage units, which Herman Miller designated as "groups," were efficient and flexible; they were all of the same depth, and could be set on legs or solid bases and placed next to each other to form extended pieces (Figure 3.23).

Rationalization could be seen in other types of wares for the home as well. Wilhelm Wagenfeld

1910 to 1930

CHAPTER 4

Design and the European Modern Movements

During the early twentieth century, radical changes were made not only in design but in all the arts, in painting and sculpture, photography, music, and literature. Subject matter, narrative, ornament— all were being rejected in the name of modernity, and simplicity and abstraction were called on as the language of a new modern movement. Artists turned from the illusionistic replication of the world as it was seen before them to an intellectualized approach that recreated the world according to the needs of art itself, evolving into a series of new styles, foremost among which was Cubism. This style developed in complex forms, spawning many offshoots, including Purism in France and Futurism in Italy. It paved the way for pure abstraction in modern art, notably in another French offshoot, Orphism, in Suprematism and Constructivism in Russia, and in the De Stijl movement in The Netherlands, and contributed to the rejection of ornament in design.

Cubism and Its Impact

Of all the modern art movements, Cubism had the broadest and longest-lived influence on design in the first quarter of the twentieth century. Almost as soon the Spaniard Pablo Picasso (1881–1973) and the Frenchman Georges Braque (1882–1963), working separately and together in Paris around 1910, developed this new, scandalous way of painting, its notoriety emboldened a number of designers to draw on it, if only superficially, as inspiration for their own work. Since the latter part of the nineteenth century, modern painting had been pushing against the burden of narrative for a discipline that emphasized the means of painting itself, the paint, the brush, the canvas. As seen in Picasso's portrait of his art dealer Daniel-Henry Kahnweiler (1884–1979), Cubist artists broke down their models into formal components, removing from the painting indications of the incidental aspects of daily life and championing an art that was said to be universal (Figure 4.1). Here, Picasso built up the figure of his dealer with faceted forms drawn from the subject but seen from different angles and pulled up to the surface of the canvas. Kahnweiler's face and hands are points of recognition but aside from the remnants of a bottle at left, the rest of the canvas is an accumulation of geometric shapes and textured paint, browns, grays, and blacks.

FIGURE 4.1. Pablo Picasso, *Portrait of Daniel-Henry Kahnweiler*, 1910. Oil on canvas.

Although the Cubist House, an installation with a faceted façade by the French sculptor Raymond Duchamp-Villon (1876–1918), was shown at the Salon d'Automne in Paris in 1912, Cubism's first true impact on design appeared abroad, notably in Prague. Galvanized by their awareness of developments in Paris, the Czech Group of Plastic Artists (Skupina Výtvamých Umělců, founded in 1911) also benefitted from Cubism at home, where the art historian Vincenc Kramář (1877–1960) had formed one of Europe's earliest collections of Cubist art. The lure of Cubism attracted not only painters and sculptors but architects and designers as well. Among them were Josef Chochol (1880–1956), Josef Gočár (1880–1945), Vlastislav Hofman (1884–1964), and Pavel Janák (1882–1956), who adopted the new angularities of Cubist painting and sculpture into astonishing ideas for prismatic furniture, ceramics, and buildings, only a small proportion of which were ever completed. In bringing Cubist form to his Hodek apartment house in Prague in 1913–14, Chochol extended rows of pyramidal facets across its entire façade, ribbons of structural fragmentation recalling the oblique planes of Picasso's and Braque's paintings (Figure 4.2).

The Cubist vocabulary was strikingly brought into advertising in 1918, when the American artist and designer Edward Mcknight Kauffer (1890–1954), then living in London, created his billboard poster *Soaring to Success—The Early Bird*, for the London *Daily Herald* (Figure 4.3). Based on a woodcut from 1916 that was probably influenced by Vorticism, a short-lived English art movement inspired by Cubism and Futurism (1913–14), the diagonal flight of birds across the yellow poster translated these compressed painting styles into a popular commercial design. Kauffer seems to have studied the impact of large billboard posters while contemplating his design for this one, and came to the conclusion that "we live in a scientific age, an age of T-squares and compasses . . . [and] the attention, therefore, is attracted to the geometric, held by the

FIGURE 4.2. Joseph Chochol, Hodek Apartment House, Prague, 1913–14.

geometric and geometric design is retained longer in the memory than the purely pictorial."

In France, Eileen Gray (1878–1976), an Irish-born designer who moved to Paris after the First World War, turned to the rich spatial ambiguities of Cubism during the 1920s. Her segmented screen from 1922, made up of movable plaques of lacquered wood attached by brass rods, shows how the angularity of Cubism could be extended to form an architectural element in space (Figure 4.4). Gray had learned the ancient and rigorous technique of lacquer over a period of many years under the guidance of the Japanese craftsman Seizo Sugawara (1884–1937), who had come to Paris to work on the restoration of traditional lacquerwork. With his

FIGURE 4.3. Edward Mcknight Kauffer, *Soaring to Success—The Early Bird*, Poster for the *Daily Herald*, 1918. Lithograph.

FIGURE 4.4. Eileen Gray, Screen, 1922. Made for Galerie Jean Désert. Lacquered wood and brass.

assistance, she began to make modern decorative lacquered furniture and figurative panels, which she sold at her Paris shop, Galerie Jean Désert, which opened in 1922.

Cubism also excited French fashion designers like Coco Chanel (1883–1971), Paul Poiret (1897–1944), and Madeleine Vionnet (1876–1975), who drew on its angularities for the cutting of their

fabrics and draping of their dresses. Sonia Delaunay (1885–1979), a Ukrainian-born textile and fashion designer and also a painter, was noted for the daring of her geometric designs. Along with her husband, Robert Delaunay (1885–1941), she pioneered the coloristic Cubist offshoot Orphism. Her patterns were drawn from Orphism's fragmented color studies, and her designs were scaled to her dresses as they would be worn, emphasizing the architecture of the body. This sheet of designs done in 1922 and 1923, from a portfolio of her work published in 1925, shows how she combined angular forms with bold color contrasts to introduce her own interpretation of Cubist fashion (Figure 4.5).

Purism took familiar type objects such as bottles and glasses as its subjects but instead of fragmenting them in the early Cubist fashion,

FIGURE 4.5.   Sonia Delaunay, Designs for Dresses, from *Sonia Delaunay: Ses Peintures, Ses Objets, Ses Tissus Simultanés, Ses Modes*, 1925. Published by Librairie des Arts Décoratifs. Pochoir print.

simplified them into flattened, emblematic images with all details removed from their representation. Co-founded by Le Corbusier and the painter Amédée Ozenfant (1886–1966), Purism is best represented by the concrete and glass Esprit Nouveau pavilion at the 1925 exhibition with its standardized furnishings and its Purist paintings, including those by Le Corbusier (see Figure 3.6, right) and Fernand Léger (1881–1955), a French artist who also belonged to the group (see Figure 3.6, left).

Cubism was the revelation of the International Exposition of Modern Decorative and Industrial Arts (Exposition International des Arts Décoratifs et Industrials Modernes), which opened in Paris in 1925, as the American critic Helen Appleton Read (1897–1974) reported. "The first impression of the Exposition is startling," Read wrote in the *International Studio*. "One comes at once upon a cubist dream city or the projection of a possible city in Mars, arisen overnight in the heart of Paris. . . its cubist shapes and futurist colors. . . looking like nothing so much as a Picasso abstraction" (Figure 4.6). The exhibition was an immediate crowd pleaser, drawing over fifteen million visitors and initiating a new style, what was originally referred to as Art Moderne but is now known as Art Deco (the popular name taken decades later from the *Arts Décoratifs* in the French title of the exhibition). Had the exhibition opened in 1916 as initially planned (but postponed because of the First World War), objects showcasing the time-honored French reverence for fine craftsmanship in updated traditional styles like those of Emile-Jacques

FIGURE 4.6. International Exposition of Modern Decorative and Industrial Arts, Paris, 1925.

Ruhlmann (see Figure 3.3) would surely have dominated the displays, but when it finally arrived a decade later, the new and fully modern Cubist style had taken precedence for the design of many of the pavilions and objects shown there.

As the twentieth century began, the superiority of French high-style design had for the first time been challenged by the new standardized products and efficient models of production being explored in Germany, which were shown to unexpected acclaim at international exhibitions, notably those in Turin in 1902 and Saint Louis in 1904. In an effort to shore up the reputation of French craftsmanship and with it, its luxury furnishings industries, the national government planned an international exhibition to showcase its modernized historic design. Following the precedent of the 1902 First International Exposition of Modern Decorative Arts (Prima Esposizione Internazionale d'Arte Decorativa Moderna) in Turin, the

organizers of the Paris exhibition established an explicit aesthetic requirement, that every object on display should be modern. The guide for exhibitors stated that the exhibition was "open to all manufacturers whose product is artistic in character and shows clearly modern tendencies." Prohibited were reproductions and period imitations, a boon to artists, designers, and craftsmen but not to larger manufacturers, whose bread and butter was the production of period styles.

Twenty-one countries in addition to France and its colonies overseas participated in the exhibition, but two were conspicuously absent, the United States and Germany. Taking the aesthetic program too strictly at its word, perhaps, the United States declined to exhibit in Paris because, as it was later stated, "American manufacturers and craftsmen had almost nothing to exhibit in the modern spirit." But the modern spirit could be interpreted quite differently, and the Art Deco exhibition included many different interpretations of it. Because of the lingering animosity between France and Germany following the bitter world war, Germany initially was not invited, and then after France relented too late for Germany to make an adequate showing, she refused to participate. This eliminated a significant representation of what was then most forward-looking in modern design, the rationalized everyday products that it had been producing, and objects such as these were considerably less in evidence in Paris than the word "industrial" in the exhibition's French title might have suggested. The few major examples of the industrial style evident in the exhibition included Le Corbusier's Esprit Nouveau pavilion (see Figures 3.5, 3.6) and the glass and concrete Russian pavilion designed by Konstantin

Melnikov (1890–1974). Also shown was a model workers' club designed by the Constructivist artist Alexander Rodchenko (1891–1956), following his principles that production work should be: "socially useful, consumer-efficient designed objects, satisfying the formal principles of creative activity, technical simplicity, functional efficacity, and economy of both execution and use" (Figure 4.7). He furnished its reading room, painted red, gray, and black, with economical wooden furniture in simple geometric shapes, some of it multipurpose and all designed for ease of manufacture and use.

Of the many Cubist-inspired ensembles at the 1925 exhibition, the lacquered smoking room created by the Swiss-born designer and coppersmith Jean Dunand (1877–1942) was

FIGURE 4.7. Alexander Rodchenko, Workers' Club, International Exposition of Modern Decorative and Industrial Arts, Paris, 1925.

FIGURE 4.8.   Jean Dunand, Smoking Room from the Society of Artist Decorators' French Embassy, International Exposition of Modern Decorative and Industrial Arts, Paris, 1925, from René Chavance, *Une Ambassade Française*, 1925.

perhaps the most tightly unified and the most glamorous (Figure 4.8). The room was created for a model French embassy installation organized by the Society of Artist Decorators (Société des Artistes Décorateurs), whose members comprised most of the well-known architects and interior designers working in France at that time. It drew on their talents to present twenty-five unified ensembles, elegant public reception rooms and more understated quarters for the imagined ambassador and his family. Dunand, a specialist in the art of lacquer, had studied its long and laborious process with the Japanese craftsman Sugawara and along with Eileen Gray led the modern French revival of this technique. He bound his small, square room in dazzling, highly reflective black-lacquered panels under a silvered ceiling, formed like a ziggurat, or

terraced pyramid. The square lacquered gaming table and chairs held the center of the room and complemented the interior completely. To bring a measure of color to the room, Dunand added red accents to pick out the corners of the ceiling, and large red decorative lacquer panels ornamented with silver leaf at two sides.

American visitors to Paris, including an official United States delegation sent to assess how these developments abroad might have an impact on the manufacturing industries at home, were impressed with what they encountered at the exhibition, and excitedly brought an awareness of this new style back across the Atlantic. For those who could not travel to Paris, the Association of American Museums organized an exhibition of some four hundred objects from the Paris exhibition, mainly in a modern traditionalist style, which opened at the Metropolitan Museum of Art in New York in 1926, traveled across the United States, and was shown in Japan in 1928. Department stores, including R. H. Macy's and Lord and Taylor's in New York and Kaufmann's in Pittsburgh, had their own more forward-looking exhibitions of this design in the following years, which had wide and long-lasting reverberations on American high style.

Perhaps the most inventive structural integration of Cubist forms into American household objects was the Ruba Rombic line of blown-glass tableware created by Reuben Haley (1872–1933), a sculptor, metalworker, and glass designer, whose shift to modern design may be attributed to his having seen the traveling exhibition of French Art Deco design in 1926 (Figure 4.9). Ruba Rombic (probably a combination of Haley's first name and the adjectival form of "rhombus," a parallelogram with no right angles) was sold inexpensively in mainstream stores and eventually included thirty-seven different pieces. This line of faceted tableware was seen by a contemporary trade journal as "the craziest thing ever brought out in glassware."

But Art Deco's most enduring impact in the United States was on architecture, both

FIGURE 4.9.   Reuben Haley, Ruba Rombic Whiskey Decanter with Glasses and Tray, 1928–32. Made by Consolidated Lamp and Glass Company. Mold-blown glass.

FIGURE 4.10.   William Van Alen, Chrysler Building, New York, 1928–30.

monumental buildings and modest ones constructed in large cities and in small towns across the country. They featured the kind of setback silhouette that had been part of a zoning legislation passed in New York City in 1916 to avoid the dark and cavernous urbanscape that comes from a profusion of soaring vertical towers. New York City's skyline was punctuated by many noted Art Deco skyscrapers, including the Empire State Building, completed in 1931 by the architectural firm Shreve, Lamb and Harmon (founded in 1929), and the Chrysler Building, erected from 1928 to 1930 by William Van Alen (1883–1954). Identified by its tiered gray tower with breathtaking sunburst setbacks, the Chrysler Building was as much about advertising as architecture, a collaboration of Van Alen and Walter Chrysler (1875–1940), head of

the automobile company that carried his name. The facade was emblazoned with allusions to the automobiles it celebrated, among them winged radiator caps and jutting eagle-head gargoyles, medieval-type figures that referred to the motif on Chrysler hood ornaments (Figure 4.10).

Art Deco architecture had its own influence on modern design with a style known as "skyscraper furniture," stepped geometrical cabinetry following New York's architectural setbacks. It was introduced in 1925 by the Viennese-born architect Paul Frankl (1886–1958), who had moved to New York before the First World War and introduced a progressive vocabulary with his furnishings. With forms such as the setback silhouette of this painted bookcase, with stacked shelves of plywood construction that

FIGURE 4.11. Paul Frankl, Skyscraper Bookcase, c. 1926. Painted plywood and brass.

Suprematism and Constructivism

Suprematism and Constructivism, two avant-garde art movements that sprang from the turmoil of Russia in the years before and after the Revolution of 1917, both had roots in Cubism and were highly influential on European design in the 1920s and 1930s. While Suprematism emerged as the personal expression of the Ukrainian-born painter Kazimir Malevich (1878–1935), Constructivism was a movement formed in Moscow in 1921 by a group that considered themselves "artist-engineers." Constructivists—including Alexander Rodchenko; his future wife, the artist Varvara Stepanova (1894–1958), and her colleague Liubov Popova (1889–1924); and Vladimir Tatlin (1885–1953), best known for his large architectural model of a never completed *Monument to the Third International* (1918–20)—rejected art for its own sake and adopted practical solutions for the creation of an ideal communist society. They went to work in industry, designing products that were based on abstract geometric forms and constructed with industrial materials, and developing graphics with bold type and striking photographic images.

Malevich's breakthrough came in his works of 1915, which featured squares, rectangles, and circles placed against a white background, among them the painting of a black and a red square ironically entitled *Painterly Realism of a Boy with a Knapsack—Color Masses in the Fourth Dimension* (Figure 4.12). These were essays in freeing art from the requirements of representation and pictorial depth, denoting for him the "supremacy of pure emotion." The graphic designer El Lissitzky (1890–1941) followed Malevich's aesthetic of abstract form in his dynamic 1920 poster *Beat the Whites with the Red Wedge*, demonstrating how Suprematist geometry could weave a symbolic narrative, here for propaganda purposes. Against a divided field of black and white, he depicted a red triangle breaking through a white circle, symbolizing the anticipated

continued above in solid steps to give the cabinet added height, Frankl's furniture joined the ranks of objects made in all manner of materials that celebrated the American skyscraper as a metaphor of the modern era (Figure 4.11).

FIGURE 4.12. Kazimir Malevich, *Painterly Realism of a Boy with a Knapsack—Color Masses in the Fourth Dimension*, 1915. Oil on canvas.

FIGURE 4.13. El Lissitzky, *Beat the Whites with the Red Wedge*, 1920. Poster for the Soviet Administration of the Western Front. Lithograph.

outcome of the Russian civil war (1917–21) when the Red Army troops would vanquish the White counterrevolutionary factions (Figure 4.13).

Malevich also turned his philosophy of pure painting and formal design into work for the Soviet society when in 1922–23 he created objects and decorations for the State (formerly Imperial) Porcelain Factory in Petrograd, which had been nationalized in 1918. Its porcelain was not intended for the proletariat but was made for official use by government agencies and was also a means of raising funds for the state when it was sold abroad. The factory took two divergent paths, issuing

agitational, or propagandistic, images painted on traditional ceramic forms, and producing avant-garde works by some of Russia's most celebrated modern designers, including Malevich and his student Nikolai Suetin (1897–1954). Malevich's designs for decorated porcelain drew on his own paintings, with geometric shapes in red and black on a white ground, but he also invented complex three-dimensional forms, including geometric teapots that were adventures in architectonic exploration as well as newly imagined ideas for a futuristic ceramic style (Figure 4.14).

The Constructivist group produced advertisements for Soviet products, agitational publications, magazines, furniture, textiles, and theatrical sets, bringing artists directly into the realm of industry and the public sphere. Schools and organizations were established to achieve these aims, including the Institute for Artistic Culture (InkHuk) and the School of Design (VKhUTEMAS), both founded in 1920 in Moscow. In 1923, Stepanova and Popova went to

FIGURE 4.14. Kazimir Malevich, Teapot , 1923. Made by State Porcelain Manufactory. Porcelain.

work for the First State Textile Printing Factory in Moscow, which like the other Soviet textile factories had seen severe declines in production since the Revolution. The factory was searching for artists to contribute to the revival of the industry by creating fresh patterns for printed cloth. The designs of Popova and Stepanova, like those of Sonia Delaunay (see Figure 4.5), represent the few truly successful translations of the art of modern painting into textile production, notably those with bold geometric patterns—circles, rectangles, triangles, and chevrons (Figure 4.15). Their dynamic patterns of crisp lines and flat forms printed in one or

FIGURE 4.15.
Liubov Popova, Textile, 1923–24. Printed cotton.

FIGURE 4.16.   Alexander Rodchenko, Poster: *Books On Every Subject!*, 1924. Published by the State Publishing House Gosizdat.

two colors were modern machinelike creations sympathetic to the mechanization programs of the Soviet state, but soon were overtaken by figurative, propagandistic designs that included such images as airplanes and tractors. Popova also created such designs using small symbolic motifs such as the hammer and sickle, the Soviet emblem standing for the socialist alliance of the industrial worker and the rural peasant.

Rodchenko, who had also been greatly influenced by the dynamic compositions of Suprematism, worked as a typographer, graphic artist, photographer, and furniture designer (see Figure 4.7). His energetic 1924 montage poster for the State Publishing House (Lengiz) placed a circular photographic detail of a woman with her hands to her mouth shouting "Lengiz, Books On

Every Subject" within a geometric composition of flat colors (Figure 4.16). Using cropped photographic images, bold modern type set at contrasting angles, geometric compositions, and pure colors, such work established a vital format for Soviet advertising and publishing design.

De Stijl

Cubism also inspired the work of De Stijl (The Style), a group of abstract painters that appeared in the Netherlands in the second decade of the century. Their goal was to seek in abstraction a new kind of universal art for modern life based on the natural harmony of vertical and horizontal forms, which became know as "Neoplasticism."

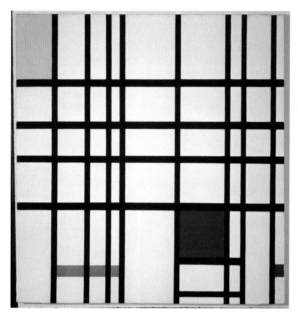

FIGURE 4.17.   Piet Mondrian, *Composition with Red, Yellow, and Blue*, 1927. Oil on canvas.

FIGURE 4.18.   Vilmos Huszár, Cover of *De Stijl*, 1917.

The name "De Stijl" was taken from that of a monthly magazine founded in 1917 by the painter Theo van Doesburg (1883–1931), the group's major theoretician. He was inspired by the spiritual values of the paintings and writings of the Russian Wassily Kandinsky (1866–1944), which he found also in the work of the Dutch painter Piet Mondrian (1872–1944), who was the best-known De Stijl artist although he lived a good part of the time in Paris. Elements of Mondrian's paintings, with rectangular grids of black lines and occasional planes of primary colors and gray and white, also appear in many works associated with other members of the group (Figure 4.17). The cover of the first issues of *De Stijl* was designed by Vilmos Huszár (1884–1960), a Hungarian artist living in the Netherlands and an early member of the group (Figure 4.18). Its abstract image is an essay in balancing black and white, giving equal value to figure and ground, that is, to positive and negative space, which met the aim of both De Stijl and Cubism to merge form and background and eliminate depth from their work. The shape of the letters continues its rigorous angularity, avoiding diagonals and curves to preserve the rectangular principles and aesthetic harmony of De Stijl.

In 1919 *De Stijl* published the image of an early, black model of the Red/Blue chair by the furniture maker and architect Gerrit Rietveld (1888–1964), although he did not know any members of the group at that time. After meeting van Doesburg and collaborating with the group (and probably on van Doesburg's recommendation), he added color to a redesigned version of the chair: red for the back, blue for the seat, black for the supporting frame, and yellow to highlight the cut edges, a palette that could be seen in paintings by Mondrian, van Doesburg, and Huszár (Figure 4.19). For Rietveld this chair demonstrated that furniture did not have to be handcrafted as his background as a cabinetmaker had taught him;

FIGURE 4.19.   Gerrit Rietveld, Red/Blue Chair, 1918 (painted 1923). Painted wood.

he realized that "a thing of beauty, e.g. a spatial object, could be made of nothing but straight, machined materials," which also made it suitable for factory production. Influenced perhaps by the plank furniture of Frank Lloyd Wright, which was well known in artistic circles in the Netherlands at that time (see Figure 3.8), Rietveld chose standard wooden components cut into modular lengths to create his unusual openwork construction. Clearly

delineated by primary colors, which emphasized the independence of each of the elements, it invited space to flow through it and was as much a manifesto of sculptural abstraction as a piece of furniture. Van Doesburg equated the act of creating the art associated with De Stijl with that of industrial design, seeing in the work of his progressive compatriots the "will to a new style" and the reformation of everyday life (see Sidebar 9).

SIDEBAR 9   Theo van Doesburg, "The Will to Style," 1922

The new spiritual philosophy of art not only saw at once its limitless potentialities for artistic expression. For a style which is no longer concerned with the production of individual pictures, ornaments or private houses, but makes a collective assault on whole districts of cities, skyscraper blocks and airports, with due consideration of the economic circumstances—for such a style there can be no question of employing hand craftsmanship. The machine is all-important here: hand craftsmanship is appropriate to an individualistic view of life which has been overtaken by progress. Hand craftsmanship, in the age of materialist philosophy, debased man to a machine; the machine, used properly in the service of cultural construction, is the only means of bringing about the converse: social liberation. This is by no means to say that mechanical production is the only requirement for creative perfection. A prerequisite for the correct use of machines is not quantity alone but, above all, quality. To serve artistic ends the use of machines must be governed by the artistic consciousness.

The needs of our age, both ideal and practical, demand constructive certainty. Only the machine can provide this constructive certainty. The new potentialities of the machine have given rise to an aesthetic theory appropriate to our age, which I have had occasion to call the "mechanical [machine] aesthetic" . . .

Let me give you some examples of the characteristics of the new style in opposition to those of the old.

Certainty instead of uncertainty.

Openness instead of enclosure.

Clarity instead of vagueness.

Religious energy instead of faith and religious authority.

Truth instead of beauty.

Simplicity instead of complexity.

Relationship instead of form.

Synthesis instead of analysis.

Logical construction instead of lyrical constellation.

Mechanisation instead of manual work.

Plastic form instead of imitation and decorative ornamentation.

Collectivism instead of individualism, etc.

The urge to establish the new style is seen in numerous phenomena. Not only in painting, sculpture and architecture, in literature, jazz and the cinema, but most significantly of all in purely utilitarian production.

1920 to 1940

CHAPTER 5

European Modernism

Modernism—a term that was only applied to this movement after the fact—developed in Europe in the first decades of the twentieth century. It set its sights on creating a better world through design, while the designer was seen as a heroic figure who would bring order to nature through rational thinking and, initially, geometric form. It took the elements of utopian design reform that had evolved in England in the nineteenth century and wove them into a body of principles to follow: objects were to be free of ornament and historic or symbolic associations; they were to be standardized and made by modern industrial methods; and finally, they would improve the lives of the masses through their logical design and their affordable prices (which rarely was achieved because most of Modernism's early products were elitist and expensive). Modernism has been largely identified with a machine style, but it was not limited to that. While the machine took center stage during the 1920s, by the early 1930s an organic style had surfaced that brought natural materials and processes and a sense of organic growth into the sphere of modernist thinking.

Modernism and the Machine Style

The machine was the determining metaphor of the industrial style that developed during the first quarter of the twentieth century. This new mode was such a pervasive expression of progressive design that by the mid 1930s, the German-born British architectural historian Nikolaus Pevsner (1902–1983) could argue in his *Pioneers of the Modern Movement* that it was the "genuine and legitimate style of our century." It embodied a completely new way of presenting form, which the Germans, from whose efforts the style mostly sprang, called the New Objectivity (Neue Sachlichkeit). This outlook was embraced by progressive architects, designers, and design schools across Germany, but it has instinctively come to be most closely associated with the Bauhaus as it redefined itself in 1923. The objective values that it demanded supplanted the emotional values of handwork that had dominated design since John Ruskin and William Morris exalted them. The elements of the New Objectivity were precisely described by the American critic Lewis Mumford (1895–1990) in his *Technics and Civilization* (1934), where he explained that "expression through the machine implies the recognition of relatively new esthetic terms: precision, calculation, flawlessness, simplicity, economy," elements that the hand could not easily achieve. "In machine work," Mumford continued, "the impersonal prevails, and if the worker leaves any tell-tale evidence of his part of the operation, it is a defect or flaw." These were the crucial features that the American photographer and sociologist Lewis Hine (1874–1940) recognized in his posed image of a worker (wielding an oversize wrench), showing the tight relationship of the components of the machine and the man subsumed by it, emphasizing mechanical flawlessness as he created a symbol of the machine aesthetic (Figure 5.1).

FIGURE 5.1.   Lewis Hine, *Steamfitter*, 1920. Gelatin silver print.

Interest in the machine as an aesthetic object manifested itself as early as the later nineteenth century and can notably be found in a talk given by the Scottish architect and teacher R. Rowand Anderson (1834–1921), who claimed that the machine itself might be raised into the realm of art. In his 1889 address to the Architectural Section of the National Association for the Advancement of Art and Its Application to Industry, of which he was president, Anderson spoke enthusiastically of the possibilities of the machine:

> The designing of machinery, whether for peace or war, has now reached such a high standard of excellence in function, form and expression, that these things are entitled to rank as works of art as much as a painting, a piece of sculpture, or a building, and also that machinery is the only true constructive art that has been produced since the decline of mediaeval architecture. That may seem to many of you a strong statement; but if you turn it over in your minds it will lose that character, and you will recognise the truth of it. Do not misunderstand me by thinking that I want to raise steam-hammers and pumps, or the work they do, to the level of a painting or a fine piece of sculpture . . . All that I maintain is that the machine itself is a true work of constructive art, and ought to be recognised as such.

Raising steam hammers and pumps to the level of art would have to wait until the twentieth century, when Lewis Hine and other photographers and artists would find inspiration for artistic expression in modern-day industry. The French artist and provocateur Marcel Duchamp (1887–1968) would also use the products of industrial design to challenge the boundaries of what could and could not be called art (in Duchamp's case, most famously, a standard-issue urinal, turned on its back and entitled *Fountain*, which he submitted unsuccessfully for exhibition in 1917).

It was not just the form of the machine but also its dynamism that stirred the artistic imagination, and this was promoted particularly by Italian Futurism, an artistic movement that evolved out of Cubism early in the second decade of the century. The Futurists, a group of artists and writers who were out to bring down the establishment, set their sights on the power and speed of the machine, primarily the automobile and the locomotive, with the poet Filippo Tommaso Marinetti (1876–1944) thundering about it in his "Manifesto of Futurism" in 1909: "We affirm that the world's magnificence has been enriched by a new beauty: the beauty of speed. A racing car whose hood is adorned with great pipes, like serpents of explosive breath—a roaring car that seems to ride on grapeshot is more beautiful than the [*Winged*] *Victory of Samothrace.* We want to hymn the man at the wheel, who hurls the lance of his spirit across the Earth, along the circle of his orbit." While Marinetti would battle the past by calling for the closing of museums and libraries and finding art and dynamism in objects of industry, by the 1920s, another Futurist artist, Enrico Prampolini (1894–1956), would raise the machine to religious heights: "Is not the machine today the most exuberant symbol of the mystery of human creation? Is it not the new mythical deity which weaves the legends and histories of the contemporary human drama?"

Machine Modernism at the Bauhaus

While Futurist artists found their symbol in the machine during the first two decades of the century, the Bauhaus, which had been founded in 1919, did not officially embrace it until the summer of 1923. At that time, pressure from Bauhaus opponents in the Weimar government led its director Walter Gropius to mount an exhibition of the students' work so that the progress of the school could be assessed. Faced by the government's

requirement, too soon from Gropius's point of view, he turned an onerous provocation into an international triumph. Although Gropius had gathered Expressionist artists who were well known in avant-garde art circles for his initial Bauhaus faculty—Itten, Kandinsky, the German-American Lionel Feininger (1871–1956), the Swiss Paul Klee (1879–1940), and the German Gerhard Marcks (1889–1981)—the school itself had achieved only limited recognition during its first four years. Now he devised a program of exhibitions and cultural events, including concerts by the most radical of musicians, which brought modern artists, architects, musicians, and others of the cultural elite to Weimar and put the Bauhaus on the map of pioneering European artistic institutions.

At the opening of the exhibition, Gropius announced that design for industrial production would now be the school's goal, and he added a motto to go with it: "Art and Technology, a New Unity!" This turnabout was triggered by the government's concerns, the school's ongoing financial difficulties, and probably by Theo van Doesburg's criticisms of the Bauhaus, which led Gropius to add practical considerations and collective solutions to the design coursework. Van Doesburg had lived in Weimar for some time during 1921 and 1922, hoping to become a teacher at the school. Thwarted in his hopes, and critical of the Bauhaus reliance on Expressionism and craft, van Doesburg offered his own independent lectures on De Stijl, including "The Will to Style" (see Sidebar 9), which were attended by a number of Bauhaus students. Direct connections with De Stijl and Rietveld's furniture (see Figure 4.19) are obvious in the wooden armchair that the Hungarian Marcel Breuer (1902–1981), then a Bauhaus student in the furniture workshop, created in 1922 (Figure 5.2). Its strictly horizontal and vertical components and its open construction leave no doubt about the source of its inspiration and the impact that van Doesburg had on the Bauhaus, when his support of industrial production also

FIGURE 5.2.   Marcel Breuer, Armchair, 1922.
Made by the Bauhaus furniture workshop. Oak with
canvas upholstery.

contributed to Walter Gropius's decision to change the direction in which the school was heading in 1923.

Espousing the machine was a critical move for the Bauhaus, for Gropius was jettisoning both the crafts, which had been at the core of its founding curriculum, and Expressionism, which had been its underlying aesthetic. This meant that the school would no longer emphasize the creativity of each individual but would push for a collaborative approach to design, and students would be expected to take into full account the technical aspects of their products along with their artistic forms. Gropius elaborated on the new direction that the school would be following in his essay "Theory and Organization of the Bauhaus," published in the catalogue of the exhibition. In a complete reversal of his founding manifesto, where he had written,

"Architects, sculptors, painters, we all must return to the crafts!" (see Sidebar 5), he declared that the Bauhaus "does not pretend to be a crafts school" and that "the teaching of a craft is meant to prepare for designing for mass production."

In redirecting the curriculum toward industry, Gropius promoted the aesthetic of the machine with all of the elements that Mumford outlined, elements that would later be recognized as a "Bauhaus style," much to Gropius's dismay because he believed that functionalist design should emerge naturally from necessity, and the designer's job was to give it a logical and impersonal form. Gropius entrusted much of the implementation of his new vision of industrial cooperation to László Moholy-Nagy (1895–1946), a Hungarian artist who had come to the Bauhaus in 1923 to work on typographic design and film. After Johannes Itten resigned from the school that year in protest against its turn toward commercial work, Moholy-Nagy took over the preliminary course and became form master of the metal workshop as well. The self-expression encouraged by Itten was replaced by the structural clarity and abstract dynamism of Moholy-Nagy's international Constructivism, a way of constructing spatial objects from simple materials, which was inspired by earlier Russian industrial examples but remained clearly within the world of art.

One of the first indications that the aesthetics at the school were changing was the dual nature of the 1923 exhibition catalogue, the cover by Herbert Bayer (1900–1985) and the interior by Moholy-Nagy. Bayer, an Austrian student who had recently completed the Expressionist-infused preliminary course under Itten, represented the aesthetic bent of the early Bauhaus, favoring intuition over a rationalized presentation in his cover design (Figure 5.3). On his hand-drawn cover, sans-serif letters vary in their width and spacing, condensed or expanded to make the lines equal in length. In grouping the letters artistically into alternating blocks of red and blue against black, he disregarded the fact that the highlighted groups would not

FIGURE 5.3. Herbert Bayer, Cover of *Staatliches Bauhaus, Weimar, 1919–1923*, 1923.

communicate as recognizable words. The title page by Moholy-Nagy is completely different, embodying a move toward clarity of visual communication through a rigorous and efficient approach to typography (Figure 5.4). The asymmetrical layout, a series of descending right angles, is hierarchical, ordered according to the importance of the information conveyed. "Bauhaus," the principal element of the title, dominates the page with its large initial letter and its vivid red color; the dates of the works in the exhibition, next in importance, are the same size but less emphatic because they are printed in black. Next, the components of the school's name, "Staatliches" (State) and "Weimar," are also the same size but subdued even more because they are striped, which sets them back visually from the plane of the page. Finally, the least important details, the facts of publication, are smaller, and at the bottom.

Jan Tschichold (1902–1974), a calligrapher who later documented the emergence of a new typographic style in Germany, had visited the Bauhaus exhibition in 1923. There, he absorbed many ideas about graphic design from Moholy-Nagy and others, which he would develop in his

own work and publish in his seminal book *The New Typography* in 1928. Bayer too would be influenced by Moholy-Nagy, and after he became a master at the school in 1925, he founded its typographic workshop, where he followed Moholy-Nagy's example in formulating an innovative, rational, graphic style for all of the school's printed matter and publicity, which he designed.

While a new typography would have been relatively easy to adopt by the Bauhaus, the change in aesthetic direction could not have spread throughout the school's workshops at once, and its handcrafted objects could not have been replaced by industrial products so quickly. But to appease his critics, Gropius contrived to make it seem that the Bauhaus workshops were already being directed toward industrial production. This was clearly reflected in metal works made by Marianne Brandt (1904–1995) and Wilhelm Wagenfeld (1900–1990), two students who entered Moholy-Nagy's workshop in 1923 after Gropius had announced his new direction for the school. Brandt, one of only a few women to have been allowed to join the metal workshop, was responsible for the remarkable Constructivist metal tea and coffee

FIGURE 5.4. László Moholy-Nagy, Title Page of *Staatliches Bauhaus, Weimar, 1919–1923*, 1923.

FIGURE 5.5.   Marianne Brandt, Tea Infuser, 1924. Made by the Bauhaus metal workshop. Brass and ebony.

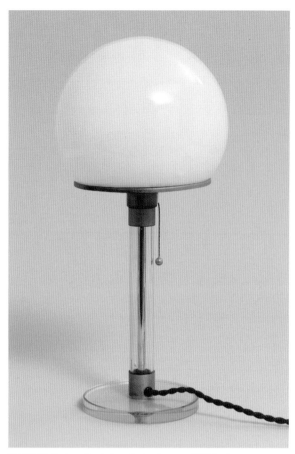

FIGURE 5.6.   Karl Jacob Jucker and Wilhelm Wagenfeld, Table Lamp, 1923–24. Made by the Bauhaus metal workshop. Glass, nickel-plated brass, and steel.

services that have become representative of the school's early machine style. Although she crafted their geometric forms by hand, the spheres, circles, and semicircles that she fashioned from both silver and non-precious metals were meant to appear as if they were made by machine, unlike earlier pieces produced in the workshop that revealed all the signs of the hand process (Figure 5.5; see also Figure 3.13).

Wagenfeld also engaged with the school's new design aesthetic, and especially Moholy-Nagy's desire to turn the metal workshop toward the creation of practical lighting design for industrial production, which achieved success only later in the decade. Wagenfeld's geometric glass and metal table lamp, which he made by revising a prototype designed by an earlier student, Karl Jacob Jucker (1902–1997), who had stayed at the school for only one year, has the appearance of a modern machine-made object even though it was fabricated by hand in the Bauhaus workshop (Figure 5.6). In 1924, to gauge the market for Bauhaus products, Wagenfeld was sent to a trade fair in Leipzig with a number of his lamps, which the metalwork students had made. Few were sold and the endeavor backfired, as

Wagenfeld reported: "Dealers and manufacturers laughed over our products. Although they looked like cheap machine products, they were in fact expensive handicrafts."

When Marcel Breuer, who became form master of the furniture workshop in 1925, designed the first piece of modern tubular-metal furniture that same year, he too was creating a handcrafted object in the guise of a machine-made product (Figure 5.7, center). A radical reinterpretation of the conventional club chair (see Figure 3.6), this light, steel-frame construction set on runners, with stretched fabric forming the seat and back, looked like nothing that had ever been seen before. Its

FIGURE 5.7.   Thonet, Brochure for Marcel Breuer's *Stahlmöbel* (Steel Furniture), 1931.

calligraphic frame was meant to appear as if it had been fabricated from a single piece of bent tube although it was made of segments of industrial metal tubing joined together. The design followed directly on Breuer's earlier experimental wooden chairs, which with their open structure and rational order were derived from the De Stijl forms of Rietveld (see Figure 4.19). But the idea of making a chair with steel tubes surfaced by chance when Breuer saw the potential in the structure of his new bicycle. Totally without knowledge of working with metal, and unsuccessful in persuading the bicycle manufacture to make a prototype for him, he went to the Junkers aircraft factory to gain the skills needed to develop a tubular-metal chair and partnered with a plumber to put the prototypes together for him. Once his tubular-metal chair proved viable, Breuer created a range of other

pieces using this material, including chairs, stools, tables, and fold-down auditorium seating. He had initially manufactured his metal furniture at the Bauhaus and then at Standard Möbel, a company he co-founded with a Hungarian partner, Kalman Lengyel (died 1945), but Standard Möbel's small-scale production caused many difficulties and by the end of the 1920s, Thonet, the giant bentwood manufacturer, took on the manufacture and sale of Breuer's metal designs.

Many of Breuer's designs were directed to fitting out the interiors of the new concrete, glass, and steel building that Walter Gropius designed in Dessau, where the Bauhaus moved in 1926 after being edged out of Weimar by its new conservative government (Figure 5.8). Not all the students and masters moved with the Bauhaus, however, including many of the women

FIGURE 5.8.
Walter Gropius,
Bauhaus, Dessau,
Germany, 1926.

in the weaving workshop, who were wary of the industrial direction in which the school was going. Wagenfeld, Erich Dieckmann, and several others stayed behind to work at the State Academy of Craft and Architecture (Staatliche Bauhochschule), the successor school, which continued to occupy the building that Henry van de Velde had designed for it. The academy was directed by the architect Otto Bartning (1883–1959), who in 1919 had helped develop the educational program that Gropius followed at the Bauhaus. The school adhered to progressive ideas, like the Bauhaus, and it too was closed by the Nazi government, even earlier, in 1930.

After the move to Dessau, the Bauhaus became more aggressive about licensing its products. In his 1926 paper "Bauhaus Dessau—Principles of Bauhaus Production," Gropius noted that the school's "laboratories" were then engaged in developing standard forms for industrial production (see Sidebar 10). Gropius, who had had considerable exposure to standardization when he was a young architect, having spent several crucial years working in the office of Peter Behrens, now espoused the idea of standard types as a "social necessity." By the end of the decade, the Bauhaus

had concluded contracts with lighting, metal, textile, and wallpaper manufacturers, mostly under the leadership of a new director, Hannes Meyer (1889–1954), a Swiss socialist architect who took control of the school after Gropius resigned in 1928. Meyer reorganized the curriculum along practical and socially relevant lines in keeping with Gropius's move toward standard types, and he expected the school to focus increasingly on technology.

It was not until 1930, however, that the weaving workshop signed its contract for the production of Bauhaus fabrics with the large manufacturer Polytextil. By this time, the architect Mies van der Rohe had become director of the Bauhaus, which he led until the school was shut down by the Nazi government in 1933. The weaving workshop was then headed by Gunta Stölzl (1897–1983), one of the first students enrolled at the Bauhaus, who became a journeyman, instructor, and then master, the only woman to have fulfilled that role at the school. From the time the Bauhaus was founded, women had not been treated equally although the guidelines stated that the school would be open to any qualified student and women could not be excluded from enrolling. But when so many women applied, the school established a

SIDEBAR 10   Walter Gropius, "Bauhaus Dessau—Principles of Bauhaus Production," 1926

The creation of standard types for all practical commodities of everyday use is a social necessity.

On the whole, the necessities of life are the same for the majority of people. The home and its furnishings are mass consumer goods, and their design is more a matter of reason than a matter of passion. The machine—capable of producing standardized products—is an effective device, which, by means of mechanical aids—steam and electricity—can free the individual from working manually for the satisfaction of his daily needs and can provide him with mass-produced products that are cheaper and better than those manufactured by hand. There is no danger that standardization will force a choice upon the individual, since due to natural competition the number of available types of each object will always be ample to provide the individual with a choice of design that suits him best.

The Bauhaus workshops are essentially laboratories in which prototypes of products suitable for mass production and typical of our time are carefully developed and constantly improved.

In these laboratories the Bauhaus wants to train a new kind of collaborator for industry and the crafts, who has an equal command of both technology and form.

To reach the objective of creating a set of standard prototypes which meet all the demands of economy, technology, and form, requires the selection of the best, most versatile, and most thoroughly educated men who are well grounded in workshop experience and who are imbued with an exact knowledge of the design elements of form and mechanics and their underlying laws.

"women's department" to avoid overwhelming the male population. This was soon transformed into the weaving workshop, where most of the female students were directed.

The new priority given to closely integrating structure and pattern in the weaving workshop at Dessau is reflected in the design for a woven geometrical wall hanging in red, black, gray, and white by Anni Albers (1899–1994), who was a Bauhaus student from 1922 to 1930 (Figure 5.9). Following the setup of her loom, she divided the work into twelve vertical strips. The pattern takes two modular rectangular units, one with bold horizontal stripes, the second solid except for a thin cross that divides it, and varies the design by alternating colors, position (sometimes joining two, three, or four striped sections together), and juxtaposition, creating an orderly, inventive, integrated composition.

The Bauhaus had signed its most lucrative industrial contract in 1929, for a Bauhaus wallpaper collection, which was set in motion by the director of the Rasch Brothers wallpaper manufacturer in Hannover. Wallpaper design was not part of the curriculum and it became the project of the mural-painting workshop, which was headed by Hinerk Scheper (1897–1957), a painter and former Bauhaus student. This was a paradoxical involvement for the Bauhaus because the modernist aesthetic renounced ornamentation of any kind. But the designs, like one created by the artist and color theorist Josef Albers (1888–1976), Anni's husband and a Bauhaus student, teacher, and then master, were very subtle (Figure 5.10). More like textured, mottled, or gridded surfaces than recognizable patterns, these papers seemed to unify interiors rather than call attention to themselves as decoration. Millions of rolls were printed, low-cost,

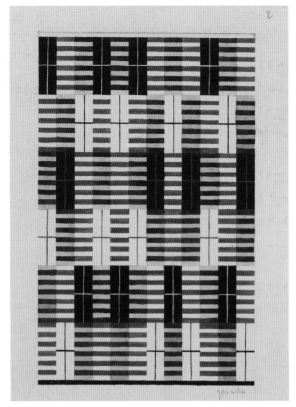

FIGURE 5.9. Anni Albers, Design for Wall Hanging, 1926. Gouache on paper.

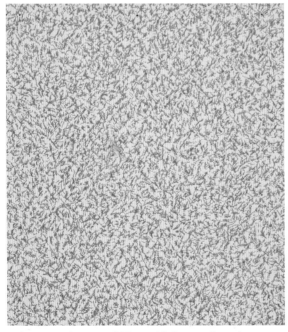

FIGURE 5.10. Josef Albers, Wallpaper Sample, c. 1929, from Bauhaus Wallpaper Collection. Produced by Rasch Brothers. Printed paper.

standard products that found a ready market for the large housing developments that were under construction throughout Germany in this time, and ultimately a justification for the Bauhaus move toward education for mass production.

Machine Modernism Elsewhere

The emergence of a full-fledged machine style was reflected at the Weissenhof experimental housing exhibition in Stuttgart in 1927. Organized by the German Werkbund, the exhibition comprised a series of striking buildings designed by some of the leading modern architects in Europe, among them Le Corbusier, the Dutchmen J. J. P. Oud (1890–1963) and Mart Stam (1899–1986), the Viennese Josef Frank (1885–1967), and the Germans Walter Gropius, Hans Scharoun (1893–1972), Max Taut (1884–1967), and Mies van der Rohe, who was the exhibition's artistic director. A number of the interiors were shown furnished and incorporated new examples of tubular-steel designs, but many were fitted out with wooden furniture, mainly bentwood models by Thonet, along with more progressive designs, including Dieckmann's modular system (see Figure 3.22) and one by Breuer.

Among the modern lighting shown at Weissenhof was that of the Dutch architect Willem H. Gispen (1890–1981). Gispen's firm had originally produced decorative metalwork, but he began to manufacture modern lamps using standardized methods and interchangeable parts in 1926 after he was introduced to new design ideas by reading *De Stijl* and other innovative art journals. Gispen developed a glass with a thin, semi-translucent coating that gave a soft, even light with little glare, which became a distinguishing feature of the lamps he sold under the brand name Giso. The company soon became a major manufacturer of modern furnishings in Europe with advertising that followed a unified house style, featuring bold contrasts of typographic scale, expressive photography by modern Dutch photographers, primarily Jan Kamman (1898–1983), and a De Stijl color palette of black, red, and white (Figure 5.11).

A number of new ideas for tubular-steel furniture appeared at the Stuttgart exhibition, including an unsettling new concept for seating, the cantilever, based on an idea originated by Mart Stam (Figure 5.12). Stam, an enigmatic utopian thinker, designed a row of model workers' houses for the exhibition but is better remembered as the designer of the cantilever chair introduced there. The chair, which was supported only by the front legs, sat on runners that formed the cantilever. This development might have seemed precarious to those who first saw it in the 1920s, although the weight of the sitter spread equally across the seat easily kept the chair from falling forward. Stam had earlier described his idea to a group of architects preparing for the Stuttgart exhibition and Marcel Breuer had lifted it for his own, more refined, version. This gave rise to a lengthy lawsuit to determine the ownership of the concept, with Stam's claim of precedence over Breuer's version being upheld by court decree. Two models of Breuer's more elegant cantilever chair

FIGURE 5.11.   W. H. Gispen, Poster for Giso Lamps, 1929. Lithograph. Photograph by Jan Kamman.

51
Stahlrohrmöbel von Mart Stam, Rotterdam

FIGURE 5.12.   Mart Stam, Steel Furniture for House No. 28 at the Weissenhof Housing Estate, Stuttgart, from *Die Wohnung*, 1927.

were illustrated along with his club chair and his line of standard chairs in a 1931 advertisement for Thonet's tubular-steel line (see Figure 5.7, upper left and bottom right). The advertisement shows that contrary to a later misunderstanding that regarded modernist designs as neutral in tonality, possibly because initial images of these products were reproduced in black and white, tubular-metal furniture could be very colorful (see also Figures 5.14, 5.15), both their frames (when lacquered) and their upholstery. In addition to chromed steel, Thonet's tubular-metal frames could be had in enameled red, brick red, lemon, cream, green, blue, violet, chocolate, silver gray, white, black, pea green, silver, and gold bronze.

While these tubular-metal works called for mass production, Mies van der Rohe designed much of his furniture as sumptuous objects of flat steel bars made for specific buildings and for limited production. The chairs (and accompanying stools) he designed for the steel and glass German pavilion at the Barcelona World's Fair in 1929, a splendid setting in which the king and queen of Spain could officially open Germany's participation at the fair, had X-shaped frames, symbols of authority that dated back to ancient times (Figure 5.13). The back and front legs crossed beneath the seat, with the back leg continuing to the floor in a fluid S curve. Rich and dignified, the chairs were gracefully composed and upholstered in regal white kid leather. Mies used a similarly elegant vocabulary for the functional but luxurious house that he built between 1928 and 1930 for the Tugendhat family in Brno, Czechoslovakia (now the Czech Republic). Like the German pavilion, it displayed a stunning wall of onyx in the sitting area of the house, and a large semicircular wall of exotic ebony surrounding the dining area, shown here in a miraculous restoration of the interior after decades of alterations and neglect (Figure 5.14). For the furnishings of the living spaces Mies created two new chairs, the squat cantilever Tugendhat model made of flat metal bars and upholstered in gray silk

FIGURE 5.13. Ludwig Mies van der Rohe, Barcelona Chair, 1929. Chrome-plated steel with leather upholstery.

in the sitting area and tubular-metal Brno chairs covered in white calfskin, which were in the dining area beyond. He also included his Barcelona chairs and stools upholstered in emerald-green leather and his cantilever chaise longue in ruby red. The startling colors set in this stark modern space were probably chosen by Mies's associate Lilly Reich (1885–1947), an exhibition and interior designer. Once again they challenge the assumption of austerity that for decades has been considered typical for an interior made of industrial materials, steel columns, large expanses of glass, and white linoleum.

For his part, Le Corbusier had hoped to use metal furniture in the two houses he built

FIGURE 5.14.   Ludwig Mies van der Rohe, Living Area of Tugendhat House, Brno, Czech Republic, 1928–30.

for the Weissenhof exhibition, but his office was unsuccessful in producing models in time, leaving him with standard metal bedsteads and bentwood furniture to complete his interiors. It may seem ironic that Le Corbusier was designing individualistic furniture in 1927 when he had argued so strongly for adopting standard types just two years earlier, but he must have felt great pressure to keep up with the other progressive architects who were exploring the possibilities offered by metal. After the exhibition closed, apparently to push this side of his work along, he hired the young French designer Charlotte Perriand (1903–1999) as an associate for the firm. Although he was hostile to her when she first came to his office in search of work ("We don't

embroider cushions here" was his response on meeting her), Le Corbusier hired her immediately after seeing an exhibition with metal furnishings that she had designed. Soon she would have the responsibility for completing all aspects of the firm's new line of metal furniture in collaboration with Le Corbusier and Pierre Jeanneret, which was introduced in a model apartment installation at the Salon d'Automne in Paris in 1929. Le Corbusier designated this installation the "Interior Equipment of a Dwelling," his definitive stand against the traditional term "decorative arts," which he had so thoroughly denounced in his book *The Decorative Art of Today* (1925). "Why," he had asked, "should chairs, bottles, baskets, shoes, which are all objects of utility, all *tools*, be called *decorative art?*"—and

FIGURE 5.15.   Charlotte Perriand, Revolving Armchair, 1928. Chrome-plated tubular steel and leather.

he now replaced the term "decorative art" with the word "equipment."

The firm's ensemble of four seating pieces, which included a swivel chair Perriand had designed independently earlier (Figure 5.15), followed Le Corbusier's ideas about standard seating types, for work or dining (Perriand's chair), for conversation, for comfort, and for relaxation. The seating type meant for relaxation was a chaise longue with a tubular-steel frame that sat freely within a sheet-metal base. It was shown with Perriand relaxing in it, face coyly averted, in her article in *The Studio* entitled "Wood or Metal?," which was published in 1929 (Figure 5.16). The designers described it in their patent application as "capable of being used equally as an armchair or ordinary chaise longue, as a seat for relaxation, as a medical seat for resting the legs [with head down and feet elevated], and finally as a 'rocking-chair,'" a fully multipurpose design. The

"chaise longue takes all positions," they observed, and "weight alone is enough to keep it in the chosen position; no mechanism. It is the true machine for resting." Perriand's article was a rebuttal to an earlier article with same title in which the English author and critic John Gloag (1896–1981) complained of the "utter inhumanity" of metal furniture. Perriand took it upon herself to set him straight about metal design, denigrating the properties of wood while praising the attributes of metal: strong, hygienic, suited to mass production, and capable of creating "new aesthetic effects." She wrote that "metal plays the same part in furniture as cement has done in architecture," and added, in Corbusian fashion, *"IT IS A REVOLUTION."*

Modernism and the Organic Style

When John Gloag posed his question "Wood or Metal?" in *The Studio* in 1929, he chose the wrong time to do it. This was exactly the moment when the craze for metal furniture was at its height, and Gloag's words were simply brushed off by Charlotte Perriand in her response to it. Although many may have agreed with Gloag that metal "is cold and brutally hard, and . . . it gives no comfort to the eye," there was little immediate outspoken support for his point of view. Soon, however, wooden designs began to edge out metal ones as designers, especially those in Scandinavia, France, and England, explored the use of natural materials and demonstrated that wood too could be a medium of modernity.

The rediscovery of wood was often linked to organic form. This went beyond simply using natural materials to borrowing from the processes of nature and to challenging the imposition of intellectually derived forms on design by the machine modernists. This approach called for a more essential strategy in which functionality might emerge within the spirit of natural growth, regardless of the materials from which an object

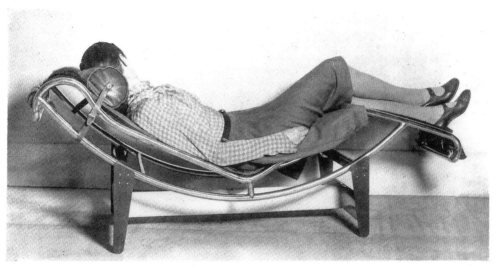

Metal Couch designed by Le Corbusier, Pierre Jeanneret and Charlotte Perriand

WOOD OR METAL?

A reply to Mr. John Gloag's article in our January issue by Charlotte Perriand who, as champion of new ideas, has adopted an original style of expressing them

METAL plays the same part in furniture as cement has done in architecture.

IT IS A REVOLUTION.

The FUTURE will favour materials which best solve the problems propounded by the new man :

I understand by the NEW MAN the type of individual who keeps pace with scientific thought, who understands his age and lives it : The Aeroplane, the Ocean Liner and the Motor are at his service ;

Sport gives him health ;

His House is his resting place.

WHAT IS HIS HOUSE TO BE?

Hygiene must be considered first : soap and water.

Tidiness : standard cupboards with partitions for these.

Rest · resting machines for ease and pleasant repose.

Beds : armchairs : chaises longues : Office chairs and tables : Stools, some high and some low : Folding chairs.

The French word for furniture, "MEUBLES" comes from the Latin "mobilis" : meaning things that can be moved about.

The only things that come into this category are chairs and tables.

We have stated the problem ; now we must solve it. . . .

MATERIAL NOW IN USE AND MATERIAL THAT OUGHT TO BE USED.

WOOD : a vegetable substance, in its very nature bound to decay, it is susceptible to the action of damp in the air. " Central heating dries the air and warps wood." Since the war, we don't get dry wood any more : it is dried by artificial means, and inadequately.

Plywood : Composition wood :

These should be used for panels, mounted on a metal framework, and allowing for " play."

METAL : a homogeneous material of which certain alloys are liable to be affected by acids in the air :

In that case protection is afforded by oxidising, or by application of paint, Duco, etc. . . .

Cupboards of beaten sheet iron :

For chairs, metal " bicycle " tubes :

A bicycle weighs only 10 to 12 kilograms. The minimum of weight, the maximum of strength :

FIGURE 5.16. Charlotte Perriand, "Wood or Metal?," from *The Studio*, 1929.

was made. The German architect and theoretician Hugo Häring (1882–1958) expressed this perspective in "Approaches to Form," an article published in 1925: "If we prefer to search for shapes rather than to propose them, to discover forms rather than to construct them, we are in harmony with nature and act with her rather than against her." And he continued: "We no longer take a motif on which we plan to base the form we create out of the geometrical world but take it instead from the world of organic forms, as we have seen that, in order to create for life, we must create as nature does, organically and not geometrically."

A modern organic sensibility appeared with the wooden furniture of Finland's leading twentieth-century architect, Alvar Aalto (1894–1949), which called on his love of his country's wooded landscape. But it was also a response to the free-form, dreamlike shapes of Surrealism, especially the work of his friend the artist Jean Arp (1888–1986), which was most directly echoed in the vase Aalto designed for the Savoy restaurant in Helsinki in 1937 and other of his works in glass (Figures 5.17, 5.18). Like Gloag, Aalto was candid with his criticism of metal once he began to use wood for his furniture, which paradoxically occurred when he was building his modern concrete and glass tuberculosis sanatorium in Paimio, Finland,

between 1929 and 1933. In step with other international modernists, he had designed several tubular-metal chairs in the later 1920s, but he came to realize that the human aspects of furniture were lost when they were made with metal. This was especially important in his work for the sanatorium, where he reconsidered all aspects of its interior furnishings and fittings in order to create a healthful and healing environment. "Tubular and chromium surfaces are good solutions technically," he explained, "but psychophysically these materials are not good for the human being. The sanatorium needed furniture that should be light, flexible, easy to clean, and so on. After extensive experimentation in wood, the flexible system was discovered and a method and material combined to produce furniture that was better for the human touch and more suitable as the general material for the long and painful life in a sanatorium."

In returning to wood, Aalto set out to replicate the structural innovations of what had already

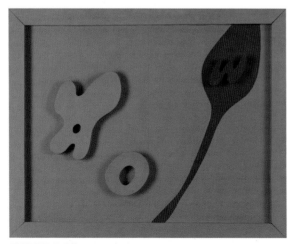

FIGURE 5.17.   Jean Arp, *Torso, Navel, Mustache—Flower*, 1930. Oil on wood relief.

FIGURE 5.18.   Alvar Aalto, Savoy Vase, 1937. Made by Karhula. Mold-blown glass.

FIGURE 5.19.   Alvar Aalto, Armchair, 1930. Made by Huonekalu-ja Rakennustyötehdas. Birch, laminated birch, and birch plywood.

become icons of 1920s design, Marcel Breuer's club and cantilever chairs in tubular metal (see Figure 5.7). The armchair Aalto designed for the lounge of the Paimio sanatorium, with its fluid wooden frame and suspended plywood seat, responded to the open geometry of Breuer's armchair (Figure 5.19). Aalto experimented extensively with his friend the furniture manufacturer Otto Korhonen (1884–1935) before they could work out the laminating and bending techniques required to give the chair adequate support and impart flexibility to its single-piece seat and back. Creating a cantilever chair in wood was even more difficult, for Aalto and Korhonen had to find a way to fabricate a bent wooden frame that had both strength and the resilience that Aalto desired (Figure 5.20).

Aalto's plywood furniture was shown in London in 1933, where it soon found a steady market. It also spurred British manufacturers, such as Isokon (established 1929) and Makers of Simple Furniture, founded by Gerald Summers (1899–1967) in 1931, to produce designs in plywood. By 1935, the difficulties of dealing with distributors abroad led Aalto and his wife, Aino Aalto (1894–1949), also an architect and designer, to take control of their own work. Along with two partners they established the firm Artek (its name put together from "art" and "technology") to distribute and market the Aaltos' designs, as it continues to do today. Like Le Corbusier, Aalto referred to his industrially produced work as standard furniture, and that is how he designated it in Artek's publicity.

FIGURE 5.20.   Alvar Aalto, Chair, 1931–32. Made by Huonekalu-ja Rakennustyötehdas. Birch, laminated birch, and birch plywood.

FIGURE 5.21.   Bruno Mathsson, Chair, 1933–36. Made by Karl Mathsson. Laminated and bent beech and jute.

The Swedish furniture maker Bruno Mathsson (1907–1988), following the ideas of Aalto and Le Corbusier, also divided his chairs into standard types in order to create optimum forms for working, sitting, and lounging. Although he had perfected his craft along traditional lines in his family's cabinetmaking business, he left this behind once he saw Aalto's wooden furniture. This set the direction for his later work, chairs that replaced conventional upholstery with hemp webbing woven around sinuous, laminated-wood frames, which he further refined as he did physiological research into human proportions and the positions of seating (Figure 5.21). He himself worked out many of the manufacturing techniques for laminating and bending the frames and legs into the fluid forms that would best serve each function. By the end of the 1930s, his chairs had attained international recognition and made his reputation as a central figure of Swedish Modern design.

In 1938, the Museum of Modern Art celebrated the achievement of the Bauhaus with a great retrospective exhibition. The same year, it belatedly recognized the work of Aalto, introducing him to the American public in a solo exhibition, with its curator, John McAndrew, sheepishly announcing the museum's new respect for the changing course of Modernism over the previous decade:

Like the designs of other men first active in the '30's, Aalto's work, without ceasing in any way to be modern, does not look like the modern work of the '20's. The younger men employ new materials and new methods of construction, of course, but these only partly explain the change. The buildings of men working naturally in an already established style are less assertive of that style's tenets than those earlier and more puristic buildings which were establishing the style with a necessarily stringent discipline. Certain materials and forms once renounced because of their association with non-modern work are now used again, in new ways or even in the old ones. To the heritage of pure geometric shapes, the younger men have added free organic curves; to the stylistic analogies with the painters, Mondrian and Léger, they have added Arp.

CHAPTER 6

Industrial Design

The 1929 Wall Street stock market crash set the stage for the meteoric rise of industrial design. By the end of the next decade it seemed that everything in the world had been redesigned, from "lipsticks to locomotives" according to Raymond Loewy (1893–1986) in his tongue-in-cheek-entitled 1951 memoir, *Never Leave Well Enough Alone*. As the economic crisis evolved into a worldwide depression, consumer confidence evaporated, orders for manufactured goods vanished, and untold numbers of workers lost their jobs, an ongoing cycle that continued to reinforce the downward turn of production. Faced with the stiff market decline, major American companies hired independent consultants like Loewy to reassess and redesign their products to appeal to the still-employed workers who might be wary of discretionary spending in troubled times. The consultants' task was to create modern, commercially appealing, mass-produced goods that would entice these consumers back to the marketplace, and in a good many instances, they effected an almost miraculous increase in sales. These multitalented designers, energetically engaged in a new profession they themselves originated, had an enormous range. They took on transportation, household appliances, radios, furniture and furnishings, exhibition and packaging design, advertising, and

corporate-identity systems, with the manufacturers essentially dividing their work among a small cadre of creative talent. Like the machine modernists, they sought to bring art into industry, but they rejected the stability of geometric functionalism for an expressive vocabulary of speed, motion, and overtly symbolic forms. It was these often criticized commercial designers who finally fulfilled the nineteenth-century dreams of producing well-designed, economical, ordinary objects, and in this case, with a distinctly American flair. In other countries the profession of industrial design was slower to take off, with engineers, inventors, and architects more likely to be the ones to give modern forms to ordinary objects than specialists in commercial design, and it was not until after the Second World War that industrial-design firms began to make inroads elsewhere.

Streamlining and Styling

American industrial designers engaged in what the New York advertising executive Earnest Elmo Calkins (1868–1964) dubbed "consumer engineering," which he defined as "shaping a product to fit more exactly consumers' needs or tastes." But for him, the real problem was "how to persuade a people to consume more goods," with one of his solutions being "artificial obsolescence," or deliberately making changes in fashion in order to spark consumer desires and spur sales. "Goods fall into two classes," Calkins wrote, "those we use, such as motor-cars or safety razors, and those we use *up*, such as toothpaste or soda biscuit. Consumer engineering must see to it that we use *up* the kinds of goods we now merely use." In this, he was picking up on the enthusiasm for obsolescence discussed by Christine Frederick in her 1929 book *Selling Mrs. Consumer*:

> America's triumphs and rapidity of progress are based on *progressive obsolescence*. We have not been aware of it, either as consumers or producers, but we have an attitude that is quite different from the rest of the world, and of late years we have been speeding it up. It appears to be a part of our new economic principle, the expansible wage fund, and its result, our increased income. It is the ambition of almost every American to practice progressive obsolescence as a

ladder by which to climb to greater human satisfactions through the purchase of more of the fascinating and thrilling range of goods and services being offered today.

While it is now recognized that using goods up quickly and replacing them with more goods is wasteful of resources and harmful to the planet, in the 1930s this method of stimulating consumer spending was seen as a positive step toward reviving the nation's economy during the Great Depression and renewing the profits of American corporations.

A significant step toward encouraging consumers to "use up" goods (or at least replace them) had been taken by the Detroit automotive industry in 1925, when the General Motors Corporation (GM) opted for its annual model-change policy. Until the mid-1920s, the industry had been dominated by the Ford Motor Company's unchanging Model T, a black and boxy vehicle with an open, buggy-shaped body (Figure 6.1). Henry Ford had introduced it in 1908 as an inexpensive vehicle for workers and he meant it to be long-lasting. "We want the man who buys one of our products never to have

FIGURE 6.1.
Model T Ford in Albany, Minnesota, 1923.

to buy another," Ford wrote in his autobiography in 1922. "We never make an improvement that renders any previous model obsolete." With this, he justified keeping the Model T just as it was; efficiently made on the first moving assembly line since 1913, it had in the best of years reached production figures of over one million cars annually. But by the mid-1920s the Model T was facing stiff competition from the more design-conscious and colorful automobiles that had come on the market, especially General Motor's stylish, closed-body Chevrolet. Ford's obstinate, and eventually disastrous, anti-design stance lingered until 1927, when in the face of plummeting sales, the Model T was replaced at great expense by the more advanced and somewhat more style-minded Model A.

The automobiles produced under General Motor's planned, or artificial, obsolescence program tempted those who wanted more style or more status than Ford's everyman's car would grant them. Each year from 1927 on, General Motors added new features, some functional improvements, some a matter of style, to its automobiles. They were trying to convince consumers to trade in their old cars, which GM expected would now seem hopelessly out of date, and replace them with new models (thus opening up a vast and lucrative secondary market in used cars). In 1927 Alfred P. Sloan, Jr. (1875–1966), president of General Motors, also hired its first automobile stylist, Harley Earl (1893–1969), to head a new Art and Colour Section (later changed to Styling), overseeing some fifty employees as they designed the yearly models for the company's five divisions. Earl's experience had been in Hollywood, where he created extravagant custom cars for Hollywood stars in his father's automobile works, and he brought an understanding of the aspirations of popular culture with him to Detroit. Although not a designer himself, Earl was able to impress his ideas onto GM's stable of designers, and his vision was demonstrated by his 1937 two-seater Buick Y-Job convertible, which is credited with giving direction to the entire American automobile industry during the later 1930s and the 1940s (Figure 6.2). Considered the first dream, or concept, car, it was a fully functioning automobile produced to test new features that might be incorporated into

FIGURE 6.2.   Harley Earl and General Motors, Buick Y-Job, 1937.

SIDEBAR 11 Norman Bel Geddes, *Horizons*, 1932

Driving to-day's motor car is a peculiar experience for one who understands in the least degree the principles of aërodynamics; for he realizes that the mechanism under his control is so inadequately designed from this viewpoint that it would be more efficient if it were operated with the rear end to the front.

Put your hand out of the window of a car traveling at thirty miles an hour, and gauge the force of the wind resistance. Do the same at sixty miles an hour. Compare, for the sake of a rough guess, the area of your hand with the total area of the car opposed to the same pressure. In this, you have the basis for a rough calculation of the tremendous inefficiency, in one respect, of to-day's motor car. Only realize, in addition, that the partial vacuum caused by projections such as lamps and fenders, abrupt steps or changes in contour such as the windshield, and the vacuum at the rear of the body itself more than doubles the resistance caused by the wind pressure at the front.

The subject of aërodynamics is anything but simple. Some applications of its principles, however, are not difficult to define. An object is *airfoiled* when its exterior surface is so designed that upon being projected through air, a useful dynamic reaction is imparted to the object by the action of the air. The lift of an airplane wing is an excellent example of a useful dynamic reaction. An object is *streamlined* when its exterior surface is so designed that upon passing through a fluid such as water or air the object creates the least disturbance in the fluid in the form of eddies or partial vacua tending to produce resistance. In other words, an object is airfoiled in order to *create* a disturbance and an object is streamlined in order to *eliminate* disturbances in the media through which they pass (Figure 6.3).

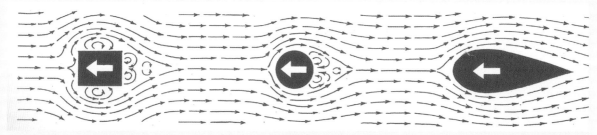

FIGURE 6.3. Norman Bel Geddes, Principle of Streamlining, from *Horizons*, 1932.

future GM models—and the public's reaction to them. The curvilinear silhouette, with its integrated fenders, flush door handles, and concealed headlights, shows the extent that automobiles had changed, from the rectangular, carriage-like body of the Model T to the streamlined, aerodynamically conceived, forms of the 1930s. This major new stylistic feature was more easily achieved with Earl's adoption of soft clay for modeling favored by custom car designers instead of following the industry practice of using hard metal for the model-making process.

In his book *Horizons*, published in 1932, Norman Bel Geddes (1893–1958) outlined the significance of streamlining for the design of automobiles as well as for airplanes, steamships, buses, and trains. Geddes had been an internationally known stage designer before moving into industrial design in 1927, drawn by the new profession's seemingly limitless creative possibilities, what he thought would be the focus of future modern artistic expression. His book offered a justification for streamlining transportation, which by introducing a teardrop-shaped vehicle aimed to reduce air or water resistance in order to attain greater speeds or more efficiency (see Sidebar 11 and Figure 6.3). He illustrated this principle with many of his own forward-looking concepts for transportation, but these futuristic forms initially met with limited interest from manufacturers, and his own streamlined Airflow automobile designed for Chrysler in 1934 was a problem-ridden failure.

About the same time, in 1933, R. Buckminster Fuller (1895–1983) and W. Starling Burgess (1878–1947) were working together to bring their own streamlined automobile to completion. Fuller, visionary designer, engineer, architect, inventor, poet, scientist, and futurist, and Burgess, an aeronautical engineer and naval architect, collaborated on building a three-wheel automobile partially based on Fuller's earlier design for a hybrid automobile-airplane. The teardrop-shaped, twenty-foot-long "Dymaxion" car—an advertiser's made-up word from bits of "dynamic," "maximum," and "tension" that Fuller adopted to describe design that was as efficient as possible within the limitations of available technology—was driven by the two front wheels and steered by the single rear wheel (Figure 6.4). Its construction followed that of a boat, with an aluminum-sheathed plywood frame and a canvas roof. Although the Dymaxion car could reach high speeds with considerable fuel efficiency, this total rethinking of the typology of the automobile was never marketed, in part because the car was involved in a freak accident when it was being shown at the Century of Progress International Exhibition in Chicago in 1933.

Perhaps the most dramatic example of streamlining was the Twentieth Century Limited locomotive designed for the New York Central Railroad by Henry Dreyfuss (1904–1972) in 1938, which brought high-speed travel between New York and Chicago into a luxury mode (Figure 6.5). Dreyfuss had trained as a designer of theatrical

FIGURE 6.4.
R. Buckminster Fuller entering his Dymaxion automobile, 1933. Designed with W. Starling Burgess.

FIGURE 6.5.   Henry Dreyfuss, Twentieth Century Limited Locomotive, New York Central Railroad, 1938. Poster by Leslie Ragan.

As streamlining was quickly catching on in the transportation industries, designers were introducing decorative derivatives as a way of styling products that did not actually move themselves. In styling, designers were most likely to favor symbolic form and futuristic ornament suggestive of the speed that their products would never attain. Such maneuvers evoked immediate censure for what critics considered the dishonesty of their forms, and in 1934, only two years after he published *Horizons*, Geddes felt the need to clarify the uses and misuses of "streamlining" in an article in the *Atlantic Monthly*:

> Originally the word "streamline" was a term of hydrodynamics. About the year 1909 the science of aerodynamics borrowed it to describe smooth flow of air as well as the form of a body which would move through air with a minimum of resistance. For some years, "streamline" in its aerodynamic sense enjoyed honorable obscurity in the physics laboratory and the shop talk of engineers. Last year, however, advertising copy writers seized upon it as a handy synonym for the word "new," using it indiscriminately and often inexactly to describe automobiles and women's dresses, railroad trains and men's shoes.

sets under Geddes, and then followed his mentor into industrial design. He shrouded the locomotive in a shell of steel, its spherical nose adorned with a vertical fin that centered the headlamp at front, but he underscored its added power and efficiency by keeping the running mechanism open and in full view on the sides. The Twentieth Century Limited achieved a unity of design by coordinating its sweep of cars with the engine, unifying them with a two-tone-gray color scheme and aluminum and blue stripes along their length. Inside, the harmonious design continued, with spare, modern metal furnishings and stage-like lighting making the dining and observation cars showpieces for what was then considered a rolling hotel.

While Geddes himself disparaged such inaccurate terminology as well as the onslaught of ornamental streamlining, his office too would lean in this direction by taking on the styling of household products, among them the chrome-plated Soda-King seltzer siphon from 1935 (Figure 6.6). A smooth curving skin hides the internal parts of the siphon, obscuring with its elegant silhouette any indication of the way it functions. The siphon was inscribed with Geddes's by then well-known name, a sales practice that became increasingly popular during the 1930s, but it was actually designed and patented by one of his partners, Worthen Paxton (1905–1977), an engineer and

FIGURE 6.6. Worthen Paxton and Norman Bel Geddes, Soda-King Siphon Bottle, 1935. Made by Kidd. Chrome-plated and enameled metal.

architect by training who quietly contributed to many of Geddes's products.

An entire chapter in *Industrial Design: A Practical Guide*, written by the early industrial designer Harold Van Doren (1895–1957), was devoted to the streamlined object. He described for the reader, whether student, designer, draftsman, or manufacturer, the how-to details of "nonfunctional" streamlining, which he defined as "the substitution of radii and fillets for sharp angles and corners." He compared two ways of working with sheet metal, the material of which most appliances were made: fabrication, which "limits you to purely geometrical forms," and stamping, which "permits much greater latitude in the development of what, for want of a better name, we shall call 'freehand forms,' that is, forms curved in two or more planes at the

same time." His own pure white Maytag washing machine, with its two simple red accents, stood as an illustration of the results he promoted in his book, its ample forms exemplifying the soft, inflated curves that could be achieved with stamping (Figure 6.7). But streamlining could do more than just alter the form of a product; it could dramatically boost its revenues, with *Time* magazine putting Raymond Loewy on its cover in 1949 and trumpeting his great success with the words "he streamlines the sales curve." Born in France, Loewy came to the United States after the First World War, skilled as an artist and with training as an engineer. His early impression of "the chasm between the excellent quality of much American production and its gross appearance, clumsiness, bulk, and noise" led him to search for work in the field of industrial design, which he attained by promoting its economic benefits to corporative executives.

FIGURE 6.7. Advertisement for Maytag Wringer Washing Machine. Designed by Harold Van Doren, 1939.

Industrial Design in the United States

The object that met with the greatest criticism for its streamlined styling was Loewy's prototype metal pencil sharpener, patented in 1933 (Figure 6.8). The aerodynamic, teardrop form of the sharpener, and its propeller-like handle alluding directly to aeronautics, made it an easy target for disdain. It was not only repeatedly criticized by modernists but was also rejected by some of Loewy's own industrial-design colleagues, suggesting an ambivalence within the profession about how

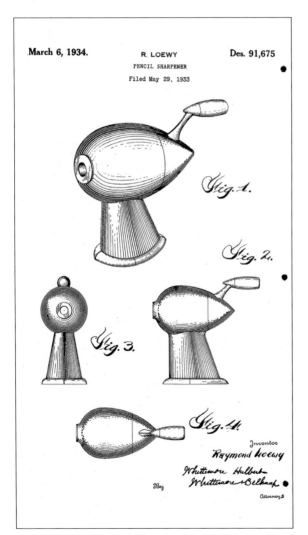

FIGURE 6.8.   Raymond Loewy, United States Design Patent for a Pencil Sharpener, 1934.

far designers might go in styling products. Even Loewy may have felt that he had gone beyond the level of public acceptance for a novelty such as this, exceeding what he called "the MAYA (Most Advanced Yet Acceptable) stage" of design (see Sidebar 12), and it was never commercially produced. Yet today, as the lure of Modernism has abated and the spell of Art Deco, streamlining, and styling has captivated our era, the design of the pencil sharpener has been vindicated, chosen to represent the designer's work in the United States postage-stamp series Pioneers of American Industrial Design.

Two factions delineated the thinking of the American design world during the 1930s: the industrial designers, who spoke for commercial styling, and the Modernists, who spoke for the abstract principles of eternal design. The elite American Modernists were, on the one hand, largely architect-designers, many Germanic in origin, who had fled the rise of Fascism and immigrated to the United States. It was their search for timeless, universal forms that became the standard in what was a recurring criticism not only of style-oriented streamlining but also of the commercialism of the industrial-design profession as a whole. These designers looked to the Museum of Modern Art's architecture and design department, newly established in 1932, for support. In 1934 the museum made its first major statement about design in the exhibition Machine Art. It showed a range of industrial products and household furnishings as exemplars of the machine aesthetic, and curiously also fragments of machinery dubbed "industrial units," such as springs and ball bearings, to demonstrate how geometry was the basis of modern design (Figure 6.9). In the foreword to the catalog, the museum's director, Alfred H. Barr, Jr., emphasized the universal aspect of its vision, suggesting that it was the direct descendant of the classical principles of ancient Greece: "The beauty of machine art is in part the abstract beauty of 'straight lines and circles' made into actual tangible 'surfaces and solids' by means

SIDEBAR 12   Raymond Loewy, "The Maya Stage," 1951

Being design consultants to one hundred and forty companies, most of them blue-ribbon corporations, and having been in very close contact with the consumer's reactions, we have been able to develop what I might call a fifth sense about public acceptance, whether it is the shape of a range, the layout of a store, the wrapper of a soap, the style of a car, or the color of a tugboat. This is the one phase of our profession that fascinates me no end. Our desire is naturally to give the buying public the most advanced product that research can develop and technology can produce. Unfortunately, it has been proved time and time gain that such a product does not always sell well. There seems to be for each individual product (or service, or store, or package,

etc.) a critical area at which the consumer's desire for novelty reaches what I might call the shock-zone. At that point the urge to buy reaches a plateau, and sometimes evolves into a resistance to buying. It is a sort of tug of war between attraction to the new and fear of the unfamiliar. The adult public's taste is not necessarily ready to accept the logical solutions to their requirements if this solution implies too vast a departure from what they have been conditioned to accepting as the norm. In other words, they will go only so far. Therefore, the smart industrial designer is the one who has a lucid understanding of where the shock-zone lies in each particular problem. At this point, a design has reached what I call the MAYA (Most Advanced Yet Acceptable) stage.

FIGURE 6.9.   Machine Art, Museum of Modern Art, New York, 1934.

of tools, 'lathes and rulers and squares.' In Plato's day the tools were simple handworker's implements but today, as a result of the perfection of modern materials and the precision of modern instruments, the modern machine-made object approaches far more closely and more frequently those pure shapes the contemplation of which Plato calls the first of the 'pure pleasures.'"

The industrial designers, on the other hand, were mainly American-born and from a diversity of professional backgrounds—art, engineering, illustration, theatrical and shop-window design, but especially advertising. Self-taught in the complexities of designing for mass production, they had little choice but to create the field themselves because no such training was available. The profession was built up through a kind of apprentice system, learned through work in the office of an established professional. The first bachelor's degree in industrial design was not given until 1936, to Maud Bowers (1913–1998) at the Carnegie Institute of Technology in Pittsburgh, one of three women and two men to receive the degree that year.

Industrial designers believed that the purpose of design was to create products that would meet the practical needs and desires of the public. Their work was more likely to be exhibited as decorative or industrial art at traditional museums, many of which had been founded in the nineteenth century with the mission of forging a connection between art and industry. Between 1919 and 1940, the Metropolitan Museum of Art held fifteen exhibitions of American industrial art. In 1934, along with decorative works by designers of art glass, metalwares, ceramics, textiles, and other traditional mediums, the thirteenth exhibition included installations by a number of industrial designers, including a corner of a music room by Gilbert Rohde, a dining room by Walter Dorwin Teague (1883–1960), and a designer's office and studio by Raymond Loewy created in collaboration with the stage-set designer Lee Simonson

(1888–1967). At the center of the replica of a corner of Loewy's own streamlined office, with its curved walls, tubular-metal furniture, and lighting that was integrated into the structure of the tables, was a model of Loewy's newly styled Hupmobile, the automobile he had redesigned in 1932 (Figure 6.10).

Teague, who had come to industrial design as a graphic artist and illustrator, promoted a distinct way of industrial styling by setting his sights on formal perfection. The language he used to describe it was not very far removed from that of the Modernists although much of his work would not have been acceptable to them. "The process of recasting our productions in forms that suit their functions and their making," he wrote in his book *Design This Day* (1940), which was subtitled *The Technique of Order in the Machine Age*, "is marked by a fresh, new simplicity, a classic elegance flowering in refinement of line and proportion, a gratifying

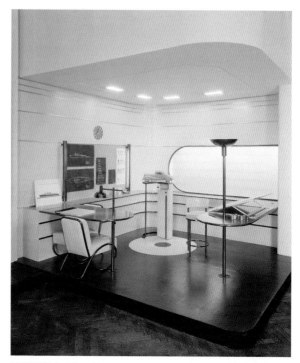

FIGURE 6.10.   Raymond Loewy with Lee Simonson, Designer's Office, Contemporary American Industrial Art, Metropolitan Museum of Art, New York, 1934.

unity attained by the rhythmic integration of all the elements involved. Here, in these products coming off our assembly lines . . . we see the harbingers of a world where simplicity, elegance, unity will not be isolated phenomena emerging in a scene of confusion: they forecast a world where serene order will bring all things into a similar gratifying harmony." This approach is clearly reflected in his design of an entirely new, basic camera for Eastman Kodak, which was marketed as the Baby Brownie (Figure 6.11). Packaged in Teague's upbeat box, it aimed at creating a young mass market for photography. Its name implied a starter model, and the simple, unified design with curved, ribbed forms for rigidity reinforced this. To manufacture the camera in large numbers, Teague depended on the economical injection-molding process of forcing molten plastic into a mold to form its Bakelite case, which paid off as millions of examples of this inexpensive model were eventually manufactured and sold.

John Vassos (1898–1985), who had founded the industrial design department of the Radio Corporation of America (RCA) in 1933, had hoped to go beyond traditional styles and materials to develop a new product type in creating the first television sets for the company. He had already designed modern radios in tubular metal and in plastic, but for this new, expensive technology with an untested audience, he was forced to temper his aspirations. He was able to abandon the shape of historicism, however, for a streamlined cabinet suited to its technical requirements. Viewers watched the picture from a mirror on the underside of the cabinet's top that reflected images from a large, vertically installed picture tube (Figure 6.12). The horizontal, ribbed accent bands on his cabinet were louvers, which at top released the extreme heat generated by the large tubes, and at bottom, sound from speakers that served both the television and a high-quality radio. The first regular American television broadcasts began in 1939 with signals sent from a transmitter on top of the Empire State Building in New York (the British Broadcasting Corporation [BBC] had begun its public television broadcasts three years earlier), but radio was already bringing the immediacy of the larger world into the home in the form of live music, drama, comedy, and news, and not until the middle of the 1950s would television displace its popularity.

FIGURE 6.11. Walter Dorwin Teague, Baby Brownie Camera and Packaging, 1934. Made by Eastman Kodak. Bakelite.

FIGURE 6.12. John Vassos, Television, 1939. Made by Radio Corporation of America. Wood.

Designers such as Russel Wright (1904–1976), influenced by the Surrealist movement for its biomorphic imagery (see Figure 5.17), took a different aesthetic path, introducing products based on eccentric organic shapes that brought informality and flexibility into American design. His American Modern ceramic table service, which was designed in 1937 but did not come onto the market until 1939, was produced until 1959, an economical and revolutionary design said to have sold over eighty million pieces during its long production run (Figure 6.13). Along with its unusual flowing forms in six mix-and-match colors were its underlying concepts of versitility and interchangeability, elements of an up-to-date lifestyle that he and his wife, Mary Wright (1922–1952), promoted in their *Guide to Easier Living* in 1951. The service was intensively advertised in newspapers, where Wright's name prominently appeared, and it was a significant factor in the American Modern mystique. With his name prominently on it, Wright's later work in melamine plastic, including his Residential service from 1953, gave status to the use of plastic for tablewares in the postwar period.

FIGURE 6.13. Russel Wright, American Modern Dinnerware, 1937. Made by Steubenville Pottery. Glazed earthenware.

FIGURE 6.14. Frank Lloyd Wright, Great Workroom, S. C. Johnson Administration Building, Racine, Wisconsin, 1936–39.

Frank Lloyd Wright brought his own form of natural, organic design to the S. C. Johnson administration building, which he constructed in Racine, Wisconsin, between 1936 and 1939. The building had a great open workroom, its glazed roof supported on a grid of tall, tapered, treelike columns with flat circular capitals, allowing natural light to enter the space (Figure 6.14). Wright designed some forty different pieces of furniture for the building, most notably the red metal desks with cantilevered wooden work surfaces, swinging drawers, and built-in lighting.

Design in Europe

With only a small market for the kinds of consumer goods that then flourished in the United States, Europe was slow to establish independent firms for industrial design, with manufacturers relying mainly on their in-house staff or occasional support from outside architects, engineers, and inventors to design new, rationalized products, many of which became celebrated for their modern forms and new technology. In Italy, the inventor Luigi di Ponti (about whom little is known) joined Alfonso

Bialetti (1888–1970), a metalware manufacturer, to create and market the cast-aluminum Moka Express coffee maker in 1933 (Figure 6.15). Ponti and Bialetti introduced a newly developed pressure system in which water was boiled in the coffeemaker's base, forced upward through a tube into a container housing the ground coffee, and then pushed into the pot at top. Apparently Bialetti had adopted his method from that of laundry systems in the town of Crusinallo in northern Italy, where he lived, in which soapy water was boiled in large cauldrons and forced up through a channel into a vessel in which clothes were being washed. Although it had a relatively slow start, once this facetted Art Deco-style coffee maker was rebranded with a mustached caricature of Bialetti, his finger held high in the air, and after it was heavily advertised in the 1950s, it became one of the best-known kitchen products ever produced.

The English engineer and inventor George Carwardine (1887–1947) held numerous patents, mainly for automobile spring suspensions and for

FIGURE 6.15.   Alfonso Bialetti and Luigi di Ponti, Moka Express Coffee Maker, 1933. Aluminum and plastic.

equipoising, or counterbalancing, mechanisms. Both interests led to the rationalized design of his Anglepoise task lamp of 1934 that allowed the arms to remain in any position placed in (Figure 6.16). The pre-tensioned springs at the base of the metal structure held the long arms of the lamp at varied angles; as its sales brochure showed, it was "*instantly adjustable*" and worked superbly to provide illumination for different activities, from dining to darning. After having difficulty manufacturing the lamp himself, Carwardine sold the rights to Herbert Terry, the manufacturer who had made the springs for his lamps and continues to produce it today. A sleeker model was developed by the Norwegian designer Jac Jacobsen (1901–1996), who in 1937 acquired access to the patent and sold it in Scandinavia, and later internationally, under the Luxo brand.

A new rationalized model for mapping transportation systems took hold in London when the new map that Harry Beck (1902–1974) designed for the Tube, or Underground railway system, was unveiled in 1933 (Figure 6.17). The earlier Tube maps produced as the Underground was growing into a complex system had imposed the highly irregular features of the train lines over the topography of the city. Instead, Beck disregarded the individual characteristics of each of the lines and of the geography of the city above (except for the River Thames, which boldly meanders across the map to orient the user) in order to design an extraordinarily usable map. Probably influenced by the electrical circuitry he was accustomed to drawing in his work as a draftsman for the Underground, he diagrammed the system geometrically using only vertical, horizontal, and diagonal lines to represent the routes. He borrowed the idea of color coding the train lines from previous Tube maps, and although it misrepresented travel times, he equalized the spacing between the stops so that the map would have a greater regularity for the ease of travelers as they planned to navigate the system. Beck's map was one element in a large graphic-identity program

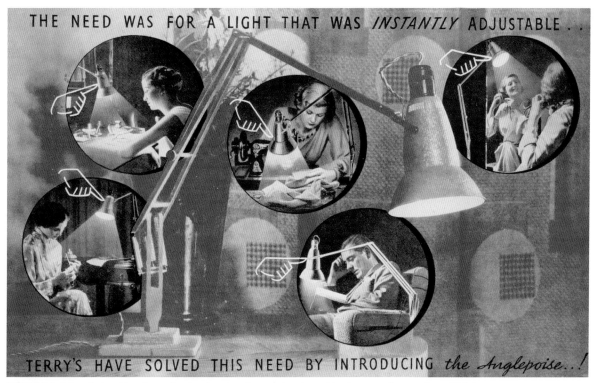

FIGURE 6.16.   Sales Brochure for Anglepoise Lamp. Designed by George Carwardine, 1934.

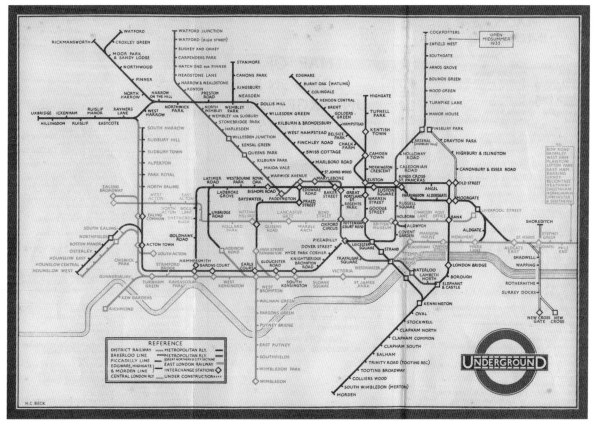

FIGURE 6.17.   Harry Beck, London Underground Map, 1933. Lithograph.

for the Tube that had been created under the direction of Frank Pick (1878–1941), its managing director. It encompassed station architecture, advertising posters, and a specially commissioned standard typeface designed by Edward Johnston (1872–1944). The familiar logo, or red roundel, seen at bottom right of the map was, however, an anonymous design, which had first appeared in 1908 and was updated later (see Figure 0.1).

The photographer and designer Herbert Matter (1907–1984) drew on Constructivist photomontage and the new typography from Germany to bring new aspects of modern graphic design to Swiss advertising. This was best seen in the travel posters he produced for the national tourist office between 1935 and 1936, relying on a different understanding of rationalization in depicting his country's mountainous landscape and the pleasures to be found there (Figure 6.18). The vertiginous scenery in this poster with a broad cobblestone road leading to Switzerland's notorious switchback roads and the mountains beyond is all artificial: he constructed the image from three different black and white photographs, cropped and recombined, with blue added for the sky and red for the diagonal caption, which boldly invited tourists to take a scenic drive through Switzerland.

In Germany after Adolf Hitler (1889–1945) came to power in 1933, his regime developed propaganda campaigns to enhance its image as dedicated to raising the lifestyle of its people. The most successful of these campaigns was for a "people's radio" (*Volksempfänger*), which was introduced that same year, increasing radio ownership by the millions, and since it could be tuned only to local stations, assuring that nothing but government-approved broadcasts could be received by the public. Hitler also supported the development of a "people's car" and was very much involved in trying to make it happen. Laying out the expectations that it would be fuel efficient and reasonably priced for workers, he expected the

country's automobile manufacturers to produce one for him. When they could not meet his cost requirements, he called in the Austrian engineer Ferdinand Porsche (1875–1951) to take charge of the project. Founder in 1931 of the automobile company that bears his name, Porsche was an automotive engineer who had built both luxury cars and military equipment. Between 1933 and 1938, Porsche developed a small, innovative, high-quality automobile with a rear air-cooled engine and streamlined body, which seated five passengers with ample space for luggage. It was taken on as a project of the Strength through Joy (*Kraft durch Freud*, or

FIGURE 6.18.   Herbert Matter, Poster for Swiss National Tourist Office, 1935. Printed by Gebrüder Fretz. Photogravure.

FIGURE 6.19. Brochure for KdF-Wagen. Designed by Ferdinand Porsche, 1938.

KdF) leisure program of the German Labor Front, a government-controlled labor organization, and in recognition, Hitler called the car the KdF-wagen. Through a barrage of publicity, the labor front pushed for subscribers to set aside funds weekly to purchase the cars once they were produced, publishing brochures that promoted the benefits of car ownership and providing instructions on how to buy one (Figure 6.19). The KdF-wagen was never mass-produced as the project was abandoned once the Second World War began, but the concept was resurrected after the war, and in 1949 the Volkswagen Beetle, a car in much the same design, arrived on the market.

The World of Tomorrow

The role of industrial design was spotlighted at the New York World's Fair in 1939, when the cream of America's designers, including Henry Dreyfuss, Norman Bel Geddes, Raymond Loewy, Gilbert Rohde, Walter Dorwin Teague, and Russel Wright, created exhibits and installations for the many civic and commercial pavilions erected there. This was a vindication of their virtuosity and the organizational skills of their offices, and the breadth of the work produced would have been unimaginable at that time without their contributions. Teague represented the profession on several of the organizing committees, serving on the board that provided oversight for design at the fair and working on developing the exhibition theme, Building the World of Tomorrow. With an uplifting message, it focused on social issues of the machine and modern culture as it presented the latest innovations from American industry.

The world's fair was laid out around its white symbols, the Trylon, a triangular obelisk, and the Perisphere, a ball-shaped exhibition space, designed by the firm of Harrison and Fouilhoux. They were depicted amid celebratory fireworks with an imaginative bird's-eye view in advance of their construction on a poster designed by the architect Nembhard Culin (1908–1990), an employee on the fair's design staff (Figure 6.20). The fair presented a variety of architectural expressions, from these geometric Art Deco theme structures to streamlined forms and functionalist designs of civic and commercial pavilions, but it was the imagination and energy behind the exhibits that broke new ground, using advanced techniques for the communication of ideas through technology.

For the Perisphere, two hundred feet in diameter, Dreyfuss designed Democracity, a utopian diorama of a city of the future, one hundred years hence. In the transportation zone of the fair, Teague conceived the installation of the Ford Motor

Company pavilion, including an exhibit with animated figures depicting the production cycle of automobiles, from the mining of raw materials to the finished car. Bel Geddes designed the exhibit that the crowds found most memorable. Called Futurama, it was designed for General Motors and subtitled "Highways and Horizons." This vast panorama of the United States landscape, seen from an aerial perspective as visitors in moving seats traversed the country overhead, forecast the world of 1960, when it was imagined that modern communications, broad superhighways, and functional structures would have replaced the outmoded fixtures of life in the 1930s (Figure 6.21). Of all such startling predictions about the world of tomorrow that the fair offered, however, only television came to pass with anything like the impact of new technology that had been foreseen.

FIGURE 6.20. Nembhard Culin, Poster for New York 1939 World's Fair, 1937. Lithograph.

FIGURE 6.21. Norman Bel Geddes, Cityscape, from Futurama, General Motors Pavilion, New York World's Fair, 1939.

1940 to 1965

CHAPTER 7
Modern Design for Everyone

The World of Tomorrow envisioned in 1939 was not the world of tomorrow that came to pass. Even before the New York World's Fair closed that October, Germany had invaded Poland and the Second World War had begun in Europe. Two years later, in 1941, with the Japanese bombing of Pearl Harbor, an American naval base near Honolulu, the United States entered the war. By this point, design and production for military needs had taken precedence across the world, with governments making great efforts to encourage civilians to aid in the war work. The United States Office of Emergency Management, for its part, commissioned a series of posters that were displayed in factories throughout the country to encourage worker production. Among them was the poster *Production: America's Answer!* by the French graphic designer and political activist Jean Carlu (1900–1997), who as artistic advisor to the French Information Service had been sent to the United States in 1940, where he was compelled to remain once the war began (Figure 7.1). With the hexagonal O in "PRODUCTION" tightened by the wrench in the gloved hand, Carlu underscored the crucial message that everyone's efforts were needed for the war effort.

But the combatant countries also had to attend to the needs of their civilian populations, which they managed to control by rationing foodstuffs and limiting the use of vital materials. At the end of the conflict in 1945, only the United States, of all the industrialized nations, had an economy and a landscape that were intact. Retrofitting the industries that had been given over to wartime use became its next challenge, but soon consumer goods were back on the market. Suddenly modern design felt relevant to many Americans, and although reproduction styles never went out of fashion, a modern aesthetic began to define new products, buildings, and interiors, much of which involved materials and processes developed or improved upon during the war, notably in the field of fibers, plastics, and plywood.

Europe had been devastated by the war, physically, economically, and politically. Postwar retooling and rebuilding was aided by the Marshall Plan, or the European Recovery Program, initiated by the United States, a reaction to the scarcities of food and industry in Europe. But it was also an effort to strengthen foreign economies as a bulwark against the threat of left-wing and Communist governments coming to power in many of its countries. From 1948 to 1952, the United States shipped agricultural and industrial products abroad and then provided economic aid to help the countries of Europe rebuild their own industries

FIGURE 7.1.   Jean Carlu, *Production: America's Answer!*, Poster for the United States Division of Information, Office for Emergency Management, 1941. Printed by the US Government Printing Office. Lithograph.

and economies, which grew at staggering rates at the beginning the 1950s. Although the tolls of war were still visible over the next decade, design and production soon exceeded prewar levels. While acknowledging its aesthetic component, the progress of modern design in Europe had deep social aims, reaching back to Modernism and its aim to better the world through design. The immense task of rebuilding Europe required innovative solutions with a more analytical approach to the needs of design and manufacture. Designers were wrestling with the realities of postwar recovery and turning toward products that would be simple and efficient and benefit the social system. Many looked to industrial

materials, unusual structures, and design systems, such as modularity and interchangeability, that carried the earlier Modernist design vision into the postwar era.

The situation in Japan was quite different. At the end of the war, the Supreme Command of Allied Powers (SCAP) led by the United States oversaw the creation of a new democratic nation. The presence of the American occupying forces, requiring large amounts of furnishings, household products, and electronic goods bought from Japanese industry, was a major factor in jump-starting its industrial recovery. American designers, including such well-known figures as Raymond Loewy and Russel Wright, traveled to Japan to advise designers there, especially with regard to creating products for export, while many Japanese students went abroad to study, particularly to the United States, where they were introduced to the practice of American industrial design.

Wartime Innovations

During the war, design innovation had concentrated on satisfying military requirements; research and development went toward munitions and transportation, to finding new materials to aid the war effort and to replacing critical materials with new ones for consumer goods. Shortages did not stop with the end of the war, continuing in some countries, like Great Britain, until the early 1950s. Britain instituted by far the severest wartime restrictions on manufacturing, particularly in the fields of furniture, ceramics, metalwares, and textiles. The Utility Design Program, introduced in 1941 under the Board of Trade, acted as

an advisory council to establish a program for manufacturing consumer goods, with the purchase of furnishings limited to newlyweds and those whose homes had been damaged in the widespread bombings. The Utility Furniture Scheme, begun in 1942, specified that furniture produced under the program, for the living room, bedroom, kitchen, and nursery, was to be utilitarian and long-lasting. It was designed in a simple style that could be called "modern" even though the products referred back to the vernacular forms of the Arts and Crafts Movement. Textile production also fell under the Utility program, where Enid Marx (1902–1998) served as a consultant and leading designer of civilian fabrics for the textile unit. She created a range of woven furnishing textiles in small-scale patterns like that of her Spot and Stripe fabric, which allowed upholstery to be pieced together with little waste of materials and for which the board, out of concern for dye restrictions, chose a limited palette of rust, green, blue, and natural (Figure 7.2).

FIGURE 7.2.
Enid Marx, Spot and Stripe Furnishing Fabric, 1945. Made for the Utility Design Program by Morton Sundour. Woven Cotton.

When after the war in 1947, the fashion designer Christian Dior (1905–1957) unveiled his first collection, he pushed back against French wartime restrictions with a design of excess, bringing feminine glamour back to the streets with an hourglass shape that was soon dubbed the "New Look" by *Harper's Bazaar* (Figure 7.3). His high-style design called for an abundance of fabric for the calf-length skirts, and he was criticized for ignoring sensible clothing for French women at a time when materials were still scarce. Enraged protesters ripped garments off women who embraced the new design, but fashion firms around the world copied his new look, and it was crucial to reestablishing the role of Paris as an arbiter of fashion. It did not take long for designers to bring an interpretation of this new style to the depiction of an American

FIGURE 7.3.   Christian Dior, the New Look: Bar Suit, 1947.

housewife, with a Westinghouse advertisement showing her in *Life* magazine late that same year with a range of domestic appliances encircling a refrigerator filled with the abundance of American agriculture (Figure 7.4).

Wartime restrictions had also meant that plywood was not available for consumer products either in Great Britain or in the United States, where its military uses included barracks for soldiers, machinery parts, assault boats, and small airplanes. The American architect and designer Charles Eames (1907–1978) worked with the United States Navy to design lightweight plywood leg splints for use on the battlefield, replacing heavier metal splints, which had proven inadequate, and he also experimented with making aircraft parts and gliders from plywood. Eames had earlier explored new technologies for molding plywood in collaboration with Eero Saarinen (1910–1961), an architectural colleague from the Cranbrook Academy of Art in Michigan. In 1939 they had designed molded plywood chairs for submission to the Museum of Modern Art's Organic Design in Home Furnishings competition and exhibition, organized by its first curator of industrial design, Eliot Noyes (1910–1977). Eames and Saarinen were trying to mold a single-unit plywood chair with curves in several planes that could be used for economical mass production, but although their chairs were awarded one of the first prizes in the competition, the seat and back units had split while being molded and upholstery had to be added to cover up the defects for the exhibition. Eames and his artist wife, Ray Eames (1912–1988), continued experimenting with molding plywood for seating during the war (Saarinen having gone off on his own), and by 1945, at war's end, they were ready to put their chairs into production, although they still had not been able to bend the single-piece plywood shells consistently without cracking. The chairs they developed (and which were exhibited by the Museum of Modern Art in 1946 in an exhibition entitled New Furniture Designed by Charles Eames) had separate seats and backs,

FIGURE 7.4. Advertisement for Westinghouse Appliances, *Life*, 1947.

which were connected to bent-metal frames with rubber shock mounts adhered with a synthetic resin that had also been developed during the war (Figure 7.5). In the end, separate seats and backs proved more economical and efficient, for they used less material, made the chairs lighter, and avoided production problems during the molding process. The chairs had originally been designed with three legs, but these proved unstable, and the Molded Plywood Division of the Evans Product Company, where Charles had experimented with plywood and become director during the war, first produced the chairs in four-legged versions with metal or plywood bases. Mass production of the plywood chairs was soon taken over by Herman Miller, which continues to manufacture them today.

FIGURE 7.5.   Charles Eames and Ray Eames, Chair, c. 1946. Made by the Herman Miller Furniture Company. Birch plywood, steel, and rubber.

Plastics was another area of heavy experimentation during the war and the material that finally allowed furniture designers to create a single-piece seating shell. Both the Eameses and Saarinen had produced them by the end of the decade, achieving this with fiberglass (plastic embedded with glass fibers), which did not come onto the market until after the war. Saarinen's molded-fiberglass shell, like the chairs that had been exhibited at the Organic Design exhibition, was covered in upholstery and lacked any visual acknowledgment of its new material, while the shell of the Eameses' chair, which entered production in 1950 after several years of design and engineering, was different. The fiberglass surface was left uncovered, introducing a startling new material for economical seating, which Edgar Kaufmann, Jr. (1910–1989), then research associate at the Museum of Modern Art, praised for its "extraordinary lustre and soft, smooth surface" (Figure 7.6). These chairs had a standard base of four legs, but they also could be ordered with a number of other bases, including wooden rockers, aluminum pedestals, and one with crossed wire struts that the Eameses called the "Eiffel Tower" base.

Among other legacies of wartime plastics were the food storage containers and serving pieces introduced by the American inventor Earl S. Tupper (1907–1983) about 1945. Tupper's products were made of polyethylene, a material he upgraded to avoid cracking, and the containers had "non-snap" lids, tops that became airtight when pressure was applied to them, a feature he also patented in 1949. But it was the new uncolored plastic material itself that fascinated reviewers when Tupper's products came on the market (Figure 7.7). *House Beautiful* told its readers in 1947 that "if you have never touched polyethylene we need to tell you that it has the appearance of great fragility and delicacy—yet has great strength. It has the fingering qualities of jade, but at the same time it reminds you of alabaster and mother-of-pearl. Held up to the light it becomes opalescent and translucent and

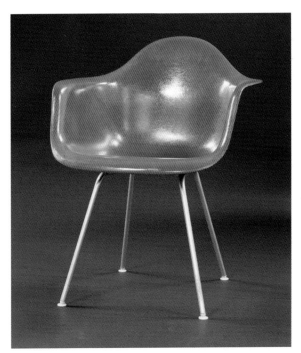

FIGURE 7.6. Charles Eames and Ray Eames, Chair, 1948–50. Made by the Herman Miller Furniture Company. Fiberglass, rubber, and steel.

has an interesting, new ability to transfer light. So these bowls look like art objects—even before you know what they do." Art objects or not, Tupper's polyethylene containers did not sell well when they were first introduced, and it was the creation of the Tupperware home party method of retailing by Brownie Wise (1913–1992), an independent saleswoman who became sales manager in 1951, that made an astounding success of Tupper's products. More than simply a sales gimmick, Tupperware parties made shopping a game, an early expression of the type of consumerist enthusiasm that would eventually become the focus of many television game shows and be reinvented as a major pastime on the World Wide Web.

While *House Beautiful* had lavished praise on the sensual characteristics of polyethylene, the French cultural critic and literary theorist Roland Barthes would see plastic in a very different way. In a series of columns written for the magazine *Lettres Nouvelles* (New Writing) between 1954 and 1956 (collected in 1957 as *Mythologies*), he examined popular culture from the point of view of an intellectual (later fodder for his contribution to the field of semiology, or semiotics, the study of signs and symbols and their interpretations). In it he gave serious appraisal to subjects that had never been thoroughly investigated in this way, analyzing the mythic hold the everyday world had on the popular imagination. In his piece on plastics, written after he had seen a molding machine disgorge cheap doodads made from this material, he described the properties of plastic as unpleasant, generalizing from his experience with a single encounter. "What best reveals it for what it is," he wrote, "is the sound it gives, at once hollow and flat; its noise is its undoing, as are its colors, for it seems capable of retaining only the most chemical-looking ones." But he wrote admiringly of the "miraculous" ability of plastic to take any form, overturning the idea that each material had a single attribute that design had to honor and questioning the principle of truth to materials that had been so important to the Arts and Crafts Movement (see Sidebar 13).

FIGURE 7.7. Earl S. Tupper, Covered Canisters, c. 1945. Polyethylene.

SIDEBAR 13   Roland Barthes, "Plastic," 1955

Until now imitation materials have always indicated pretension, they belonged to the world of appearances, not to that of actual use; they aimed at reproducing cheaply the rarest substances, diamonds, silk, feathers, furs, silver, all the luxurious brilliance of the world. Plastic has climbed down, it is a household material. It is the first magical substance which consents to be prosaic. But it is precisely because this prosaic character is a triumphant reason for its existence: for the first time, artifice aims at something common, not rare. And as an immediate consequence, the age-old function of nature is modified: it is no longer the Idea, the pure Substance to be regained or imitated: an artificial Matter, more bountiful than all the natural deposits, is about to replace her, and to determine the very invention of forms. A luxurious object is still of this earth, it still recalls, albeit in a precious mode, its mineral or animal origin, the natural theme of which it is but one actualization. Plastic is wholly swallowed up in the fact of being used: ultimately, objects will be invented for the sole pleasure of using them. The hierarchy of substances is abolished; a single one replaces them all; the whole world *can* be plasticized.

Good Design

The postwar period began as the age of American design. Looking back at the senseless war in Europe, many lost faith in traditional values and began to question the relevance of the past; when consumers in the United States faced the prospect of buying new objects after the war, choosing a modern style suddenly seemed to make sense. As early as 1949, the prolific writer, editor, architect, and designer George Nelson (1908–1986) announced in an article in *Interiors* magazine, somewhat optimistically perhaps, that modern design was selling, explaining that at last the designer felt "compelled to produce shapes that fit appropriately into his world. And his world, lest we forget, includes Radar, Waring mixers, rocket propulsion, ball point pens, Picasso, and that well-known formula E=MC². There is another factor that has contributed significantly to the mushroom growth of modern furniture design: There is now a market. There is a market because more and more individuals are recognizing the designer's world as their own; they feel more comfortable in modern houses and modern interiors, and they are buying the fabrics, china, glass—and furniture—that fit."

Such were the products of the German-born inventor Peter Schlumbohm (1896–1962), who brought his design of the crystal-clear hourglass-shaped Chemex coffeemaker with him when he immigrated to the United States in 1936 (Figure 7.8). With a special dispensation from President Franklin Delano Roosevelt (1882–1945) himself, prompted by an erudite appeal from Schlumbohm, production of the flask in Pyrex, a critical material, by Corning Glass (established 1851) was not interrupted by the war effort after the coffee maker was introduced in 1941. Incorporating a filter-paper system that he had already patented in Germany, the coffee maker was one component of what Schlumbohm referred to as the "Chemist's Kitchen." Like the industrial objects used by Le Corbusier and other European modernist designers in their interiors, these were type forms of laboratory glassware, which here Schlumbohm adapted by adding a channel so the coffee could be poured outside the filter paper and softening its mechanistic aura with a hardwood collar and the natural rawhide lace that held it in place.

The new allure of simple modern styles was reflected in an advertisement that appeared in 1952 in *House and Garden* showing an upscale

FIGURE 7.8.   Peter Schlumbohm, Chemex Coffeemaker, 1941. Made by Chemex. Glass, wood, and leather.

living room with a tag line that asked "Where do you put radiators in a room this modern?" (Figure 7.9). With the words "this modern," the advertisement established a baseline for what the height of modernity was then thought to be. Seen on a sunny spring day, when metaphorically a new lifestyle was being born, this bright living room with its understated furnishings and inconspicuous baseboard heating units, new to domestic interiors, suggested that in the postwar era, modern was a style that everyone would desire. Several of the furnishings are easily identified: from left, the corner of a modular storage system with a round speaker unit (1946) by Nelson, a steel-and-cord indoor-outdoor lounge chair and ottoman (1946) by the Los Angeles firm Van Keppel-Green, and a free-form coffee table (c. 1947) by the sculptor Isamu Noguchi (1904–1988). But the room also includes other features that contributed to the typical modern interior at midcentury: a large

Where do you put radiators in a room this modern?

FIGURE 7.9.
Advertisement for Crane Radiators, *House and Garden*, 1952.

window wall, printed fabrics for curtains, solid wall colors, a sectional sofa, woven-grass floor matting, a rubber plant on a metal stand, a conical hanging lamp, and organic pottery forms.

Signifying modernity, these features were not restricted to any one economic level, and modern design made inroads across economic lines. It could be seen in the homes of the well-off, as reflected in the radiator advertisement, as well as in those of the lower-income families who had taken advantage of cheap mortgages to buy houses in newly built suburban communities. The model living room of a house in the Levittown community in Pennsylvania, which was begun in 1952, shared a similar spare ambience and many mannerisms with the living room in the radiator advertisement. It too had a large window wall, solid wall colors,

plain undecorated furniture, conical lampshades, ornamental houseplants, and possibly even the same curtain fabric (Figure 7.10).

What defined much of modern design in the immediate postwar period was its practicality, a middle ground between the rigors of Modernism on the one hand and streamlining and styling on the other. This was most clearly represented by the products shown in a series of exhibitions entitled Good Design, which were organized between 1950 and 1955 by the Museum of Modern Art and the Merchandise Mart in Chicago, a center for the country's wholesale design and consumer-product trade. Other museums were also exhibiting products with a similar aesthetic, including the Akron (Ohio) Art Institute, Buffalo (New York) Fine Arts Academy, and the Walker Art Center in

FIGURE 7.10.   Model Living Room, the Levittowner, Levittown, Pennsylvania, about 1953.

Minneapolis. The Good Design exhibitions took a pragmatic approach. Products were selected, according to Edgar Kaufmann, director for the project at the Museum of Modern Art, with regard to their "eye appeal, function, construction and price, with emphasis on the first." They were mostly objects for the home, chosen with aesthetics in mind as Kaufmann noted, ranging from furniture and lighting to brooms, housewares, and appliances. Manufacturers and retailers whose products were exhibited could use the Good Design label as a certificate of reassurance for those buyers who might be uncertain about their own judgments of quality in modern design (Figure 7.11). Because

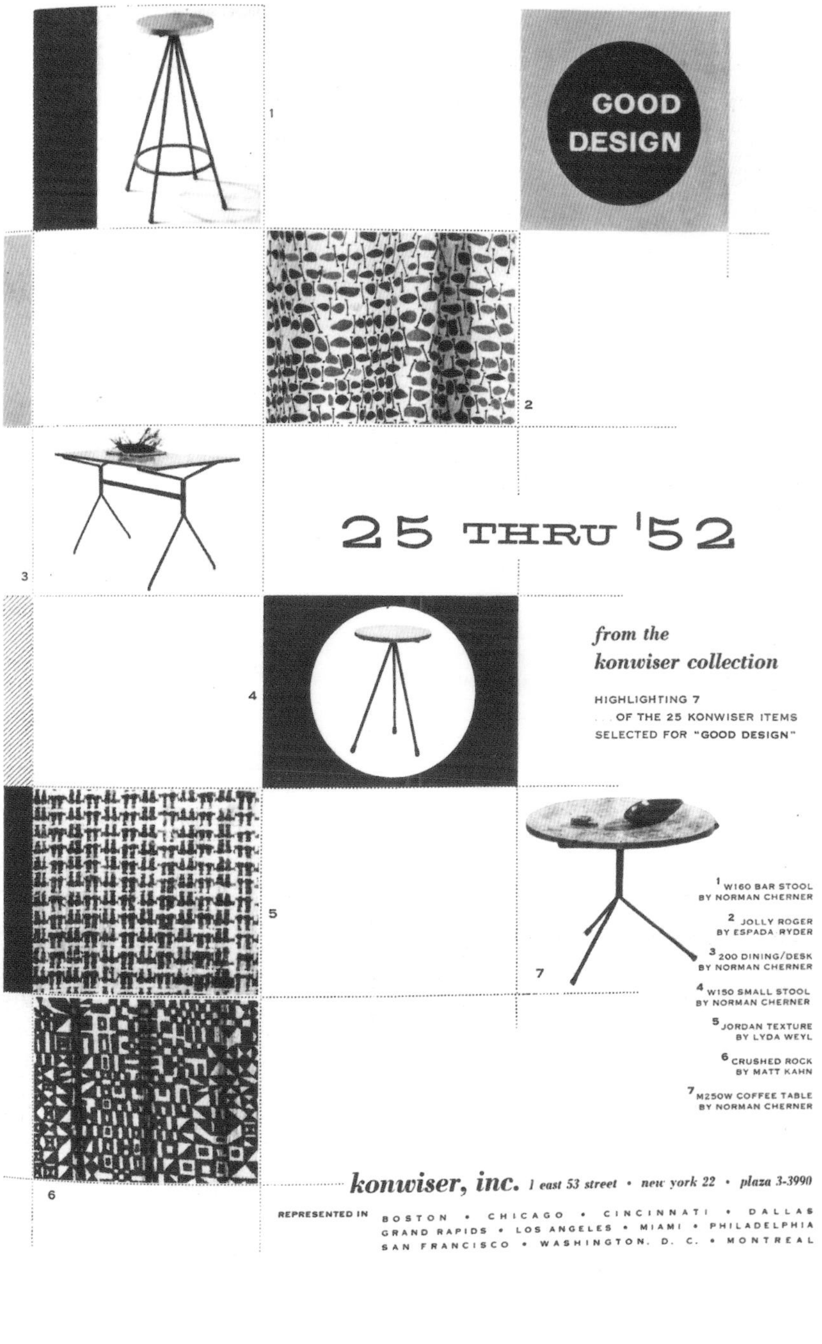

FIGURE 7.11.
Advertisement for Konwiser Furniture Company with Good Design Label, *Interiors*, 1952.

the museum was collaborating with industry, it tempered its reluctance to show objects with applied (not integral) decoration, which had been forbidden by Modernism, and by 1953 Good Design included some dinnerware with ornamental patterns, the museum having softened its position since its elitist Machine Art exhibition of 1934 (see Figure 6.9). The call for the abstract beauty of objects in Machine Art was supplanted by an approach that was more relaxed and egalitarian, broadened to embrace the realities of everyday life. This had already been evident in a series of straightforward exhibitions in which the museum had shown useful household objects, from those costing under five dollars in 1938 to under ten dollars in 1942, to those of "fine design" at under one hundred dollars in 1948, a natural lead-in to the Good Design exhibitions.

In his booklet *What Is Modern Design?*, published by the museum in 1950, Kaufmann compiled a list of "Twelve Precepts of Modern Design" based on the principles of reform that had developed since the middle of the nineteenth century (see Sidebar 14). He had made up the list somewhat reluctantly, pressured by schoolteachers who wanted to be able to explain modern design to their students. His precepts clearly outlined the path that design should follow if it were to be modern in the postwar era. While it recapped many of the nineteenth-century principles of design reform, the list put a greater emphasis on aesthetics and on the humanistic and scientific advances of the period. The principles that Kaufmann outlined indicated that modern design had come of age, and this would have been seconded by most up-to-date designers whether or not they were following them strictly. Although Precept 11 stated that modern design should "master the machine," neither the museum nor retailers or the public rejected handcraftsmanship, for this would have been impossible at a time when so many modern designs still relied on small workshops for their manufacture.

By the later 1950s, when the boom in new housing waned in the United States and the

SIDEBAR 14 Edgar Kaufmann, Jr., "Twelve Precepts of Modern Design," 1950

1. Modern design should fulfill the practical needs of modern life.

2. Modern design should express the spirit of our times.

3. Modern design should benefit by contemporary advances in fine arts and pure sciences.

4. Modern design should take advantage of new materials and techniques and develop familiar ones.

5. Modern design should develop the forms, textures and colors that spring from the direct fulfillment of requirements in appropriate materials and techniques.

6. Modern design should express the purpose of an object, never making it seem what it is not.

7. Modern design should express the qualities and beauties of the materials used, never making the materials seem to be what they are not.

8. Modern design should express the methods used to make an object, not disguising mass production as handicraft or simulating a technique not used.

9. Modern design should blend the expression of utility, materials and process into a visually satisfactory whole.

10. Modern design should be simple, its structure, evident in its appearance, avoiding extraneous enrichment.

11. Modern design should master the machine for the service of man.

12. Modern design should serve as wide a public as possible, considering modest needs and limited costs no less challenging than the requirements of pomp and luxury.

market for new home furnishings slacked off, Good Design lost much of its egalitarian cross-section, with designers turning for their commissions to large corporations, which were then building new headquarters. It now favored expensive designs for executive suites and furnishings that could be manufactured in large quantities for outfitting entire offices and even complete buildings. Charles and Ray Eames's entry into the corporate market was signaled by their luxurious lounge chair made of expensive rosewood plywood and upholstered in leather (Figure 7.12). Eero Saarinen also turned to upscale, elegant forms for his Tulip series of fiberglass pedestal chairs and tables, which he designed between 1955 and 1957 for Knoll Associates (Figure 7.13). The use of the

FIGURE 7.12.   Charles Eames and Ray Eames, Lounge Chair and Ottoman, 1956. Made by the Herman Miller Furniture Company. Rosewood plywood, aluminum, and rubber with leather upholstery.

FIGURE 7.13.   Eero Saarinen (Interior Design by Alexander Girard), Living Room, Miller House, Columbus, Indiana, 1953–57, with Saarinen's Tulip Table and Chairs. Fiberglass and aluminum, 1955–56.

pedestal, he said, was "to clear up the slum of legs" that in "a typical interior makes an ugly, confusing, unrestful world," and as demonstrated in the dining room he furnished with the textile and interior designer Alexander Girard (1907–1993) for his Miller house in Columbus, Indiana, his concept worked perfectly. Although Saarinen had hoped to manufacture these chairs as one-piece units of plastic, it was an impossible goal at that time, when fiberglass had not yet proved its strength to be applied in this way. Instead, he chose cast aluminum for the flowing pedestal and lacquered it white like the plastic shell to make the chair appear as if it were made of a continuous one-piece construction.

At this time, European Modernist furniture from the 1920s was being revived for use in modern corporate interiors. Mies van der Rohe's Barcelona chair had already been reintroduced in 1948 by Knoll to provide him with furniture for the new buildings he was designing. The furniture of Le

Corbusier, Pierre Jeanneret, and Charlotte Perriand came back on the market in 1958 and Marcel Breuer's in 1962. Florence Knoll (1917–2019), architect, designer, and wife of the founder of the company, Hans G. Knoll (1914–1955), used Mies's furniture in many of the office interiors she designed for the Knoll Planning Unit, which she had founded. She selected Barcelona chairs and stools for the executive reception room in Eero Saarinen's headquarters for the Columbia Broadcasting System (CBS) in New York, supplementing them with the necessary fill-in pieces—sofas, tables, and cabinets—that she herself created to complement the works of Mies and Knoll's other notable designers (Figure 7.14).

The International Business Machines Corporation (IBM), taking as its model Olivetti, the Italian business machines company, which since its inception in 1908 had made design a significant factor of its corporate vision, instituted a similar

FIGURE 7.14.   Florence Knoll, Executive Reception Room, CBS Building, New York, 1962.

FIGURE 7.15. Eliot Noyes, Selectric Typewriter, 1961. Made by IBM. Aluminum.

program in the United States during the 1950s. Thomas Watson, Jr. (1914–1993), son of the head of the company, hired the architect and former Museum of Modern Art curator Eliot Noyes as a consultant. Noyes designed a revolutionary typewriter for IBM, called the "Selectric," which used revolving type balls that were interchangeable and offered different fonts and sizes, doing away with the moving carriage to create a more compact form (Figure 7.15). Configured with an organic silhouette and offered in several colors, the Selectric brought a friendlier machine to the American office landscape. Noyes recommended several other consultants to the company, among them Charles Eames for communication projects— films, multimedia presentations, exhibitions, and museum work—which he developed with his wife Ray, although she did not always receive sufficient recognition for her collaborations with him, and the graphic designer Paul Rand (1914–1996) for visual communications, with Rand redesigning and updating the IBM logo and the company's graphic image. "In the IBM Company," Watson later said, affirming his faith in the efficacy of design, "we do not think that good design can make a poor product good, whether the product be a machine or a building or a promotional brochure or a business

man. But we are convinced that good design can materially help make a good product reach its full potential. In short, we think that good design is good business."

Beyond Good Design

The chasm between Good Design products and those of popular culture could be narrow, and although standards were no longer as clearly outlined as they had been in the previous century, those in the design establishment and those who followed it seemed to know what was acceptable and what was not. Many designers turned to bright, shiny, and extreme organic designs, often at the request of manufacturers who were trying to attract middle America to modern styles, like the playful Town and Country dinnerware designed by Eva Zeisel (Figure 7.16). A Hungarian-born American designer known for her eccentric ceramic and glass designs, Zeisel dove deeply into biomorphic experimentation with her service, which was commissioned by the Red Wing Pottery in Minnesota in 1946. Its thick pieces took unprecedented forms for a utilitarian service, and its unusual color combinations found a remarkable resonance in the popular market while retaining an affiliation with Good Design principles.

FIGURE 7.16. Eva Zeisel, Town and Country Pitchers, 1946. Made by Red Wing Potteries. Glazed earthenware.

When the Museum of Modern Art organized its 10 Automobiles exhibition in 1953, however, it left the economical, everyday aspects of American Good Design behind. Chosen "primarily for their excellence as works of art" that depended on the "designer's mastery of sculptural problems," the exhibition catalogue explained, these cars thumbed their noses at the American automotive industry. By likening automobiles to art and ignoring their popular symbolism, the museum turned a blind eye to their primacy in American culture and to the realities of the marketplace. Only one of the ten cars in the exhibition was a standard American model, Raymond Loewy's renegade 1953 Studebaker Commander V-8 Starliner Coupe (Figure 7.17). The catalogue, following the museum's Eurocentric bias, praised it precisely because it was the "first American mass-produced car to adapt design characteristics of European automobiles." Few American automobiles would have fit the museum's standards of modern design, and only by showing automobiles as fine sculptural forms did the exhibition have any validity.

But the machines that molded much of American life had values other than sculptural; they were markers of status and individuality.

Manufacturers encouraged this by increasing the number of options opened to buyers and offering them a wide degree of customization during the 1950s. Many different exterior colors and color combinations could be ordered, while intriguing interior fabrics and appointments put together mostly by women designers who were newly hired as stylists were offered to entice wives to join their husbands in the adventure of buying a new car. Like the stylists in other fields who exploited snob appeal and luxury in advertisements, automobile manufacturers blatantly reinforced this. Still, it was the husband's car, as is clearly shown in an advertisement for the 1957 Cadillac 60 Special One (Figure 7.18). While the text attempted to justify the purchase of this costly car by emphasizing its practicality, the image massaged his ego and his aspirations by associating Cadillac ownership with a lifestyle well beyond that of most of its buyers. This pink convertible was outfitted with the ever-increasing tail fins inspired by the tail booms of the Lockheed P38 airplane (1937), which had been introduced by Harley Earl on the 1948 Cadillac models, although by this time he was no longer with GM, having left the company in 1955.

FIGURE 7.17.
Raymond Loewy, Commander V-8 Starliner Coupe, 1953. Made by Studebaker.

There Are Some Secrets a Man Can't Keep ...

... when he is seen in the driver's seat of a new 1957 Cadillac. And not the least among these is the fact that he is a man of unusual practical wisdom. For it is widely recognized that when a motorist selects the "car of cars", he selects one of the soundest of all motor car purchases. The original cost of a new Cadillac, for instance, is remarkably modest—in view of the great beauty and luxury and performance it represents. Cadillac's marvelous economy of operation and its extraordinary dependability are without counterpart on the world's highways. And Cadillac's unsurpassed resale value assures its owner a greater return on his investment than any other automobile in the land. If you would like to enjoy these many practical benefits in *your* next motor car—then you are looking for Cadillac! The car is waiting for you in your dealer's showroom—and this is the perfect moment to make the move quickly and economically. CADILLAC MOTOR CAR DIVISION • GENERAL MOTORS CORPORATION

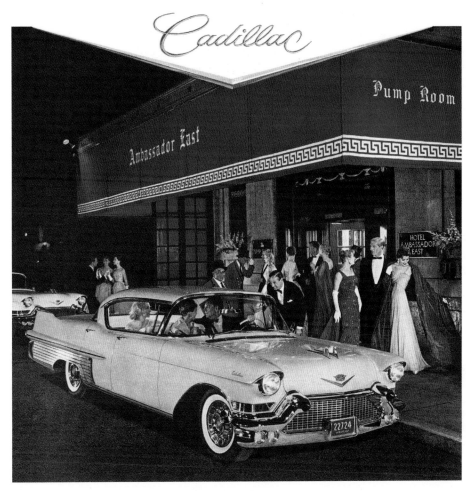

FIGURE 7.18.
Advertisement for Cadillac 60 Special One, 1957. Made by General Motors.

By the middle of the 1950s, automotive criticism was beginning to look more seriously at American cars. Modernists were still using architectural standards to analyze their design, following Le Corbusier, who in his book *Towards a New Architecture* saw automobiles of the 1920s as type forms, comparing them to Greek temples such as the Parthenon (see Sidebar 8). But the British critic Reyner Banham (1922–1988) had a different outlook, introducing a kind of criticism that was based on an understanding of popular culture developed through his association with the Independent Group in London. Formed in 1952 to study American mass media, the Independent Group is credited with giving the name "Pop" to the products of mass culture. It looked to familiar imagery, including those in advertisements and comics, to gain its insights, with Banham explaining the difficulty of coming to terms with these popular influences from the marketplace: "In aesthetics we still have no formulated intellectual attitudes for living in a throwaway economy." Those who

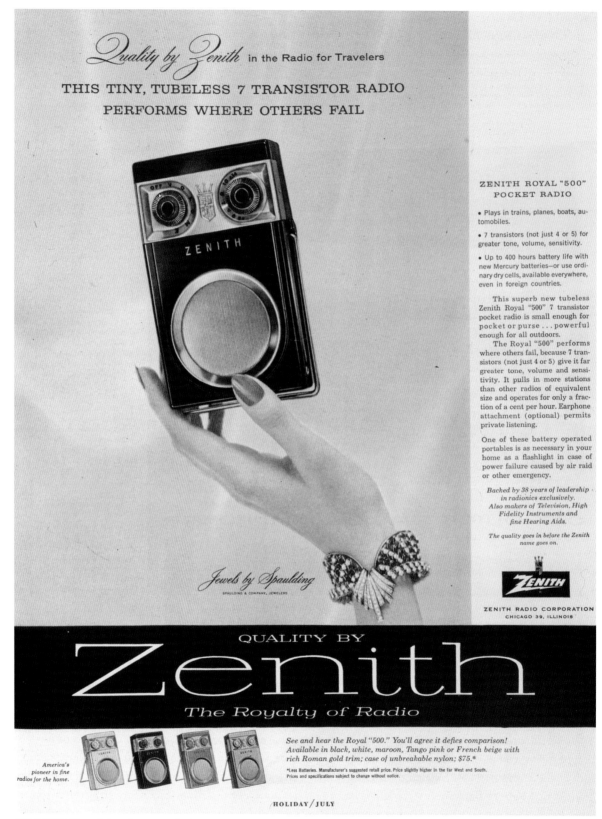

FIGURE 7.19. Advertisement for Zenith Royal 500 Pocket Radio, *Holiday*, 1957.

were critical of American automobiles, with their challenging colors, abundance of chrome, and rocket symbolism, had not understood the design perspective of the automotive body stylists, who, according to Banham, gave

> their creations qualities of apparent speed, power, brutalism, luxury, snob-appeal, exoticism and plain common-or-garden sex. The means at their disposal are symbolic iconographies, whose ultimate power lies in their firm grounding in popular taste and the innate traditions of the product, while the actual symbols are drawn from Science Fiction, movies, earth-moving equipment, supersonic aircraft, racing cars, heraldry and certain deep-seated mental dispositions about the great outdoors and the kinship between technology and sex. Arbiter and interpreter between the industry and the consumer, the body-stylist deploys, not a farrage of meaningless ornament, as fine art critics insist, but a means of saying something of breathless, but unverbalisable, consequence to the live culture of the Technological Century.

Symbolism like this was used in advertisements for other objects, like the miniaturized Zenith Royal 500 pocket radio in 1957 (Figure 7.19). In this case, the connection of the radio, the manicured disembodied hand, and a bracelet by Spaulding, the prestigious Chicago jeweler, seemed to say that this radio was fit for a king or queen. Its face-like case, much like the grinning chrome sneer of the pink Cadillac and other automobiles, attempted to add a personality to the object in a way that Modernism decried.

Design in Europe and Japan

Good Design, as exemplified by the exhibitions organized by the Museum of Modern Art, had a wide appeal. As an approach that favored aesthetics, it was noticed abroad, and soon inspired the undertaking of government and commercial initiatives promoting the modern aesthetic across the globe. These included the creation of the Design Centre in London in 1956, which was organized by Britain's Council of Industrial Design for the display of exemplary British products; and the Japanese G-Mark (good) design awards, created by the Ministry of International Trade and Industry (MITI) and inaugurated in 1957 by the Design Promotion Council.

Japanese postwar design seemed to go in two directions: on the one hand it fell under the influence of the United States, with its new industrial design firms following the image of American ones, while on the other hand, there was a tendency to retain aspects of the understated Japanese aesthetic in industrial products. Seeking products for export, many new companies saw a future in the development of electronics and photographic equipment. The company that eventually became known as Sony was an early entrant in the electronics field, founded in 1946 as the Tokyo Telecommunications Engineering Corporation by Masaru Ibuka (1908–1997) and Akio Morita (1921–1999). Unlike many Japanese firms that had their start by imitating foreign designs, the young company set out to make their products distinctive, as Ibuka said at the opening of the firm, to "strive for unique combinations that other companies cannot emulate. We cannot compete by doing the same thing as other companies. There are plenty of technical opportunities. We must do what large companies cannot do and take part in the reconstruction of our country through the power of technology."

Sony would build up its brand through the introduction of transistors, which were invented at Bell Telephone Labs in New Jersey in 1947 by the future Nobel laureates John Bardeen (1908–1981), Walter Brattain (1902–1987), and William Shockley (1910–1989). Successful in arranging a license for manufacturing transistors in 1953, Sony found a new use for them by replacing the large vacuum tubes in conventional radios with the small transistors, starting a push in the industry

FIGURE 7.20.   Tokyo Telecommunications Engineering Corporation, Sony Radio, 1957. Plastic.

FIGURE 7.21.   Sony, Television, 1959. Metal.

for extreme miniaturization. After producing the first Japanese transistor radio in 1955 and its first miniaturized pocket-size radio in 1957, the company followed it up in 1958 with a more elegant tapered version influenced by American styling that made great inroads in international sales and established Sony's name as a new competitor in the industry (Figure 7.20). With its dials for volume and tuning on the right side at top, the radio could be efficiently operated while it was in a shirt pocket using only one thumb. Sony adopted a different aesthetic for its next major innovation, the first all-transistor portable television set, which was introduced in 1959 (Figure 7.21). Reduced to an eight-inch screen with a case that fit snugly around the picture tube, the television took a pragmatic approach to design that required form to follow the miniaturized components of its function directly. With a hood added to reduce glare for an appliance that might be used out of doors, it followed a practical Japanese aesthetic, responding to the particular circumstances of the product by locating

the buttons and grills close to the inner workings with which they were connected.

Modern design was one of the priorities of the Festival of Britain, which celebrated both the country's recovery from the war and the centenary of the Crystal Palace exhibition at a site on the South Bank of the River Thames in London in 1951. The Council of Industrial Design, which had been founded by the Board of Trade in 1944 and was led by the designer and manufacturer Gordon Russell (1892–1980), took complete control of design at the Festival, emboldened by the success of the Utility Furniture Scheme in coordinating the wartime production of goods. Everything from architecture to street furniture to the products displayed in the various exhibits had to pass muster by the council, and an overriding promotion of modern aesthetics, however idiosyncratic, was strongly in evidence. Notable among the modern furnishings was the outdoor Antelope seating designed by Ernest Race (1913–1964), one of Britain's foremost early postwar furniture designers (Figure 7.22). With its wiry white enameled-steel frame sitting on ball feet and its plywood seat inspired by the experiments of Charles and Ray Eames (see Figure 7.5) and painted in one of the

FIGURE 7.22. Ernest Race, Antelope Chair, 1951. Enameled steel and painted plywood.

Festival colors, yellow, red, blue, or gray, it added a fresh look to a landscape just newly released from the burden of wartime restrictions.

The combined designs at the exhibition came to be considered a unique, Festival style. Contributing to this style was one of the most unusual coordinated efforts put forth for design, an attempt to create an ornamental style for the modern era based on patterns made by crystals, conceived to demonstrate how new developments in science might contribute to contemporary design. Called the Festival Pattern Group, these designs were distilled from X-rays that crystallographers made of various minerals and provided to a group of designers as diagrams of their atomic structures. They became the basis of designs for textiles, carpets, china, wallpaper, and linoleum, many used at the exhibition and some commercially produced. The screen-printed rayon fabric designed by Susan Slade (1918–?) was based on the atomic structure of the mineral afwillite as diagrammed by the Irish crystallographer Helen Megaw (1907–2002), mastermind of the Festival Pattern concept (Figure 7.23). Of all the minerals used, afwillite gave the

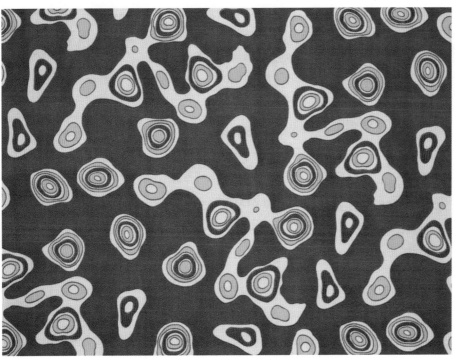

FIGURE 7.23. Susan Slade, Afwillite 8.45 Crystal Pattern Fabric, 1951. Made by British Celanese. Screen-printed rayon.

liveliest results, free forms that could be compared to those of Surrealism (see Figure 5.17) and that easily suggested the spirit of organic modern, or "contemporary," design, as it was known in Britain.

As much as the Festival of Britain had spurred interest in modern design across British society, contemporary furnishings remained economically out of reach of much of the population. But when inexpensive wallpapers and textiles decorated with natural organic shapes such as Slade's or with everyday objects associated with modern life such as free-form vases, cocktail shakers, and potted plants appeared, and when the inexpensive Homemaker dinnerware designed by Enid Seeney (1931–2011) was introduced in 1957, working families could share in the modern style (Figure 7.24). Seeney, an in-house designer for Ridgeway Potteries, set a group of modern-style objects on a background of thin linear tracings, a wiry element that reverberated in many designs of the 1950s. Some of the objects depicted in the plate were works that Seeney had seen in shops or design magazines, although the designs were adapted and polka dots and patterns added to liven them up: at

top, a reclining chair with metal legs by the English designer Robin Day (1915–2010) from 1952; bottom left, a two-seat sofa by the Swedish designer Sigvard Bernadotte (1907–2002), co-founder of Denmark's first industrial design firm, Bernadotte & Bjørn, from 1954; and bottom right, a cabinet possibly designed by the British architect David Booth (1908–1962) and the Dutch-born Judith Ledeboer (1901–1990). Here, too, the furniture is rounded out with typical midcentury accessories: a houseplant on a metal stand; a biomorphic, boomerang-shaped coffee table; and sleek cutlery and bar tools.

In France, a reaching out to broader audiences had begun when the progressive Union of Modern Artists (UAM), whose members included Le Corbusier, Charlotte Perriand, and the metalworker and furniture designer Jean Prouvé (1901–1984), initiated a series of exhibitions in 1949 entitled Useful Forms (Formes Utiles) intended to show that French design was more than just elitist. One issue that had been on the minds of international architects since the late 1920s was minimal housing, that is, creating affordable dwelling units that satisfied the needs of a family efficiently in a very limited space. This was at the core of Le Corbusier's designs for a series of apartment houses that he built after the war, the earliest being the Unité d'Habitation in Marseilles (1947–52). Le Corbusier conceived this as a social experiment, attempting to make his complex into a community with the inclusion of social services, schools, shops, recreational facilities, and other amenities for its inhabitants. To help fit out the interiors efficiently, Le Corbusier rehired Charlotte Perriand (who had left the firm at the beginning of the Second World War) to create a modular kitchen for the apartments. She developed a kitchen of oak cabinets with colored sliding plywood doors and aluminum and ceramic tile counter tops (Figure 7.25). It included many of the storage and utilitarian features of the Frankfurt Kitchen designed by Margarete Schütte-Lihotzky in 1926–27 (see Figure 3.20), but Perriand's cabinetry was part of a totally

FIGURE 7.24. Enid Seeney, Plate from Homemaker Service, 1956–57. Made by Ridgeway Potteries. Glazed ceramic with transfer-printed decoration.

FIGURE 7.25.
Charlotte Perriand, with Le Corbusier, Kitchen from the Unité d'Habitation, Marseille, c. 1952.

integrated U-shaped unit. Perriand did more, however, than build a kitchen; she made a stab at changing the dynamics of the French household by integrating the kitchen into the living space with its open construction and pass-through, which allowed the housewife to participate more fully in the life of her family.

In Italy, the 1920s and 1930s had seen a synthesis of traditional, nationalistic design with a move toward rationalism, with products taking on the logic of industrial production. Gio Ponti (1891–1979), a pioneering rationalist architect and founder in 1928 of Italy's most influential design magazine *Domus*, developed his Superleggera (super lightweight) chair in 1957 after years of engineering experiments undertaken to reduce its mass and make it extremely light but sturdy enough for use. It was inspired by a type of vernacular chair with a cane seat that had been developed during the nineteenth century in the vicinity of Chiavari, a town in Liguria in the north of Italy (Figure 7.26). He was following both an aesthetic and a structural tendency that was emerging in Italian design, which he identified as a "shift from heavy to light, from

FIGURE 7.26. Gio Ponti, Superleggera (Super Lightweight) Chair, 1957. Made by Cassina. Ash and cane.

opaque to transparent, from costly to convenient." Like the design of the chair, its fabrication was both modern and traditional, the frame being made in a factory and the cane seat finely handwoven by women in the company's workshops, a duality of industrial and craft production then common to Italian manufacturing.

A movement toward organicism had also emerged in Italy after the war, bringing with it a new style-oriented design such as the sculptural office machines and appliances of Marcello Nizzoli (1887–1969). A significant change in the Italian lifestyle occurred almost instantaneously with the introduction of the organic Vespa (wasp) motor scooter, which brought immediate stature and a new mobility to those who could acquire it (Figure 7.27). The scooter was unlike any existing means of transportation, a new type object conceived by the aeronautical engineer Corradino D'Ascanio (1891–1981) for the firm of Enrico Piaggio (1905–1965), a former aircraft manufacturer. D'Ascanio had joined Piaggio in 1932, and in 1946 created the Vespa motor scooter for the company, which was looking for new products to manufacture. Turning from the conventional, raw, industrial motorcycle,

FIGURE 7.27.
Corradino D'Ascanio,
Vespa Motor Scooter,
1946. Made by Piaggio.

D'Ascanio imagined a scooter that was softer, rounder, and more sensual in appearance, a safe means of transportation for a consumer who had never driven a scooter before. Its machinery hidden, the vehicle was practical and easy to drive, with a large front shield that would protect passengers from the dirt of the road.

The Danish craftsman and architect Hans Wegner (1914–2007) combined rational and traditional qualities in the manufacture of his furniture. He designed his works for quality factory production, emphasizing their natural materials, simple organic forms, and roots in traditional and vernacular design. His armchair of 1949, modern in its organic simplicity, reflected traditional materials and forms, its subtle curves reminiscent of the handles of common tools such as axes and scythes (Figure 7.28). In its rationalized production, the various components of the chair were made in factories, finished separately, and then joined with strong handmade zigzag joints, integrated closely so that all the elements seemed to flow seamlessly into one another. Once his chairs began to be distributed abroad in the 1950s, his name became closely associated with a growing appreciation for Danish modern design.

An early Finnish rationalized design, the Kilta (guild) tableware that Kaj Franck (1911–1989) created for industrial production by the Arabia ceramics company in 1952 was an affordable dinner service free of decoration and the attachment to age-old rituals of the table (Figure 7.29). Franck saw design as socially positioned, supporting Modernist ideas of the anonymous designer and producing tablewares that were inexpensive, simple in form, multifunctional, and suited to mass

FIGURE 7.28.   Hans J. Wegner, Armchair, 1949. Made by Johannes Hansen. Beech and cane.

FIGURE 7.29.   Kaj Franck, Kilta Tableware, 1952. Made by Arabia. Glazed earthenware.

production. He reduced the standard service to a series of basic components, eliminating many of the distinctive dinnerware shapes that were becoming outmoded. Choosing the ideal Modernist forms for the series—square, circle, and rectangle—he introduced multipurpose pieces in mix-and-match colors and maximized their stacking and storage functions, important for the smaller spaces of postwar housing. But with the canted rims of the dishes, the use of cork for the stoppers on jugs and bottles, and the woven handle of the sugar bowl, the pottery still retained an underlying image of independent craftsmanship.

A rational, and in this case mathematically oriented, system of graphic design emerged in Switzerland, especially at the design schools in Basel and Zurich, where a new international typographic style made its mark on the postwar period. The work of such designers as Armin Hoffman (born 1920), who taught in Basel, and Josef Müller-Brockmann (1914–1996), in Zurich, was a late modern expression of objectivity that had moral and political dimensions as well (see Sidebar 15). These designers brought a sense of order to the page with the use of rational layouts depending on sans-serif type and on complex grids (mathematically determined underlying spatial divisions) as the organizing principle of their compositions, with straightforward photography for their illustrations. Müller-Brockmann presented this style devoid of any suggestion of the designer's emotions, seeking a dispassionate approach that he had found in the works of such designers as László Moholy-Nagy and Herbert Matter. Müller-Brockmann is best known for posters with arresting photographic images for public-service use and a long-standing series in collaboration with the Tonhalle (concert hall) in Zurich with music-inspired layouts beginning in the mid-1950s. His poster for the Musica Viva series from 1957 has four mathematically placed columns of type above, and below, a sequence of black, slanted, horizontal lines of different lengths that

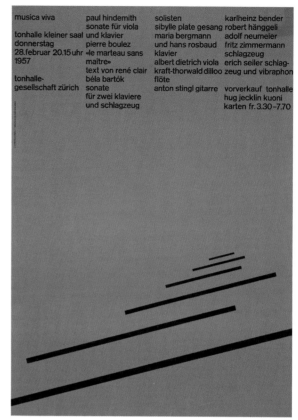

FIGURE 7.30.   Josef Müller-Brockmann, Poster for Musica Viva Concert, Tonhalle (Concert Hall), Zurich, 1957. Printed by Bollman. Photolithograph.

seem to recede in space as they suggest the tenor of the modern music that was to be performed in the concert (Figure 7.30).

A determined Modernism remained essential to Germany's design pathways although its first important postwar statement was the diminutive and unassuming streamlined Volkswagen, retrieved from the prewar people's car (see Figure 6.19) and reengineered for its release in 1949. The most significant design proponent was an institution billed as a new Bauhaus, the College of Design (Hochschule für Gestaltung) that opened its doors in the city of Ulm in southern Germany in 1953

SIDEBAR 15   Josef Müller-Brockmann, *Grid Systems in Graphic Design*, 1981

Constructive design which is capable of analysis and reproduction can influence and enhance the taste of a society and the way it conceives forms and colours. Design which is objective, committed to the common weal, well composed and refined constitutes the basis of democratic behaviour. Constructivist design means the conversion of design laws into practical solutions. Work done systematically and in accordance with strict formal principles makes those demands for directness, intelligibility and the integration of all factors which are also vital in sociopolitical life.

Working with the grid system means submitting to laws of universal validity.

The use of the grid system implies

the will to systematize, to clarify

the will to penetrate to the essentials, to concentrate

the will to cultivate objectivity instead of subjectivity

the will to rationalize the creative and technical production processes

the will to integrate elements of colour, form and material

the will to achieve architectural dominion over surface and space

the will to adopt a positive, forward-looking attitude

the recognition of the importance of education and the effect of work devised in a constructive and creative spirit.

Every visual creative work is a manifestation of the character of the designer. It is a reflection of his knowledge, his ability, and his mentality.

(and continued until 1968). Initially, the school in Ulm followed Bauhaus precepts, with the former Bauhaus masters Johannes Itten and Josef Albers on the teaching staff along with the Dutch industrial designer Hans Gugelot (1920–1965) and the German graphic designer Otl Aicher (1922–1991). Its first director was the Swiss artist and designer Max Bill (1908–1994), a former Bauhaus student, who led the school until 1957, when he left because of changing ideas about teaching and the downgrading of the role of art in design. He was replaced by the Argentinean Tomás Maldonado (1922–2018), who turned the school toward the systematization of design through mathematics and science. The wider, amended curriculum of the school was described in the first issue of its

journal *Ulm*, initiated in 1958, soon after Bill had left: "The school . . . educates designers for the production and consumer goods industries as well as for present-day means of communication: press, films, broadcasting, television, and advertising. These designers must have at their disposal the technological and scientific knowledge necessary for collaboration in industry today. At the same time they must grasp and bear in mind the cultural and sociological consequences of their work."

"In order to achieve this goal," the journal continued, "it was necessary, as it was for its Bauhaus antecedent, to bring income to the school from the collaboration with industrial companies." The firm with which the College of Design had its closest connections in its early years was that of the radio manufacturer Max Braun (founded 1921), and it was instrumental in establishing a company aesthetic that recaptured the Modernist ethos of the 1920s. Members of the faculty set out to work with Braun's own designers, including Gerd Alfred Müller (1932–1991) and Dieter Rams (born 1932), to create a cool, objective, and minimalist product line reinforced by a corporate-identity program directed by the graphic designer and photographer Wolfgang Schmittel (1930–2013). Rams was hired by Braun in 1955 and would become director of design in 1968, creating hundreds of products over his decades at the firm. But Rams's designs were by no means all of the company's output, and Braun employed numerous other designers working simultaneously on electronic products, although the aesthetic they implemented was determined by the Ulm sensibility and Rams's vision. The work that Rams did for Braun staunchly carried the banner of simplicity that William Morris had preached, to which he added his own mantra: "Good design for us means: As little design as possible" (see Sidebar 16).

Among the first fruits of the collaboration with Braun was the Phonosuper radio and phonograph, designed in 1956 by Rams with the aid of Hans Gugelot, which introduced a new concept for audio equipment (Figure 7.31). Housed in a white cabinet made of bent sheet metal with wooden sides and a transparent plexiglass cover, this radio displayed the intuition for simple functionality and respect for details that have became connected with Braun's name. Underlying the design was a deep consciousness of formal relationships, notably those of the rectangular and cubic grills on the front with the position of the white turntable and arm, and gray push buttons and dials on top. A separate coordinated auxiliary speaker was produced a year later, introducing the concept of product families, which, along with the transparent top, soon became standard in high-end audio equipment.

Such product systems following on Ulm ideas distinguished other Braun's products besides audio equipment, among them Gerd Alfred Müller's Kitchen Machine food processor from 1957 (Figure 7.32). Like such earlier appliances as Sunbeam's popular Mixmaster mixer, introduced

SIDEBAR 16   Dieter Rams, Speech at the International Marketing Meeting, 1976

Good design for us means: As little design as possible. Not for reasons of economy or convenience. It is surely one of the most difficult tasks to arrive at a really convincing, harmonious form by employing simple means. The other way is easier (and often—as paradoxical as it may seem—cheaper). More complicated, unnecessary forms are nothing more than designers' escapades, which have the function of self-expression instead of expressing the product functions. The reason often is that design is used to do nothing more than polish up things and make them chic. That is not design—it's packaging styling and a poor example of it at that. The economy of Braun design is a rejection of this type of design: It leaves away everything superfluous to emphasize that which is more important. The contours become more placid, soothing, perceptible and long-living. Today, "more design than necessary" is almost always modish styling. The rapid change in fashion makes them age just as fast.

FIGURE 7.31.   Hans Gugelot and Dieter Rams, Phonosuper Radio and Phonograph, 1956. Made by Braun. Metal, wood and plexiglass.

in the United States in 1930, it was a multipurpose machine with different attachments, including a shredder slicer, juicer, meat grinder, and coffee mill. Müller, whose sculptural approach deviated from the geometry of most Braun products, divided the casing into three sections indicated by two parallel cuts. Its rounded all-white plastic housing was accentuated with a round greenish dial to operate the processor and a small black company logo. The underlying order and efficiency of its design were testaments to the strength of the Braun aesthetic, which the company persistently followed over the next decades despite radical developments in design elsewhere.

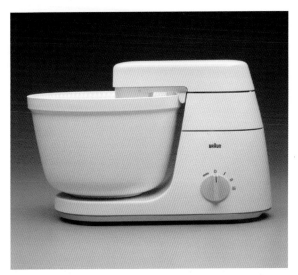

FIGURE 7.32.   Gerd Alfred Müller, Kitchen Machine Food Processor, 1957. Made by Braun. Polystyrol.

CHAPTER 8

Revolutionary and Postmodern Design

As the 1950s ended, it seemed that Good Design had set a solid path for the future with its well-mannered mixture of functionality and formalist aesthetics and its diversity of products for domestic and corporate clients. But early in the next decade, design took an unexpected turn; its creative center shifted back to Europe, especially to Italy, where with the adoption of new materials, exaggerated, expressive forms, and the influence of popular culture, a creative assertiveness materialized. This was a revolutionary moment when innovative thinking rejected conventional forms, replaced with objects and graphics that were forceful, colorful, and controversial. Such designs frequently transgressed the precepts of Modernism and those set out by Edgar Kaufmann (see Sidebar 14) by embracing aspects of irrationality, narrative, and humor, closing the door on Modernism's narrow definition of objectivity and functionality. This new aesthetic defined many of the fashionable consumer products that were cited as expressions of a distinctive Italian style at the Milan Triennale (Triennial) design exhibitions during the period, at least until 1968, when student protests against establishment political and social systems forced its postponement,

with future Triennale exhibitions concentrating on design with broader social goals.

Many found support for the questioning of Modernism in *Complexity and Contradiction in Architecture*, a treatise written by the American architect Robert Venturi (1925–2018) and first published in 1966 (but not translated into Italian until 1980), in which he proposed a design free of orthodoxies. Instead, his ideal was "a complex and contradictory architecture based on the richness and ambiguity of modern experience." This became one of the most influential architectural texts of the twentieth century, and for many it justified a move toward Postmodern design and a reconsideration of ornamentation and the historic styles, however ironic they may have been. Venturi was not alone in his respect for the past. The Victorian Society, for example, was found in England in 1958 to crusade for the preservation of nineteenth-century buildings and in 1966, the American Victorian Society was established directly upon the demolition of Pennsylvania Station in New York, a powerful example of the architecture of McKim, Mead & White from 1910. Modernism itself was also repositioned, notably by the High-Tech movement, a trend in design that repurposed everyday industrial forms and turned buildings inside out to reveal their inner workings.

Cutting-Edge Materials and Processes

Enjoying a period of economic boom in Europe, manufacturers explored cutting-edge materials and processes during the 1960s, largely in the field of plastics, to bring the creations of a new breed of designers to market, many of whom began to question the hold that consumerism had over society. Such experimentation was much more suited to the practice of small European manufacturers, who with their skilled craftsmen had no need to tool up for large production runs, unlike those in the United States, where large-scale industrial production was the norm. In reviewing the year in 1960, the American magazine *Industrial Design* noted that it had already seen an "astonishing, though expected, progress in the development of new materials and processes, and especially in the invasion by plastics of product areas ordinarily preempted by other materials." These products ranged from plumbing fixtures and building materials to furniture and household goods. With chemistry continuing to open up new areas for these oil-based compounds, the applications of plastic only grew more widespread over the next years. In 1973, however, when the international oil cartel Organization of the Petroleum Exporting Countries (OPEC) reduced its production and set up an embargo on oil for the United States, the price of oil rose to such a level that became uneconomical for much of manufacturing, and producers had to look elsewhere for substitute materials (prices remained higher even after the embargo ended a year later).

Plastic, which Roland Barthes had characterized as formless and featureless in his 1955 essay (see Sidebar 13), now took on a strong physical identity. With the use of hard and tough substances with bright finishes (some integral to the plastic itself, some with lacquered color added), the pale colors and odd sounds that Barthes had described proved to be only two characteristics of a medium with considerably more possibilities than he had imagined. Each plastic had its own particular properties, allowing designers to choose among them for those that satisfied their technical and aesthetic requirements. Fiberglass (glass-reinforced plastic, or GRP), for example, provided strength and durability at low cost. It was essential for designs like the wobbly Gyro rocking chair created in 1968 by the Finn Eero Aarnio (born 1932), which was made in two sections and could revolve in a complete circle (Figure 8.1). ABS (acrylonitrile-butadiene-styrene) plastic was tough, easy to mold, and yielded bright, integral colors, facilitating the vivid red of the Valentine portable typewriter designed in Italy by Ettore Sottsass, Jr. (1917–2007), in collaboration with the English designer Perry King (born 1938) in 1969 (see Figure 8.8).

Polypropylene (PP) afforded products that were light, sturdy, and easy and inexpensive to produce

FIGURE 8.1. Eero Aarnio, Gyro Chair, 1968. Made by Asko. Fiberglass.

by injection molding, requiring little costly finishing and resulting in minimum waste (although the start-up costs for making the molds were very high). Robin Day chose polypropylene for its strength and economy of manufacture when he was working out the engineering of his widely used stacking chairs in 1962–63 with the furniture manufacturer Hille (established 1906) (Figure 8.2). Polypropylene, which had only been invented in 1954, was so unusual that this design became popularly called by the name of its material, the Polyprop chair. Day had learned of the advantages of polypropylene when judging a competition for designs made from this recently developed plastic, and was one of the first designers to apply it to the mass production of furniture. Its sturdiness stood the chairs well for the rough use they had as one of the decade's most popular pieces of furniture for schools, restaurants, and government and industrial settings, and it led to the long-standing collaboration with Day that made Hille the leading British postwar manufacturer of modern design.

The difficulty of using this young medium to introduce unusual forms was demonstrated by the long experimental period required to produce the audacious cantilever chair designed between 1960 and 1967 by the Dane Verner Panton (1926–1998) (Figure 8.3). Eero Saarinen had faced similar problems of designing ahead of technology during the 1950s when he attempted to create his Tulip chairs using only plastic (see Figure 7.13). When it was introduced after seven years of gestation, Panton's chair became the first molded single-piece seating successfully manufactured by industry, but Panton was not completely satisfied with the initial model, which was developed with the German furniture manufacturer Vitra. Different production versions were tried over the three following decades, first a chair of rigid cast polyurethane foam coated with synthetic polymer paint; then of Luran-S plastic (acrylate-styrene-acrylonitrile), an alternative to ABS plastic; and then of injection-molded polystyrene. Only when Vitra introduced its fourth version of this striking chair, in injection-molded

FIGURE 8.2.   Robin Day, Polyprop Chairs, 1962–63. Made by Hille. Polypropylene.

FIGURE 8.3.   Verner Panton, Chair, 1960–67. Made by Vitra. Polypropylene.

polypropylene in 1999, just after Panton's death, was it finally deemed a success.

The French designer Pierre Paulin (1927–2009) created equally audacious furniture by turning to soft latex foam instead of hard plastics, upholstering his highly sculptural designs with a new synthetic stretch fabric that had become popular for form-fitting bathing suits. A work such as his Ribbon chair, created in 1967, could only have been achieved with the use of this newly developed material from the fashion industry, which allowed the upholstery to be fit tightly to its complex shapes (Figure 8.4). The chair had an inner tubular-metal structure, which was covered with stretched rubber sheeting and foam, and then upholstered with a type of slip cover, which could easily be changed with the seasons or when it showed signs of wear. In its most celebrated version, the chair was upholstered with a stretch fabric in the sinuous Momentum Blue Flame pattern created by the dean of American textile designers, Jack Lenor Larsen

(born 1927). Publicity photographs showing the Ribbon chair on a runway as a jet takes off above it highlighted the modernity of Paulin's organic forms and the vibrating colors of Larsen's Op (optical) Art patterns.

Stretch fabric and foam were also the materials used for the Up seating designed in 1969 by the Italian Gaetano Pesce (born 1939). Included among the seven pieces in the series was his Lady armchair, conceived as a voluptuous female form and frequently attached with a cord to its companion ottoman, often seen as a symbol of feminine subjugation (Figure 8.5). Still, the series was essentially an essay in process as Pesce introduced a completely new concept of furniture production and transportation. Unlike Paulin's furniture, Pesce's chairs had no internal structure but depended on the ability of high-density foam to retain its shape. These pieces were first fashioned of polyurethane foam and then tightly upholstered, after which they were compressed in a pressurized vacuum chamber where all the air was removed from the foam (which, in fact, is mostly air). The flattened pieces were then heat-sealed between vinyl sheets and put into flat boxes, which allowed them to be shipped

FIGURE 8.4.   Pierre Paulin, Ribbon Chair, 1967. Made by Artifort. Momentum Fabric by Jack Lenor Larsen. Tubular steel, latex foam, stretch fabric, and painted wood.

FIGURE 8.5.   Gaetano Pesce, Up 5 (Lady) Armchair and Up 6 Ottoman, 1969. Made by C & B Italia. Expanded polyurethane foam and stretch fabric.

economically, solving a continual problem faced by the furniture industry. When the buyers removed the flattened chairs from their wrappers, the chairs naturally filled up with air, reaching their original dimensions in about an hour (the process could not be reversed, however). Pesce's concept was not taken further at that time, but a similar process is used today for producing and shipping mattresses.

The more explicit appropriation of recognizable forms for design and social comment appeared at a large scale when the Pop art movement had its first showing in Italy in 1964 at the Biennale (Biennial) art exhibition in Venice. There, its ironic, larger-than-life replications of common objects, like the soft sculptures by the Swedish-born American artist Claes Oldenburg (born 1929), had a great impact on international design. Perhaps the most fitting interpretation of this new approach to design was that of the German designer Ingo Maurer (born 1932), his Bulb of 1966, which set a standard lightbulb inside a foot-high replica of it; unlike most Pop art transformations, it followed the same function as the original it copied

(Figure 8.6). The Pillola (pill) lamp from 1968 by Cesare Casati (1936–2015) and C. Emanuele Ponzio (1923–2015) took a very small, common object, an inch-long medical capsule, and enlarged it enormously, magnifying it in ABS plastic to almost two feet high (Figure 8.7). With five shiny, multicolored lamps teetering at different angles next to each other as its promotional image showed, they brought humor to their product through their use of an unexpected source and the idea of taking objects out of their cultural contexts.

Equally subversive was the red ABS plastic Valentine portable typewriter designed by Sottsass and King, who were then consultants to the Olivetti business-machine company (Figure 8.8). It too had a personal narrative, a stylish design masquerading as a social statement. It was made, according to Sottsass, "for use any place except in an office, so as not to remind anyone of monotonous working hours, but rather to keep amateur poets company on quiet Sundays in the country or to provide a highly colored object on a table in a studio apartment. An anti-machine machine, built around

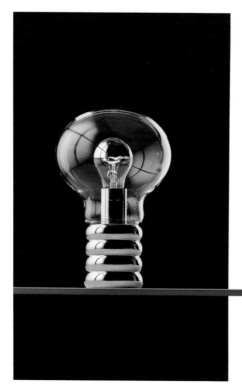

FIGURE 8.6. Ingo Maurer, Bulb, 1966. Chromium-plated metal and glass.

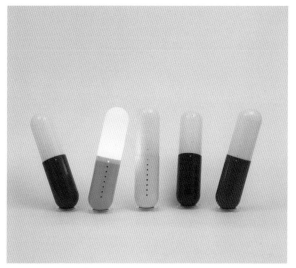

FIGURE 8.7. Cesare Casati and C. Emanuele Ponzio, Pillola (Pill) Lamp, 1968. Made by Nai Ponteur. ABS plastic and acrylic.

the commonest mass-produced mechanism, the works inside any typewriter, it may also seem to be an unpretentious toy"—and with its two yellow typewriter-ribbon spools looking like the eyes of a robot, it could easily have been mistaken for one.

The Grillo (cricket) telephone was also toylike, a new instrument of ABS plastic commissioned from Marco Zanuso (1916–2001) and Richard Sapper (1932–2015) by the Italian national telephone service Italtel in 1966 as an alternative to the conventional telephone (Figure 8.9). The commission had called for a small, simple device, and the designers reduced their design to half the

FIGURE 8.8. Ettore Sottsass, Jr., with Perry King, Valentine Portable Typewriter, 1969. Made by Olivetti. ABS plastic.

size of the standard model. This reticent object was meant to be friendly, suggesting a pet or the harmless creature that inspired its name. It could fit in one hand, and when it was not in use, the hinged mouthpiece section was folded over to serve as the base of the telephone, concealing, not revealing, its structure and function.

FIGURE 8.9. Marco Zanuso and Richard Sapper, Grillo (Cricket) Telephone, 1966. Made by Italtel. ABS Plastic.

FIGURE 8.10.   Joe Colombo, Tubo (Tube) Seating, 1969. Made by Flexform. PVC plastic, polyurethane foam, and fabric.

At the same time, other designers were embracing design that was not limited to isolated objects but was created in the context of a changing environment, introducing systems with endless possibilities like those explored at the College of Design in Ulm. Modularity and interchangeability, what for many other modern products had been ancillary features, now became the substance of system design. A multiplicity of uses and the involvement of the user in deciding what those would be was also fundamental to these products. Joe Colombo (1930–1971) advanced the concept of functional flexibility in a series of modular designs that included his Tubo (tube) group of 1969 (Figure 8.10). Made of four upholstered foam-covered PVC plastic tubes of different diameters that nested inside each other, they could be hooked together or kept separate, inviting the user to change their arrangement at will.

The unstructured Sacco (sack), or beanbag, chair, a relaxed, adaptable, and flexible object designed in 1968–69 by the Gatti, Paolini, Teodoro firm (established in Turin in 1965), stands as a prime expression of freedom from preexisting boundaries (Figure 8.11). Designed originally as a

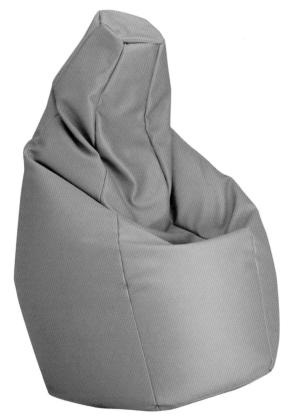

FIGURE 8.11.   Gatti, Paolini, Teodoro, Sacco Seating, 1968–69. Made by Zanotta. Leather-covered polystyrene.

bag of leather stuffed with polystyrene beads, it had no form except the one that it took at any moment. Not surprisingly, its simple design was immediately knocked off, with numerous imitations and versions in different materials coming onto the market and many found there to this day. "It is adaptable to any body, on any surface," the designers explained. "It assumes the form and position of the body resting on it, with its original shape being unrecognizable when it is in use. Thus it is an ambiguous, mimetic, anti-formalist object, and because of these characteristics, it can be part of any environment." With this narrative element, they attempted to humanize what was essentially a small, light, and completely anonymous form, adding that it could be "loaded into a car and transported anywhere, to a meadow, under a tree, for sleeping, for reading, for making love."

These unconventional and liberating designs emerged at a particular moment of social upheaval when there was a call for autonomy and the breaking down of hierarchical structures across daily life. They mirrored the striving of many of the antiestablishment groups in the news in 1968, students at the barricades in France, protesters against the Vietnam War (1954–75) marching in the United States, and the nonconformist dropouts and hippies who had centered in California in the mid-1960s. Distinguished by drug use, loose social arrangements, psychedelic art, and a resurgence of do-it-yourself activities and crafts, the hippie movement also enabled a new rock-music scene, which gave rise to the vibrant work of such graphic artists as Milton Glaser (born 1929) and Peter Max (born 1937) and the animators of *The Yellow Submarine*, the 1968 film by the Beatles (1960–69), the British rock band. With concerts at the Fillmore Auditorium in San Francisco and music festivals across the country, including the mammoth Woodstock, New York, festival in 1969, these American venues showcased young new groups who were promoted (and soon supported) by the sales of drug-inspired, psychedelic posters. Some, like the poster for a concert by the Youngbloods designed by

Victor Moscoso (born 1936), a Yale graduate much influenced by the color studies of his teacher Josef Albers, were almost unintelligible (Figure 8.12). They seduced viewers to look more closely in order to decipher their content, to engage actively with a complex typography that the graphic designer and typographic theorist Dan Friedman (1945–1995) would soon applaud as "readable," opposing it to the simple, orderly, and passively received Modernist typography, which he deprecated as merely "legible." The counterculture Punk movement that emerged in England in the late 1970s was similarly centered on underground music and alternative clothing styles, expressed in irreverent graphic designs for rock bands, such as the record covers of Jamie Reid (born 1947) and Neville Brody (born 1957), and in the fashions of Vivienne Westwood (born 1941).

FIGURE 8.12. Victor Moscoso, Poster for Youngbloods Concert, 1967. Lithograph.

High-Tech

The 1970s saw a return to the materials of Modernism in what became known as the High-Tech style, with consumers and designers looking to everyday products from hardware stores, kitchen supply houses, and office furniture suppliers to find shiny objects that could be adapted for domestic interiors. The term "High-Tech," coined by the American journalists Joan Kron (born 1928) and Suzanne Slesin (born 1944) and used as the title of their 1978 book, stood for an industrial aesthetic that was then being reborn, even if the way it was interpreted may sometimes have transgressed Modernist principles. Front and center to what Kron and Slesin saw as a new movement, and a great influence on the architecture and design of its time, was the Centre Georges Pompidou in Paris, a museum and cultural center and an industrial masterpiece designed by the British architect Richard Rodgers (born 1933) and the Italian architect and engineer Renzo Piano (born 1937) between 1971 and 1977 (Figure 8.13). With no continuous outer façade but a mass of exterior ducts, steel struts, and glass creating its boundaries and supporting its uninterrupted reinforced-concrete floors, the building was a paragon of revealed design. Its four major components for "circulation" were clearly visible and identified by their strong colors, with blue covering the ducts for air circulation, yellow for electricity, green for water, and red for people, the last named identifying the means of human circulation with a great public escalator outside on its façade and the elevators and escalators within.

This new aesthetic was frequently elaborated by ad-hoc assemblages, the appropriation and repurposing of industrial components for new and stylish aims. This unusual approach, both practical and intellectual, characterized one aspect of the work of the brothers Achille Castiglioni (1918–2002) and Pier Giacomo Castiglioni (1913–1968), whose designs defined lighting in Italy in the second

FIGURE 8.13.   Richard Rogers and Renzo Piano, Centre Georges Pompidou, Paris, 1971–77.

half of the century. Their Toio floor lamp from 1962, an engaging assemblage of "found" elements, had as its centerpiece an automobile headlamp mounted on a shiny metal pole in a red stand, which stabilized the piece and held the transformer that was needed for the light to function (Figure 8.14). Its electrical wire was loosely draped and coiled, held to the pole by the round guides from a fishing rod. Each element, drawn from a separate environment, was transmuted as it served its specific function in this assemblage, creating a design with a witty sense of rightness through its expressive act of communication

The Castiglioni brothers insisted on pushing forward with such singular experiments without

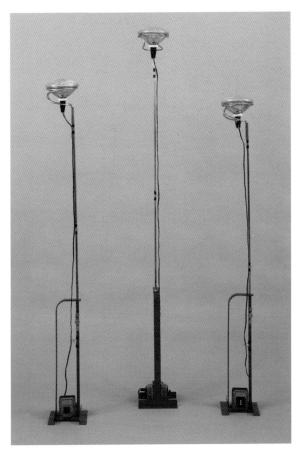

FIGURE 8.15.   Richard Sapper, Tizio Table Lamp, 1970–71. Made by Artemide. ABS plastic and aluminum.

FIGURE 8.14.   Achille Castiglioni and Pier Giacomo Castiglioni, Toio Floor Lamps, 1962. Made by Flos. Automobile headlight bulb, steel, enamel, transformer, rubber, plastic.

regard to their commercial feasibility. "Design is, or ought to be, always a negation or contestation of the existing set-up," Achille wrote. "It is this attitude that some semiologist has called a 'deviation from the norm.' In other words, the design always tends to go beyond the threshold of expectation of both client and market" (see Sidebar 17). Unlike Raymond Loewy and his conciliatory MAYA (Most Advanced Yet Acceptable) principle (see Sidebar 12), Castiglioni believed that it was the designer's role to push the limits of the market by bringing pioneering products to the public. For him, quality was irreconcilable with the views of market

researchers; had the brothers' Toio lamp been subject to their deliberations, it would probably never have been produced.

Richard Sapper's high-tech matte-black Tizio task lamp from 1970–71 fully exploited the stylish aspects of its industrial aesthetic, an update of George Carwardine's Anglepoise worktable lighting (Figure 8.15; see also Figure 6.16). Red accents signaled the points of the pivoting arms, which counterbalanced each other, and which along with a red switch on the top of the base revealed the way the object functioned. The lamp used new technology, a recently developed low-voltage, high-intensity, halogen bulb, and its cool elegance was a by-product of its engineering: with the new bulb requiring little voltage, the metal arms could conduct the low power to the bulb, and without the need for cables within the arms, they could be made very thin.

SIDEBAR 17   Achille Castiglioni, Design Survey, 1965

The choice of the functions is, therefore, the first act in designing, and it remains decisive right to the end of the creative process. We feel that it is at this level that the designer can and must exercise to the full his powers of interpretation and freedom. The powers of interpretation are applied essentially to the identification of certain objective functions (technological, practical, commercial, economic, etc.). Sometimes, for example, we choose a form that may seem to have an established traditional significance, but in reality we use it in ways quite unrelated to that significance. In this case we want to communicate with the observer, to stimulate his powers of understanding, his knowledge of the object, and to disregard formal appearances.

This relationship could be described as one of reciprocal curiosity. Besides, an unprejudiced use of an expressive detail may lead us to rediscover the original rationality of certain forms that, precisely because they have always been part of our education, are never questioned. In this case understanding a familiar form means discovering its significance; and communicating this discovery means, in the last analysis, charging the object with a rational expressiveness. We feel that this play of "appearances" is important, partly because it is within these margins of freedom that the designer can express the broader significance of his "sense of his age" and it may, at times, confer a cultural value on an expression of taste.

Radical Design

In his introduction to the catalogue of the Museum of Modern Art's 1972 exhibition Italy: The New Domestic Landscape, its curator, the Argentine architect and social activist Emilio Ambasz (born 1943), distinguished between "three prevalent attitudes toward design," approaches that he called "conformist," "reformist," and "one of contestation," or argument (see Sidebar 18). For a number of environments of contestation commissioned specifically for the exhibition, the designers "were asked to explore the domestic landscape with a sense for its places, and to postulate the spaces and artifacts that give them form, the ceremonies and behaviors that assign them meaning. Special attention was to be paid to new forms and patterns of use emerging as a result of changing life styles, more informal social and family relationships, and evolving notions of privacy and territoriality; as well as to the exploration of new materials and techniques of production." With this in mind, Joe Colombo created his prototype Total Furnishing

Unit as compact modular system with all the necessities for living packed in tightly (Figure 8.16). Beds, fixtures, facilities, and storage were all accessed by opening doors, lifting up shelves, or pulling out elements from the central unit. For Colombo, it was "necessary to create a dwelling unit that more closely approximates the actual life style of today and tomorrow, but that is also closer to man's true requirements, and thus less restricting and less representative of taste, prestige, and so forth . . . The space within this unit should be dynamic; that is, it should be in a continual state of transformation, so that a cubic space smaller than the conventional norm can nevertheless be exploited to the maximum, with a maximum economy in its interior arrangement."

In addition to commissioning environments, the museum arranged for the collaboration of design groups considered part of the Radical Design movement, Archizoom and Superstudio among them. The term "radical" was first applied to architecture, but it was eventually given to any object or event that seemed to represent anti-design

FIGURE 8.16.
Joe Colombo, Total Furnishing Unit, Italy: The New Domestic Landscape, Museum of Modern Art, New York, 1972.

or counter-design sentiments in the later 1960s and early 1970s. In inviting these designers, the museum was implicit in the further elaboration of a period of radical rejection of the status quo, legitimizing the counterculture objectives of Italian designers by inviting them to showcase a range of controversial ideas through polemical presentations in the exhibition. Their work, the museum's brief said, was to emphasize "the need for a renewal of philosophical discourse and for social and political involvement as a way of bringing about structural changes in our society."

Superstudio was an anti-design group founded in Florence in 1966 by two recent architectural graduates, Cristiano Toraldo di Francia (born 1941) and Adolfo Natalini (born 1941), pioneers of architecture as a conceptual practice, expressed through exhibitions, installations, films, and collaged images of a fraught future world without architecture or design. For the museum's exhibition, they proposed an imaginary installation that described their ideas for an endless, unbuilt environment demarcated only by a neutral universal grid. This offered "a critical reappraisal of the possibilities of life without objects. It is a reconsideration of the relations between process of design and the environment through an alternative mode of existence, rendered visible by a series of symbolic images." Their submission was illustrated with images showing humans wandering in an alien future world, with a gridded ground, where nomadism, the lack of attachment to a particular

SIDEBAR 18   Emilio Ambasz, Introduction, *Italy: The New Domestic Landscape*, 1972

By the first, or conformist, approach, we refer to the attitude of certain designers who conceive of their work as an autonomous activity responsible only to itself; they do not question the sociocultural context in which they work, but instead continue to refine already established forms and functions . . .

The second, or reformist, attitude is motivated by a profound concern for the designer's role in a society that fosters consumption as one means of inducing individual happiness, thereby insuring social stability. Torn by the dilemma of having been trained as creators of objects, and yet being incapable of controlling either the significance or the ultimate uses of these objects, they find themselves unable to reconcile the conflicts between their social concerns and their professional practices . . . Convinced that there can be no renovation of design until structural changes have occurred in society, but not attempting to bring these about themselves, they do not invent substantially new forms; instead, they engage in a rhetorical operation of redesigning conventional objects with new, ironic, and sometimes self-deprecatory sociocultural and aesthetic references . . .

The third approach to design . . . reveals itself in two main trends in Italy today, each trying to get to the root in very different ways. The first is by commitment to a "moratorium" position and an absolute refusal to take part in the present socioindustrial system. Here, "antiobject" literally means "not making objects," and the designers' pursuits are either confined to political action and philosophical postulation, or else consist of total withdrawal.

Those following the second tendency share with the preceding group the disbelief that an object can be designed as a single, isolated entity, without regard for its physical and sociocultural context. Their reaction to the problem, however, is not one of passive abstention but rather one of active critical participation. They have thus come to conceive objects and of their users as an ensemble of interrelated processes, whose interaction results in constantly changing patterns of relationships. To the traditional preoccupation with aesthetic objects, these contemporary designers have therefore added a concern for an aesthetic of the uses made of these objects. This holistic approach is manifested in the design of objects that are flexible in function, thus permitting multiple modes of use and arrangement.

place, was the mode of living (Figure 8.17). "The designing of a region free from the pollution of design is very similar to a design for a terrestrial paradise," their statement concluded.

With a sense of futility about the future of objects during a time of continued social turbulence, a period of semi-stasis and reassessment followed, with a number of Italian radical designers and groups leaving the design of products behind and offering alternative visions for the future. Ettore Sottsass, Jr., for one, imagined creating for a post-consumer society, hoping that "it may occur to someone working in design to produce objects that are of no use to industrial civilization as it is set up at present but that serve to release creative energies, to suggest possibilities, to stimulate awareness, to bring people's feet back onto the planet." Sottsass and many other designers joined together in 1973 to create an experimental design laboratory, which they called Global Tools. They intended to provide informal classes to reeducate architects and designers, returning to basic forms, craftsmanship,

A Journey from A to B

There will be no further need for cities or castles.
There will be no further reason for roads or squares.
Every point will be the same as any other
(excluding a few deserts or mountains which are in no wise inhabitable).
So, having chosen a random point on the map,
we'll be able to say my house will be here
for three days two months or ten years.
And we'll set off that way (let's call it B)
without provisions, carrying only objects we're fond of.
The journey from A to B can be long or short,
in any case it will be a constant migration,
with the actions of living at every point along the ideal line
between A (departure) and B (arrival).
It won't, you see, be just the transportation of matter.

These are the objects we'll carry with us:
some strange pressed flowers,
a few videotapes, some family photos,
a drawing on crumpled paper,
an enormous banner of grass and reeds interwoven with
old pieces of material which once were clothes,
a fine suit, a bad book...
These will be the objects.
Someone will take with him
only a herd of animals for friends. For instance:
a quartet of Bremermusikanten,
or a horse, two dogs and two doves
or twelve cats, five dogs and a goat.
Yet others will take with them only memory,
become so sharp and bright as to be a visible object.
Others will hold one arm raised, fist clenched.
Someone will have learnt a magic word and will take it with him
as a suitcase or a standard: CALM, COMPREHENSION, CONFIDENCE,

247

FIGURE 8.17.
Superstudio, *Journey from A to B*, Italy: The New Domestic Landscape, Museum of Modern Art, New York, 1972.

and hand production using natural materials. Global Tools was supported by Alessandro Mendini (1931–2019), one of its founders and the influential editor of *Casabella*, who used the magazine to document and publicize the laboratory's activities.

By the mid-1970s, however, Global Tools and many other radical groups had lost their steam, and a performance by Mendini in 1974, in which he set his Lassù (up there) chair ablaze in a mountainous setting, seemed to call an end to the style-based Italian design that had been dominant since the early 1960s (Figure 8.18). A performance executed as a cover photograph for *Casabella*, it was a self-referential act that demonstrated that design and experience had somehow merged. Mendini himself claimed that he was mourning for the fate of the designed object, and that he "wanted to show that even objects have a life, and that it can be tragic. Their trajectory goes from conception, to birth, through their years of life, and finally death—which

FIGURE 8.18.   Alessandro Mendini, Destruction of the Lassù (Up There) Chair, 1974.

can be ritual. It would be nice if every object, even the simplest and most utilitarian, were used in a ritual manner. This would mean that every action we perform purposefully would have its own dignity."

Postmodernism

Postmodern was a style that probably had as many definitions as practitioners and critics, but it was generally agreed that decoration was an essential element of it. The term first appeared in a significant architectural context in *The Language of Post-Modern Architecture*, written in 1977 by the American theorist and architect Charles Jencks

(born 1939). But he, like many others, had trouble defining the term, saying that "all it admits is the minimum information that certain architects and buildings have moved beyond or counter to modern architecture." Robert Venturi had made an early, energetic move with his book *Complexity and Contradiction in Architecture*, in which he spoke out against the intimidation that many architects still felt from the precepts of Modernism (see Sidebar 19). Although by then some designers had left Modernist principles behind, a good number of architects still held on to them, following the example of Mies van der Rohe and his commitment to a "less is more" attitude about design.

In reintroducing ornament and historicism, Postmodernism seemingly rejected the principles of modern design that had been discarded earlier in the century. But it never seriously meant to transgress these principles, and the perpetuation of the modern aspects of design was generally assured through simplification and the abstraction of the decorative motifs and historical elements it reintroduced, often with an ironic nature. The label "Postmodern" itself was disavowed by both Venturi and Ettore Sottsass, Jr., those designers most closely associated with its beginnings, Venturi because critics considered it merely a decorative movement without any of the critique of modern society that he felt it implied, and Sottsass because he thought it involved historicism, which his Memphis design group never embraced.

Despite the broader basis of Postmodernism in the language of philosophy and semiotics (the study of signs and symbols and their interpretations), Postmodern design played itself out primarily through visual means, although those were not immune to metaphorical and symbolic expression. The exhibition Signs of Life: Symbols in the American City, which Venturi, his wife and partner Denise Scott Brown (born 1931), and their associate Steven Izenhour (1940–2001) organized for the Smithsonian Institution in Washington, DC, at the time of the American Bicentennial in 1976, showed that there was more to objects than their immediate appearance. They had earlier

SIDEBAR 19   Robert Venturi, "Nonstraightforward Architecture: A Gentle Manifesto," 1966

Architects can no longer afford to be intimidated by the puritanically moral language of orthodox modern architecture. I like elements which are hybrid rather than "pure," compromising rather than "clean," distorted rather than "straightforward," ambiguous rather than "articulated," perverse as well as impersonal, boring as well as "interesting," conventional rather than "designed," accommodating rather than excluding, redundant rather than simple, vestigial as well as innovating, inconsistent and equivocal rather than direct and clear. I am for messy vitality over obvious unity. I include the non sequitur and proclaim the duality.

I am for richness of meaning rather than clarity of meaning; for the implicit function as well as the explicit function. I prefer "both-and" to "either-or," black and white, and sometimes gray, to black or white. A valid architecture evokes many levels of meaning and combinations of focus: its space and its elements become readable and workable in several ways at once.

But an architecture of complexity and contradiction has a special obligation toward the whole: its truth must be in its totality or its implications of totality. It must embody the difficult unity of inclusion rather than the easy unity of exclusion. More is not less.

FIGURE 8.19.   Venturi and Rauch, Signs of Life: Symbols in the American City, Smithsonian Institution, Washington, DC, 1976.

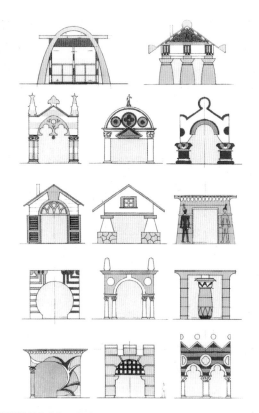

FIGURE 8.20. Robert Venturi, *Eclectic Houses*, 1977. Watercolor (lost).

investigated the meaning and relevance of signs in their study of popular and contemporary vernacular design in *Learning from Las Vegas*, published in 1972. Signs of Life, an exhibition mounted not for academics but for the public, offered visitors insights into how the riches of the past infused their own lives. Examining several typical middle American interiors, they showed that furnishings had associations that people "use to communicate with others about themselves. The communication is mainly about social status, social aspirations, personal identity, individual freedom, and nostalgia for another time or place." These historical connections were highlighted in the exhibition through labels in speech balloons above the objects, although many visitors might not have had sufficient knowledge of past styles to understand the specifics of these associations (Figure 8.19).

Venturi drew on his fascination with historical styles in his *Eclectic Houses* drawing depicting three columns of colorful elevations of architectural fantasies from the time of the Egyptians to the present (Figure 8.20). Capping off the chart is one

FIGURE 8.21.
Robert Venturi, Chairs, 1978–84. Made by Knoll. Bent and laminated wood. In the exhibition *Out of the Ordinary*, Philadelphia Museum of Art, 2001.

of McDonald's golden arches, a presence in the popular mind that in every way seemed to equal the importance given to styles from the past. Similarly looking back to the flow of styles from the past was Venturi's early foray into historicizing design, a series of dining chairs created for Knoll between 1978 and 1984. His nine chair designs, representing familiar styles from the early eighteenth century to the 1930s—Gothic Revival, Art Nouveau, Art Deco, Empire, Chippendale, Biedermeier, Sheraton, Hepplewhite, and Queen Anne, as seen from right to left in the illustration (Figure 8.21)—captured the essence of each style in silhouette and in selected details and ornament but ironically left the rest abstracted and simplified. In suggesting the program in 1978, Venturi had outlined his concept to the Knoll organization: "What I propose is chairs, tables, and bureaus that adapt a series of historical styles involving wit, variety, and industrial process, and consisting of a flat profile in a decorative shape in a frontal dimension. Like a building with a 'false' façade, you see the 'real' structure from the side and you attribute a symbolic rather than an authentic quality to the ornamental surface in front. For this reason I consider this furniture to be a variety of Modern furniture, an evolution within the Modern movement." By leaving the layers of the plywood visible when seen from the side and relating this to the plywood furniture of Alvar Aalto (see Figures 5.19, 5.20), he could justify these chairs as "modern" forms and dodge the label "Postmodern" for his work. The chairs were manufactured with solid finishes, or with selected ornamentation like the laminate on his Sheraton chair, which replicates in a flat pattern the sculptural details of the model it imitates (Figure 8.22), or with his allover Grandmother pattern, a blended motif also used by Venturi for fabrics, china, and other objects (Figure 8.23). He derived the pattern from an old fabric, which he then partially obliterated and devalued by overprinting it with the camouflage marks found inside business envelopes.

FIGURE 8.22. Robert Venturi, Sheraton Chair, 1978–84. Made by Knoll. Bent and laminated wood.

FIGURE 8.23. Robert Venturi, Grandmother Pattern Dinner Service, 1982–84. Made by Swid Powell. Glazed porcelain.

Venturi's historicist venture for Knoll overlapped with an international project for the design of luxury tea and coffee services commissioned by the Italian metalware firm Alessi (founded 1921) in 1980. Venturi was one of eleven leading architects to receive this commission, among whom were the Americans Michael Graves (1934–2015), Charles

FIGURE 8.24.   Michael Graves, Portland Building, Portland, Oregon, 1979–82.

Jencks, and Richard Meier (born 1934) and the Italians Mendini and Aldo Rossi (1931–1997). The project had been initiated by Mendini himself, who had been brought in the previous year by the new director of the Alessi family firm, Alberto

Alessi (born 1946), to make design a high-profile endeavor at the company. The eleven silver services in the series, each consisting of a teapot, coffee pot, sugar bowl, and creamer on a tray, were to be designed on the theme of buildings laid out around a piazza, or city square, the source of its title, Coffee and Tea Piazza.

Michael Graves was one of the designers of the Piazza services who was then taking inspiration from the historical past, calling up ideas from the classical world and reinventing the vocabulary of antiquity, initially in his Portland (Oregon) Building, designed and built between 1979 and 1982 (Figure 8.24). This was the first important attempt to bring classical elements back into American architecture, and in cladding its façades with symbolic elements, including colossal fluted pilasters and giant keystones, he made a decisive argument for the new type of historicism that became known as Postmodernism. His square Piazza vessels, looking like fortified buildings bound by engaged columns and surmounted by conical tops, made up a brilliant service in silver and imitation ivory (plastic) with spheres of lacquered aluminum impersonating semiprecious stones (Figure 8.25). While all the Piazzas were made of silver and destined for collectors and museums, Graves's service played up its luxury to the greatest degree, and it was the best selling of these services.

FIGURE 8.25.
Michael Graves, Coffee and Tea Piazza, 1983. Made by Alessi. Silver, lacquered aluminum, plastic, and glass.

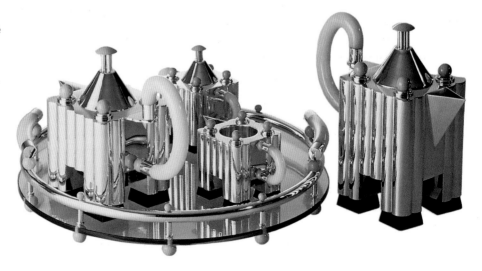

By 1978, Mendini's earlier pessimism about the future of design had turned into critique with a series of ironic redesigns of Modernist icons, among them Thonet's bentwood chair (Figure 8.26; see Figure 1.2). For his redesign of the Thonet chair, he added colorful appendages, a baby-blue, squiggly shape tacked onto its back, and balls in primary colors affixed to it on wires. Mendini's original designs at that time took a decorative path, clearly seen in his hand-painted Armchair for Proust, which was made by Studio Alchimia (Alchemy), a design collective founded in 1976 to which Mendini belonged (Figure 8.27). The armchair can be seen as a continuation of his redesigns of works from the past. The concept emerged from Mendini's musings about what kind of chair the French novelist Marcel Proust (1871–1922) would have sat in. With no facts to be found that would satisfy him, he decided to craft a chair that would reflect the writer's time and his interest in Impressionist painting. Appropriating a late Victorian revival armchair, he covered the upholstery and the robustly carved wooden frame with an allover pattern using daubs of paint, "pointillist" brushstrokes taken from Neo-Impressionist paintings such as those by Georges Seurat (1859–1891) and Paul Signac (1863–1935), in this case projected onto the chair from slides of a work by Signac. Each of Mendini's iterations of Proust armchairs, and his other objects that were later adorned with pointillist brushstrokes, was individually painted and unique, a rebuff to the factory model that then was still considered the ideal production method for modern design. With its appropriation of a historical object, its decoration, and its hand production, this armchair stood as an important precedent for the emergence of Postmodern design.

About the same time, in 1979, the designer and architect Michele De Lucchi created a series of prototype domestic appliances in dull pastel colors for exhibition at the Milan Triennale, shown under the theme of the decorated house (Figures 8.28, 8.29). De Lucchi clearly described

FIGURE 8.26. Alessandro Mendini, Redesign of Modern Movement Chairs: Thonet, 1978. Wood.

FIGURE 8.27. Alessandro Mendini, Armchair for Proust, 1978. Made by Studio Alchimia. Painted wood and upholstery.

his thinking about these pieces: "Everything today, from a TV set to an iron, a stereo system to a gas-lighter," he wrote,

> is designed to accentuate the technical advantages of the industrial product. So a poor sweet lady is forced to dry her hair with an object that looks more like a laser-ray gun than a hair-dryer. For these reasons and because in designing electrical appliances nobody seems to have noticed how sad it all is, I decided to invent different, newer and more fanciful, simpler, amusing and friendly electrical appliances. I chose commonplace toy-like forms, those of funny, uncomplicated objects. In this way my electrical appliances have become a little less symbolic of the technological civilization, and a little more like household objects to be used and loved with

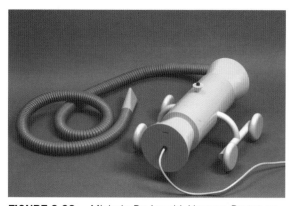

FIGURE 8.28.   Michele De Lucchi, Vacuum Prototype, 1979. Painted wood.

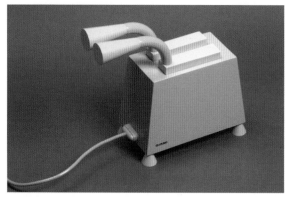

FIGURE 8.29.   Michele De Lucchi, Flat Iron Prototype, 1979. Painted wood.

joy. I believe that to overcome the cold moods of rationalism and functionalism this is an important step.

These were designed for the Italian appliance manufacturer Girmi but were immediately considered too advanced to be put into production.

Without such precedents as De Lucchi's prototypes, one can hardly imagine the pink and purple plastic form of the first commercial G Force vacuum created by the British engineer and designer Sir James Dyson (born 1947) in 1983 (Figure 8.30). Dyson tells how it took five difficult years and 5,127 prototypes to work out the engineering of a bagless vacuum cleaner that retained its suction by collecting dust particles from the air by centrifugal force. But its expressive features may have been more important than its functional achievement for its reception in Japan in 1986, when it was first sold there at a high price and became an object of great status. These features included a window that let users see how well the device was picking up the dust, inserted to give psychological satisfaction to the user, and a series of tubes that suggested space-age technology, which was mitigated by its unusual soft colors. Dyson's initial success with this vacuum allowed him to launch his own firm, and in 1993 he introduced his updated vacuum iconography, a gray, futuristic upright model with bright yellow accents and more fantastic futuristic hoses and rocket shapes that were meant to underscore the efficiency and power of his cyclonic technology.

The Postmodern Memphis group, which Ettore Sottsass initiated in 1981 and led until its dissolution in 1987, took its name from a line in the song *Stuck Inside of Mobile with the Memphis Blues Again* (1966) by the American singer-songwriter Bob Dylan (born 1941). But in choosing the title Memphis: The New International Style for its first show in Milan that same year, Sottsass was also referencing the concrete and glass architecture of Modernism introduced as the International Style by the Museum of Modern Art in 1932, which Sottsass's new international style was meant to

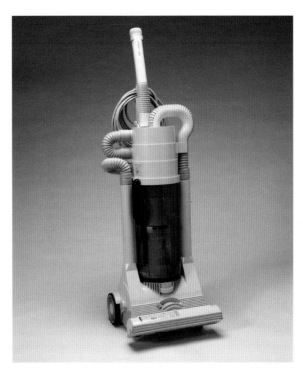

FIGURE 8.30.   Sir James Dyson, Force G Vacuum Cleaner, 1986. Made by APEX. Plastic.

replace. Unlike the Studio Alchimia, this was not just an organization set on the critique of design but a young, enthusiastic group set on energetically making a name for itself with its unlikely aesthetic, and a serious business determined to create objects that could be produced in quantity. Memphis involved many different approaches but relied on its own craftsmen and a partnership with the plastic firm Abet to execute the designs. It opened up design to a truly international and popular world, communicating with a wealth of new, radical sources from "unorganized areas of culture, like suburbs or cultures in movement, in gestation," as Sottsass noted in the second Memphis catalogue in 1982 (see Sidebar 20).

The works shown at the Memphis debut were decisively different, totally independent of what had been done before. What disconcerted many was that the sources for the forms and decorations, and thus their meanings, could not be immediately identified, which seemed just fine with Sottsass. Memphis was truly an international style, with furniture in the first collection from Austria, by Hans Hollein (1934–2014); Great Britain, by the graphic designer Terry Jones (born 1945); Japan, by Shiro Kuramata (1934–1991) and Umeda Masanori (born 1941); Spain, by Javier Mariscal (born 1950); and the United States, by Michael Graves and the artist Peter Shire (born 1947); and with lighting from France by Martine Bedin (born 1957), one of the founders of the group. The second Memphis collection was more diversified, and in

SIDEBAR 20   Ettore Sottsass, Jr., Interview, 1982

The signs that distinguish the new design, especially that of Memphis, are the fact that there is no organized catalogue of signs. All stylistic cultures have an organized catalogue of signs, like the French Enlightenment's Encyclopedia; an attempt to compile signs, to arrange metaphors in such a way that they would make sense and so that this sense would represent the more general framework which the compilers wanted to give to public culture. What I am saying is that this encyclopedia of ours does not yet exist, and the novelty lies precisely in the fact that a definitively organized encyclopedia today is neither foreseeable nor foreseen. If there is an encyclopedia it concerns no stylistic package of signs ever seen: it is not the fruit of quotations and it is perhaps not yet co-ordinated. If there are any quotations and metaphors they are taken from zones which are themselves unco-ordinated, from unorganized areas of culture, like suburbs or cultures in movement, in gestation. The reason for this is that we can't go on producing nothing up-to-date, nothing of any use, by digging up the same old heavily codified previous cultural organizations.

FIGURE 8.31. Memphis Catalogue, 1982. Logo by Christoph Radl and Valentina Grego.

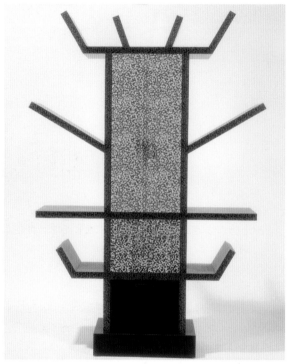

FIGURE 8.32. Ettore Sottsass, Jr., Casablanca Sideboard, 1981. Made by Abet for Memphis. Wood and plastic laminate.

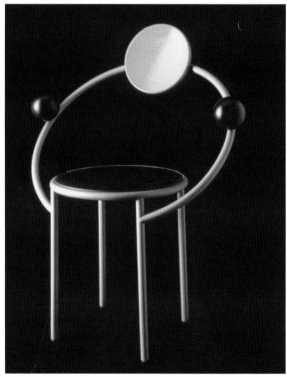

FIGURE 8.33. Michele De Lucchi, First Chair, 1983. Made by Memphis. Lacquered metal and wood.

addition to furniture, fanciful objects of ceramic, glass, marble, and metal, lamps and smaller tabletop items were introduced (Figure 8.31).

Memphis furniture reversed the modern insistence on conventional functionality with shelves and structural members set at abrupt angles. Sottsass's Casablanca sideboard spread its angled arms widely, limiting the practical capabilities of a sideboard to hold and display objects (Figure 8.32). Covered in colored, patterned, plastic laminate, a material associated with cheap popular design from the 1950s, it was the archetype of Memphis production. Not all Memphis objects followed this decorative style, however. Michele De Lucchi's First Chair from 1983 was made of simple materials, tubular metal and wood (Figure 8.33). But its design was disconcerting, quite distinct from the logic of Modernist objects, which De Lucchi was surely poking fun at. Its cantilevered back, open and angled with spheres for arms, appeared even more precarious than the legs of Marcel Breuer's cantilever chair of 1927 (see Figure 5.7), causing dismay about how one would actually sit in it. This curious object must be seen as a polemic against the style that Postmodernism expected to succeed, but De Lucchi's latter-day act of rebelliousness, like that of his domestic appliances, demonstrated how Modernism and functionalism still had a hold on design a half century later.

1980 to 2000

CHAPTER 9

Design and the Consumer

By the 1980s it had become clear that the modern world had changed, succeeded by a world that was now postmodern. It was not easy to put one's finger exactly on all that the term involved, but it avowed pluralism and individual expression and rejected absolutes, such as those that had dictated what was good or bad, or high or low, in art and design. Yet, as late as 1983, the British critic and curator Stephen Bayley (born 1951) could organize an exhibition at the Victoria and Albert Museum's Boilerhouse gallery entitled Taste: An Exhibition about Values in Design, which with its judgments on what was good and what was bad in design in many ways reprised a century later Sir Henry Cole's exhibition of objects he considered to have been created on "false principles" at the Museum of Ornamental Art in London.

"Postmodern" meant that everyday objects as well as high-end products would now receive design consideration, with everything from the trash can to the tea kettle in line for makeovers. It would now embrace digital technology, mass customization, niche marketing, globalization, outsourcing of manufacture, designer-makers, and the rise of celebrity designers who created user experiences along with products. Moreover, design would now regard consumers as individuals or members of interest groups, each of whom had different desires and needs, and manufacturers began to target their products for them.

Expressive Design

The profession of design grew broadly through marketing and publicity in the 1990s, with a number of designers, like Michael Graves in the United States and Philippe Starck (born 1949) in France, becoming celebrated internationally for their unusual and expressive works. In addition to sanctioning symbolic language, personality, humor, historical allusions, and unlikely forms, the Postmodern era gave designers a new status with which to negotiate the production of their creations. Unlike the American industrial designers of the 1930s, who were hired by large corporations to "fix" their products, designers were now more likely to partner with manufacturers who saw the niche design market as a way of establishing their own product categories, as Alessi, for example, has done so successfully. Following up on its Coffee and Tea Piazza program (see Figure 8.25), Alessi commissioned Richard Sapper in 1983 to design a stainless-steel tea kettle for the Italian mid-range

FIGURE 9.1.   Richard Sapper, Tea Kettle, 1983. Made by Alessi. Stainless steel, brass, and plastic.

housewares market, which became the first in its series of popular whistling products (Figure 9.1). Sapper's design, with its shiny domed shape, wavy black handle, and three-note brass whistle sounding like it came from a train, turned into a top-selling item for the company.

Building on this success, in 1985 Alessi asked Michael Graves to design a tea kettle specifically for the American market (Figure 9.2). Graves was captivated by Sapper's train whistle and decided to include a bird whistle in his design. His kettle also drew on other elements of Sapper's model, especially its thick plastic handle, but he then introduced several features that alluded to classical design and eighteenth-century objects. The regular line of dots around the base of the conical kettle referred to the rivets that a metal vessel would have had in classical times, and perhaps also to the precedent of Josef Hoffmann's then well-known tea services (see Figure 2.22), while the bird was reminiscent of those that often appeared atop neoclassical tea urns. Despite criticisms that the plastic handle had a tendency to burn and that steam poured forth dangerously when the whistling bird was removed (similar to earlier criticisms of Sapper's kettle), sales numbers for Graves's expensive design reached into the millions within a decade. It became a decorator's favorite, and

hardly was a photograph of a kitchen published that did not have Graves's tea kettle on the stove. This prominence did not go unnoticed, and in 1999 Graves was asked to produce a line of housewares for Target, the large American retailer, which gave broad access to Graves's personal brand and allowed mid-level buyers to acquire objects that for them had a status value equal to that of the original Graves kettle. By the time of his death in 2015, his firm had produced over ten thousand separate items for Target, which raised its image and its bottom line as well.

Alessi was also expanding its product line by introducing small, expressive, plastic tabletop items that were quirky, lovable, and friendly—and relatively inexpensive. They belonged to a new line that Alessandro Mendini introduced in the Alessi catalogue, which he entitled the FFF, or Family Follows Fiction, series. It replaced the long-dismissed Modernist precept "Form Follows Function" with a postmodern idea, feel-good products that looked like toys and toyed with the psychological and emotional needs of the consumer. These emotionally charged objects formed a family of characters that had no hidden meanings, and it seems that the designers rejected a deeper reading of their products for the simple joy of creation.

FIGURE 9.2.   Michael Graves, Tea Kettle, 1985. Made by Alessi. Stainless steel and plastic.

These products easily entered the world of novelty and fashion and were accepted internationally as just one more stage in the evolution of a particularly Italian approach to style. When its market for these objects grew appreciably, Alessi, following the success of the Vitra furniture manufacturer in selling miniatures of its modern furniture, created a series of miniature replicas of its own products to allow patrons "the chance to complete their private collections of authentic objects and with considerable savings in terms of both space and expenditure." If any question remained that a practical function was essential to the definition of design, these collectibles quashed it.

Many of these winsome pieces were designed by the architects Stefano Giovannoni (born 1954) and Guido Venturini (born 1957), founders of the King-Kong group, which between 1985 and 1989 brought such cartoonish characters to product design. An object such as Giovannoni's translucent-plastic Magic Bunny toothpick holder, designed in 1989, which cutely dispenses toothpicks when the rabbit is pulled out of the hat, could easily have been confused with a tabletop item found in a neighborhood trattoria in Rome, or with the type of design that elitist commentators considered in poor taste and denigrated as "kitsch" (Figure 9.3). With the Alessi name attached to them, however, one could not write off these colorful character objects so easily, and the concept of kitsch was in any case then systematically being questioned. Taste now began to be seen in a more egalitarian light, as described by the German design historian Gert Selle (born 1933), whose work values everyday objects as a counterpart to the type of classic design discussed here (see Sidebar 21). The Magic Bunny was not the ironic gesture that some might have wished it to be but an attempt by Alessi to search out more inclusive realms, like those of Target's customers, who had become newly aware of the field of design. Criticism from design purists about the loss of Modernist standards would have been especially problematic for the Magic Bunny because of its affinities with the large, stainless-steel balloon rabbits that the American artist Jeff Koons (born 1955) had been creating. Accepted as high art and given serious consideration by critics, collectors, and museums, they were at the same time being embraced by popular culture and ironically, were later returned to balloon format as an entrant in the annual Macy's Thanksgiving Day parade in New York (Figure 9.4).

FIGURE 9.3.   Stefano Giovannoni, Magic Bunny Toothpick Holder, 1989. Made by Alessi. Thermoplastic resin.

FIGURE 9.4.   Jeff Koons's Rabbit Balloon in the Macy's Thanksgiving Day Parade in New York in 2007.

SIDEBAR 21   Gert Selle, "There Is No Kitsch, There Is Only Design!," 1984

The kitsch concept is an invention of the nineteenth century—taken into use at a time when bourgeois culture was already going downhill and positions had to be firmly established. However, this bourgeois high culture has vanished today, except for remnants. Therewith ends at least the old necessity of culture delimitation. The parvenus know themselves what is suitable, and their measure of suitability has, as a new standard, taken the place of temperate restraint. To this extent the kitsch concept is obsolete; it no longer holds, despite the fact that many educated persons have at their disposal a learning history that is laden with this antiquated value concept and that permits them in their own life context to classify their personal environment according to such criteria.

However, it seems extremely doubtful whether a classification of the esthetic manifestations of contemporary product culture into *kitschy* or *non-kitschy* is a performance of insight. Taste judgments are standpoint judgments. It is from a value awareness that one observes and judges. Where a fixed coordinate system for social and individual value decisions is lacking, however, this judgment is irrelevant and noncommittal. One should at least first try to determine for oneself the position one objectively occupies: "To follow one's taste means to *sight* the goods that are objectively allocated to one's own social position and which harmonize with one another because they are approximately of equal rank," writes [the French sociologist Pierre] Bourdieu.

Such an attempt would also make it possible to understand other people's positions and values. A sort of social-esthetic empathy would be needed in situations in which old, internalized value systems again and again play tricks on us. There simply is no absolute "good taste." It exists only in relation to a basis of social points of departure, that is, everyone who lives according to his taste *has* a "good taste," which, of course, can be distinguished from another "good taste." In the pluralistic permissive esthetic of our everyday, this is already experienced by countless individuals, while the guardians of the once-leading good taste do not trust their eyes.

The French designer Philippe Starck also gained unprecedented popularity during the 1980s and 1990s as the man who with Postmodern self-assurance put humor, narrative, and historic styles back into design. Starck has been in the public eye since the early years of his career in the 1970s; his exuberant personality, his unconventional objects, and his edgy interiors for restaurants and boutique hotels have made him the face of French design over the last decades. For a photograph from the 1990s, Starck took the pose of the Hindu god Shiva, his many hands holding examples of the products he designed for a number of his many manufacturers (Figure 9.5). From top right, he is shown with a sport shoe for Puma (1990s), water bottle for Saint Georges (1998), Excalibur toilet brush for Heller (1993), Dede doorstop for Alessi (1995), To Yoo telephone for Alessi (1995), and Miss Sissi table lamp for Flos (1989). Starck gained a wider international reputation through his collaboration with the American hotel developer Ian Schrager (born 1946), who had introduced the concept of the boutique hotel and made Starck his major designer in the late 1980s, beginning with his redesign of the Royalton Hotel in New York. Starck's interior for the Saint Martin's Lane Hotel in London (1999) shows his unexpected fusions, with extreme changes of scale, pieces drawn from exotic cultures, and enlarged recognizable objects, creating not only a design but also a destination experience worth remembering (Figure 9.6). "My job is like that of a film director," he explained. "I tell stories and

FIGURE 9.5.   Philippe Starck as the Hindu god Shiva with examples of his own products held in his hands, 1990s.

FIGURE 9.6.   Philippe Starck, Interior of the Saint Martin's Lane Hotel, London, 1999.

offer the public the most complete spiritual notion possible of the spaces they visit. Public spaces are above all about emotions and experiences."

Starck's designs repeatedly brought him wide publicity, but his Juicy Salif lemon squeezer with its inexplicable name brought him an unanticipated notoriety (Figure 9.7). Like Loewy's aerodynamic pencil sharpener (see Figure 6.8), Starck's lemon squeezer became one of the most maligned, as well as one of the most discussed, products when it was introduced in 1996. Its functionality was a big issue. Many consumers complained that the juice squeezed from its organic, overscale, squid-like form did not drip easily into a glass set below it and that there was no way to avoid having the lemon pips collect with the juice. But they missed the point. For Starck, functionality was not necessarily found in how in a product worked but in how it was perceived by consumers and the stories it could conjure. This was especially true

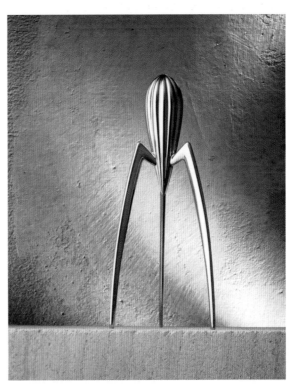

FIGURE 9.7.   Philippe Starck, Juicy Salif Lemon Squeezer, 1996. Aluminum.

for those who would receive his objects as gifts, for many of Alessi's upscale products appealed to that specialized market. To dispel criticism of his Juicy Salif, Starck fashioned a creation myth for it, a narrative of designing it as a conversation piece. Regardless of its functional inefficiency, he suggested, it would make a perfect wedding present, setting up his own story of the poignant moment in which a new bride bonds with her mother-in-law as they get together for the first time after the wedding and inspect this curious gift.

Engaging Materials, Forms, and Technology

Because most of us have now had the experience of listening to music through ear buds attached to an iPod or a cell phone, it may be difficult to comprehend how revolutionary Sony's Walkman audio-cassette player was when it was launched in 1979 (Figure 9.8). Not until then had music been truly personal, with listeners able to enjoy intense sound privately through a miniaturized mobile player. This was the beginning of a new culture, the device being targeted to a previously unexplored youth market, with an impact that grew steadily over the years. The idea of a personal cassette player was questioned at first at Sony, where there was concern that users would not want to listen to music by themselves. Two jacks were included in the first version to allow two users to enjoy the sound together, while a bright orange button was added to pause the tape if they wanted to talk to each other. In later versions, the second jack and pause button were eliminated after Sony's research had demonstrated that the device was mostly being used by one person alone. Sony formulated its program for a product that would once again draw on American styling, and its success was so immediate that improvements and specialized products for niche markets soon followed, such as a bright yellow Solar Walkman with an FM radio feature, a Sports Walkman, and a children's version, called My First Sony.

Equally revolutionary was the beige Macintosh from Apple Computer, the concept of the company's co-founder Steve Jobs (1955–2011) (Figure 9.9). His idea had been to make the computer complete in itself instead of expecting consumers to put together a system from separate components as was then customary. This was a user-friendly, all-in-one, ready-to-go device, made for everyone, not just professionals, and users did not have to know how to write computer code to access it. The Macintosh was announced in a now-famous advertisement broadcast during the American Super Bowl football championship in 1984, in which the future of conformity described in *1984*, the novel by the English author George Orwell (1903–1950), was dispelled. The Macintosh arrived in the guise of an Olympic athlete wielding her sledgehammer and smashing an archetypal image of Orwell's Big Brother to bits, which was seen by many as Apple's challenging of the dominance of IBM in the personal computer (PC) market.

FIGURE 9.8. Sony, Walkman Portable Cassette Player, 1979. Plastic and metal.

FIGURE 9.9. Apple, Macintosh Computer, 1984. Plastic.

The Macintosh had many new features: its own keyboard, drawing and word-processing programs, a slot for a "floppy" memory disk, and a graphical user interface (GUI) on which Apple's future preeminence in the field of graphic design would depend. The GUI enabled the user to click on a mouse, an input device that had been invented in 1964 by the computer engineer Douglas C. Engelbart (1925–2013), which moved a cursor on the screen that interfaced with graphic icons like folders and trash cans on a desktop, making recognition of their functions intuitive by replicating real-life situations of working in an office. These now-universal icons were the creation of the graphic designer Susan Kare (born 1954), who also designed a range of simple digital typefaces for the computer. Along with the PageMaker program from Aldus and Apple's LaserWriter printer, both introduced the next year, the Macintosh computer facilitated the first phase of desktop publishing, a way for users to communicate directly, becoming their own

designers, typesetters, and printers and creating letterheads, newsletters, and brochures without having to outsource their work to professional firms. Graphic designers benefitted from the computer also with a new creative device that allowed them to manipulate images and type fonts freely, and to draw their own typefaces, an activity that previously had taken months or even years.

The American April Greiman (born 1948) was one of the first graphic designers to exploit the creative possibilities of digital technologies, using computers, fax machines, and video to generate designs for the print medium. She put the Macintosh and Apple's new graphics software MacPaint, MacDraw, and MacVision to the test in an extraordinary project for the magazine *Design Quarterly* in 1986. Greiman had studied in Basel with Wolfgang Weingart (born 1941), a designer who in the 1970s had broken the bounds of the mathematically based Swiss graphic style with a free, expressive layering of type and images that was seen as a "new wave" in Swiss design. Greiman worked for over a year to create her issue of *Design Quarterly*, a two-sided, six-foot-long poster, which she entitled "Does It Make Sense?" This took the form of a complex, layered composition using a nude, life-size, digitally printed image of herself on one side and images from space and a variety of texts that yielded a profusion of information about the history of technology and about the methods she had used to execute the poster itself on the other (Figure 9.10). With the capabilities of the Macintosh, Greiman was able to print the components of the poster from computer files using a LaserWriter printer. She was hampered by the length of time needed to print what were then considered extremely large image files but nevertheless took satisfaction in the low-resolution graphics and rudimentary elements of the new technologies instead of creating highly finished mechanical artwork, as was the previous method of readying a design for printing.

Among the most innovative designers working at this time was Ingo Maurer, whose low-voltage Ya Ya Ho lighting from 1984, one of the earliest cable systems, produced an open installation of lights that appeared as if they came from nowhere (Figure 9.11). It was an infinitely flexible and interchangeable arrangement that users could install according to their own needs. Based on the concept of connecting each unit directly to the main electric source, which was inspired by an outdoors Caribbean celebration where Maurer saw electricity being drawn directly from overhead power lines, it allowed light to be placed anywhere users wanted it and included different types of fixtures and bulbs for different illumination effects. The system retained a sense of its celebratory origins with glowing lights suspended immaterially in the air.

A quite different expression of immateriality was Shiro Kuramata's How High the Moon armchair from 1986, which took the high-tech

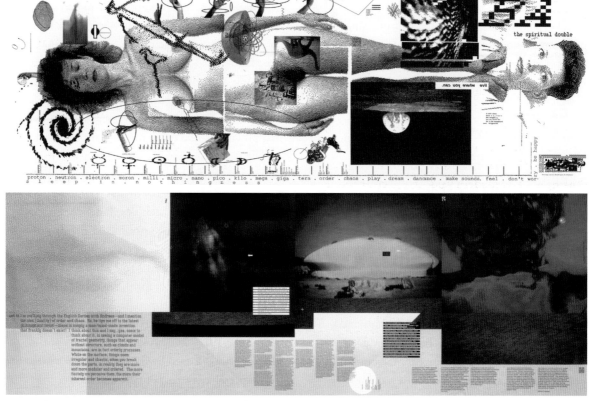

FIGURE 9.10.   April Greiman, "Does It Make Sense?," *Design Quarterly*, 1986.

FIGURE 9.11. Ingo Maurer, Ya Ya Ho Lighting System, 1984. Made by Design M Ingo Maurer. Glass, ceramic, metal, and plastic.

element of expanded steel mesh and turned it into an unexpectedly sensual material (Figure 9.12). In this latter-day club chair devoid of the soft leather upholstery of its earlier precedents (see Figure 3.6), Kuramata emphasized Modernist lightness and openness in what could only counter the functionalist concept of honesty to materials, since these expectations were not in accord with the conventional understanding of hard steel. He saw it as more than just material, however; he saw it as his "own style of decoration," adding an ornamental Postmodern value to the chair through the repetitive pattern of mesh.

Just as Kuramata showed that materials such as steel no longer had to meet instinctive expectations of what they should look or feel like, Marcel Wanders (born 1963) challenged the definition of what a material could do with his Knotted chair from 1996. Wanders was one of a group of designers in the Netherlands who joined the Droog Design collective soon after it was founded in 1993 by the art historian Renny Ramakers (born 1946) and the jeweler and industrial designer Gijs Bakker (born 1942). In line with the

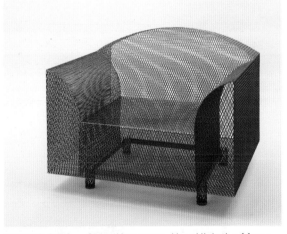

FIGURE 9.12. Shiro Kuramata, How High the Moon Armchair, 1986. Made by Vitra. Painted steel.

group's name, which in Dutch means "dry" as in "witty," their products usually had an amusing and extraordinary originality to them, bringing a flood of international publicity to them. Droog designers distinguished their work from the slick technical aesthetic of conventional commercial products by using unpretentious objects, traditional techniques, and industrial materials. Wanders created this chair from a pliable, modern high-tech fiber worked in the age-old low-tech macramé method (Figure 9.13). In macramé, cords are hand-knotted to create decorative patterns, and the fact that one could sit on a chair made of knotted cords contradicted every expectation of a fiber construction. In creating the chair, Wanders used aramid, a strong, synthetic fiber, which was wrapped around a core of carbon. It was first knotted into an open mesh weaving, then soaked in epoxy and draped over a mold; when the fibers dried, the chair could stand alone and have the necessary strength for someone to sit in it. Another Droog designer, Hella Jongerius (born 1963), also chose an unlikely material when she designed her Pushed Washbasin in 1996. Instead of the cold, hard porcelain typically used for sanitary fixtures, she molded her sink of polyurethane, a translucent plastic with a soft surface and warm color (Figure 9.14).

The Canadian-born American architect Frank Gehry (born 1929) chose an unusual material

for architecture, titanium, taking advantage of its coloristic possibilities to complete his dazzling Guggenheim Museum in Bilbao, Spain, which was unveiled in 1997 (Figure 9.15). He formed its bold organic shapes with thousands of titanium panels, which responded to the environment by billowing in the wind. Using his customary method, Gehry conceived the building by making models in paper and cardboard, which were only later digitized and engineered for its complex construction. The unprecedented architectural forms and the thin titanium sheets that sheathed them drew cultural tourists from around the world, opening up a new type of tourism for the modern era, which led to the revitalization of the entire city, whose economy had declined after its manufacturing base was lost.

The 1990s had already seen a ready return to organic form, best exemplified by the works of the Egyptian-born Karim Rashid (born 1960), a prolific Canadian designer who coined the term "blobism" for these shapes. His translucent Garbo trash cans

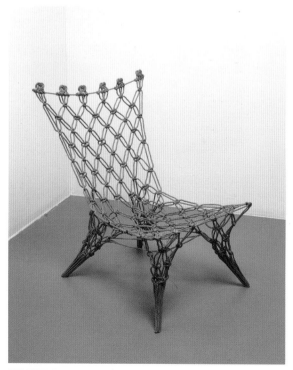

FIGURE 9.13. Marcel Wanders, Knotted Chair, 1996. Made by Droog Design. Carbon, aramid fibers, and epoxy.

FIGURE 9.14. Hella Jongerius, Pushed Washbasin, 1996. Made by Droog Design. Polyurethane and metal.

FIGURE 9.15.   Frank Gehry, Guggenheim Museum, Bilbao, Spain, 1997.

from 1996, gracefully fashioned and widely noticed, continued to excite an infectious enthusiasm for the most minor of household products as long as they were designed in new, elegant, and expressive forms (Figure 9.16). But with its minimalist shape easily molded from polypropylene so that large numbers could be produced economically, the trash can was part of a continuing environmental dilemma about the proliferation of plastic products. Although Rashid strives today to make his products sustainable, this issue did not seem so important in the past century, when he like many designers at the time valued other aspects of design, believing that it was not just "about solving problems, but about a rigorous beautification of our built environments. Design is about the betterment of our lives poetically, aesthetically, experientially, sensorially, and emotionally."

The New Beetle, Volkswagen's revival of the 1940s adaptation of Ferdinand Porsche's "people's car" from the 1930s (see Figure 6.19), also appeared with a bulbous shape (Figure 9.17). Based on its

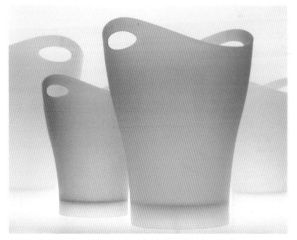

FIGURE 9.16.   Karim Rashid, Garbo Trash Cans, 1996. Made by Umbra. Polypropylene.

fabled ancestor but not looking quite like it, the Beetle was conceived in the company's California design studio by the American J Mays (born 1954), an automobile designer who had spent his early career in Germany with Audi and who first envisioned it as a concept car in 1994. The

FIGURE 9.17. J Mays,
New Beetle, 1997.
Made by Volkswagen.

car was then engineered in Volkswagen's German headquarters and released in the United States in 1997. The New Beetle came with a lot of nostalgia, even for those who were not around for its previous existence; this included a vase for a flower on the dashboard (punning on the 1960s "flower-power" movement), the lovable Beetle's baggage of jokes, and films (including *The Love Bug*, 1968) with legends to support it, and its enormous success led to a retro craze in the automotive industry.

Choices

Just as appealing was Apple's translucent-plastic iMac personal computer, which made its debut in 1998 soon after Steve Jobs had returned as head of the company following a twelve-year hiatus (Figure 9.18). Design had always been central to the psyche of Apple, defined by Jobs as the way for the company to distinguish and brand itself. For this new polycarbonate computer, he chose the British designer Jonathan Ive (born 1967), who had been employed at Apple since 1992, to carry out his vision, both men having discovered a shared

sensibility to the smallest details of form. Similar to Apple's earlier Macintosh computer with its all-in-one ready-to-connect concept (see Figure 9.9), the iMac was internet ready, a breakthrough at a time when surfing the World Wide Web was still foreign to most of the population and less than a decade after the English computer scientist Sir Tim Berners-Lee (born 1955) had invented it as a medium for sharing documents and information. This and the computer's friendly Bondi blue color, a name meant to conjure the popular surfing destination Bondi Beach in Sydney, Australia, spurred a large volume of sales. Apple soon added other colors to the line, following an international trend in which everything from irons to telephones to office supplies came in a variety of bright pigments. Apple's translucent colors were particularly brilliant and consistent, having been perfected through consultation with a number of manufacturers of hard candy. The iMac's fruit colors were labeled blueberry, grape, lime, strawberry, and tangerine, with tongue-in-cheek advertisements playing up their delicious "flavors" and even suggesting that consumers "Think Different" and "Collect all five."

FIGURE 9.18.
Jonathan Ive and
Apple, iMac Computer,
1999. Made by Apple.
Polycarbonate.

The tyranny of one-size- and one-color-fits-all seemed out of place as the new millennium was approaching. With the arrival of computers, businesses were able to introduce flexible manufacturing systems and control their inventories more closely in order to create products that targeted specific areas and groups, combating the effects of globalization and fragmentation in the marketplace through what has been called "mass customization." The large Dutch appliance firm Philips did this in the 1980s when it was losing its international market share and began to direct its products to serve different demographics and reflect their cultural values. Its Roller radios, from 1986, fun plastic objects produced in bright colors with two engaging large round speakers, emerged from a realization that young buyers in Europe found Philips's products dull and were turning to Japan for exciting design (Figure 9.19). To recapture this market, Philips began to focus on lifestyle design, as Sony had done with its Walkman (see Figure 9.8), which anticipated a new move for advertising and marketing in the firm. The Roller radios led to a broad youth-directed campaign at Philips entitled Moving Sound, which according to its then director of design, Robert Blaich (born 1930), "indicated that the radios were portable (moveable) and that they Moved You (Emotionally)."

FIGURE 9.19. Philips, Roller Radio, 1986. Plastic.

Another tactic was to give consumers a sense of constant choice, as the Finnish manufacturer Nokia, the leading producer of cellular telephones in the 1990s, did in a very competitive market. In 1998, Nokia began to sell its telephones with replaceable skins, which it called Xpress-on covers, allowing users to choose different colors and patterns for their devices and change them at will (Figure 9.20). Almost immediately, a lively business with entrepreneurs selling their own faceplates emerged, figurative and decorative designs that seemed to be made by everyone and sold everywhere, from electronics stores to kiosks in train stations to flea markets, individualizing design even further. The idea of replacing product components like fashion accessories extended even to automobiles, notably the Smart car. This small, light, easy-to-park vehicle was conceived by Nicholas Hayek (1928–2010), who had founded the Swatch brand (named from a combination of "Swiss" and "watch") in 1983 and who partnered with Daimler Benz to launch this new endeavor in 1998. Like Swatch watches,

which come with many choices and interchangeable elements, the automobile was conceived with plastic exterior panels that could be switched for different colors (or replaced if damaged) at a service station in about ninety minutes. And like Swatch watches, they have been showcased in glass towers not unlike the revolving glass cabinets in which jewelry and watches were conventionally displayed (Figure 9.21).

But the most effective way to offer consumers choices was to allow them to customize their purchases before they were made. Customization, which had always been a segment of consumer production, especially in the area of high-end clothing, was a more focused, and egalitarian, way of selling a personal product. As the World Wide Web developed, consumers were able to surf manufacturers' websites in order to choose an entire range of features for their purchases, which were then made and delivered to their homes quickly, giving them control over their new products within predetermined frameworks. NikeiD, a program

FIGURE 9.20.   Nokia, Discarded Cell Phone Faceplates, about 2006.

FIGURE 9.21.   Smart Car tower at a dealership in Cologne, Germany, 2001.

developing their real product, their brand. This has generated worldwide controversy about the compensation of their workers and their rights, environmental pollution, and so forth, issues taken up in 1999 in the anti-globalization book *No Logo: Taking Aim at the Brand Bullies* written by Naomi Klein (born 1970). Today, offering customization through the internet is a common way of doing business, a development that was foreseen as early as 1980 by the American futurist writer Alvin Toffler (1928–2016) in *The Third Wave*, where he predicted that the consumer would soon be "so integrated into the production process that we will find it more and more difficult to tell just who is actually the consumer and who the producer."

Low-Tech

Not every product in the late twentieth century depended on new materials, techniques, and the computer. Frank Gehry's organic maple chairs for Knoll were low-tech designs, calling on the traditional skills of handcraftsmanship to bend them into their shape (Figure 9.22). Designed in 1990, they are each named with a hockey term, such as Slap Shot and Power Play, emphasizing the fact that the chairs are made of sturdy wood like that of hockey sticks. The chairs are made of seven layers of maple veneer and assembled with high-bonding glue. Gehry explained that his chairs differed from typical bentwood chairs, such as those of Thonet (see Figure 1.2), which have a separate structure and seat, because in his bentwood version, the "structure and the seat are formed of the same incredible lightweight slender wood strops which serve both functions. The material forms a single and continuous idea. What makes this all work and gives it extraordinary strength is the interwoven, basket-like character of the design."

begun in the late 1990s, sold sport shoes that could be customized on the Web and which were manufactured overseas with delivery promised in three to five weeks. In the process buyers could choose their own combinations of colors, patterns, and materials for their shoes, involving themselves in a game of designing and redesigning until they were satisfied with their own creations, a practice that continues on Nike's and other manufacturers' sites to this day. These products would then be assembled in developing countries from components fabricated in factories in different parts of the world, where labor was cheaper than in industrial countries.

Outsourcing has become the model for many large corporations, which have no manufacturing plants of their own but move the production of their goods to factories abroad. With considerably less financial outlay, they can concentrate on

The bottles that Hella Jongerius created of glass and ceramic components in 2001 were put together by hand with plastic caution tape, an unexpected and unconventional found material that took on

FIGURE 9.22. Frank Gehry, Chairs, 1990–91. Made by Knoll. Maple.

an ornamental as well as a practical function in the process (Figure 9.23). She could justify this unusual synthesis by the fact that its two components, glass and porcelain, soften and harden at different temperatures and cannot be fused together, so that the bottles could only have been completed if some means of adhesive had been used, although her choice need not have been as provocative as this one. The tape also gave additional meaning to the bottles; on the one hand, it emphasized the fragility of the two materials, and on the other, it called into question the way high value is ascribed to certain materials and low value to others. Jongerius is known for designs that focus on imperfection, abandoning flawless and repetitive processes for

those that create individual variations and draw expressiveness from the layering of ideas, even if they may be made by industrial methods.

The latter-day chest of drawers designed by Tejo Remy (born 1960) and entitled You Can't Lay Down Your Memories, which was designed in 1991 and made by Droog Design, was also a pushback against the dominance of slick manufacturing techniques and digital technologies. In line with Droog's preference for unassuming materials, Remy collected different types of drawers from discarded furniture, which he recycled, encasing them in finely crafted maple boxes (some of his later versions included television sets and wine racks) and joining them together with a mover's strap (Figure

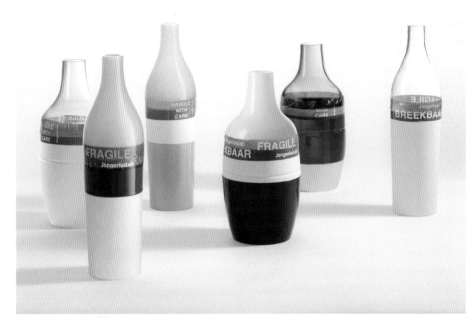

FIGURE 9.23.
Hella Jongerius,
Bottles, 2000. Glass,
porcelain, and plastic
packing tape.

9.24). He then photographed the stacked drawers,
disassembled them, and shipped the chest of
drawers to the buyers, leaving it up them to decide
if they should follow his arrangement as shown
in the photograph or create their own format to
customize the chest of drawers for themselves. If
they did it themselves, they perhaps would be more
likely to remember where they had stored their
possessions, disputing Remy's sly title for these
assemblages.

The ultimate statement against the modern
designer's reliance on digital technology and the
increasing inconspicuousness of the hand of the
graphic artist appeared as a poster by the Austrian-
born New York–based Stefan Sagmeister (born
1962) for a talk he was to give to the Detroit
chapter of the American Institute of Graphic Arts
(AIGA) in 1999 (Figure 9.25). In creating the
image for this photographic poster, he turned his
back on any stylistic element from the past (his
motto, as seen in the poster itself, is "style=fart"),
eschewing mechanical or digital typography for
handwriting, but a handwriting executed in a

FIGURE 9.24.   Tejo Remy, You Can't Lay Down
Your Memories Chest of Drawers, 1991. Made
by Droog Design. Recycled drawers, maple, and
shipper's strap.

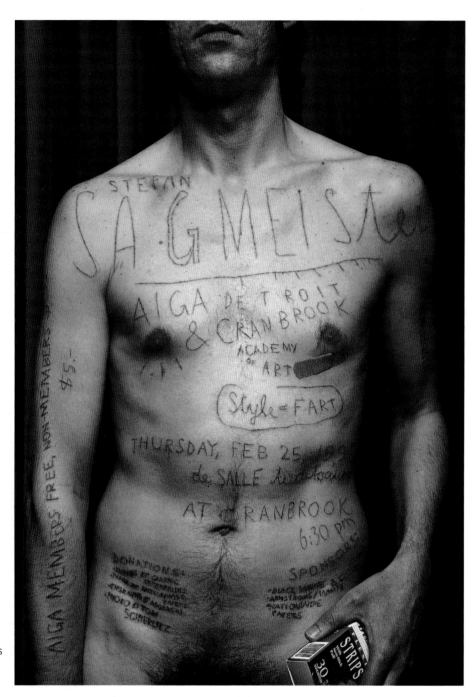

FIGURE 9.25. Stefan Sagmeister, Poster for a Talk to the American Institute of Graphic Arts (AIGA), Detroit, 1999. Lithograph.

scary way. To put himself on the line and show his personal commitment to direct design, he said he "tried to visualize the pain that seems to accompany most of our design projects" by having an associate cut the entire promotional message, and all the tedious information about the talk, into his skin (after he was unable to do it himself). This

was not meant simply as a personal statement but as a call to graphic-design professionals to reinsert themselves into their work, suggesting perhaps with the small box of adhesive bandages he holds in his hand that it might really not hurt them too much to do so, although he later admitted, "Yes, it did hurt real bad."

CHAPTER 10

Responsible Design

A number of forces came together around 1970 to raise a strong critique of design as it was then practiced internationally and to call for responsibility within the design profession. Critics questioned the morality of consumerism; they attempted to broaden design, to turn it away from its narrow focus on form, manufacture, and sales in order to face important issues that had come forward at that time. Product safety, the endangered environment, shrinking resources, and the need of access for all to the physical and virtual environment—these called on designers to find technological solutions to such societal issues. Others turned away from the capitalist design establishment to live and work independently, attempting to return to a preindustrial lifestyle in do-it-yourself environments (Figure 10.1). Design equality for all individuals became a major issue during the 1990s. Legislative acts mandating accessible design for those with disabilities officially recognized that everyone has different needs, and universal, or inclusive, design (design that was usable by everyone, including those with disabilities) was soon adopted as a reasonable route for design in the future.

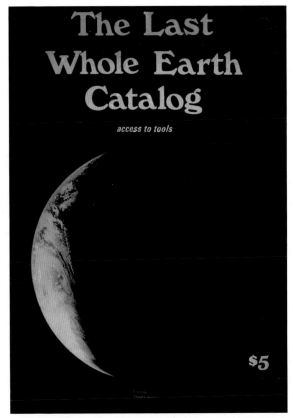

FIGURE 10.1. Cover of *The Last Whole Earth Catalog: Access to Tools*, 1971.

Critique of Industrial Design

The severest criticism of design came in 1971 from the American Victor Papanek (1927–1998), a Viennese-born designer and academic whose book *Design for the Real World: Human Ecology and Social Change* condemned the profession in its entirety. "There are professions more harmful than industrial design," he wrote, "but only a very few of them. And possibly only one profession is phonier. Advertising design, in persuading people to buy things they don't need, with money they don't have, in order to impress others who don't care, is probably the phoniest field in existence today. Industrial design, by concocting the tawdry idiocies, hawked by advertisers, comes a close second." For Papanek, the design profession had never seriously faced the challenge of creating objects that made sense in an efficient and economical way, that would serve universal human needs, be appropriate for the elderly, disabled, and impoverished as well as for those in developing countries, and be free from the talons of big business. His book was as much about the excesses of the consumerism that he saw around him as about the methods of industrial design itself, pointing out in example after example how industrial designers fed the pocketbooks of manufacturers and mocking the mentality of those out to con the acquisitive consumer. He was criticized by reviewers for the many misunderstandings that appeared in his book, and for the narrow application of examples drawn from the work of his students, which although idealistic did not always recognize the cultural values of the groups for whom they were designed, yet *Design for the Real World* has become a classic text about the ethics of design.

Today much progress has been made in designing for underserved communities, although the way that this is done with regard to cultural differences remains a major issue. By the beginning of the new millennium, through what became known as "leapfrogging," where people in developing countries jump ahead of local technology to gain access to advanced digital systems, the cellular phone had become a major player in micro-economies across the world. But there were still relatively few computers in most developing countries (and fewer people who knew how to use them). To make computers accessible to children in these countries, the American architect and professor at the Massachusetts Institute of Technology (MIT) Nicholas Negroponte (born 1947) founded the nonprofit One Laptop Per Child (OLPC) project in 2005. Its goal was "to empower the world's poorest children through education" by providing them with free computers. Negroponte brought in the Swiss industrial designer Yves Béhar (born 1967) to create a simple, portable computer with a manufacturing cost below one hundred dollars (a goal that could never be reached). With singularly restrictive and yet untested requirements because of the extreme and varied conditions under which these instruments were to be used, Béhar produced the first XO computer in 2006, with mass production and distribution to schools starting in 2007 and reaching over three million laptops worldwide within a decade (although not without facing technical problems and cultural conflicts). An acid-green nine-by-nine-inch laptop with flip-up antennas, it was an almost weatherproof and indestructible device made of injection-molded ABS plastic, designed to run on solar energy and to be intuitive so that children with no knowledge of computers would understand how to use it (Figure 10.2). Emblazoned on the backs were differently colored X and O combinations so that each child's computer could be easily identified.

The problems that Papanek saw in industrial design did not go away, and one of the issues that continued to plague products was the seeming unconcern designers had for how consumers interacted with what they designed, especially objects of advanced technology. Ever since the invention of the transistor in 1947 and its expanding application in the 1950s, the word

FIGURE 10.2. Yves Béhar, Laptop, 2005–8. Made for One Laptop Per Child. ABS plastic.

"technology" has instinctively been attached to electronic products, although it may be defined simply as the application of scientific knowledge to the creation of machinery or equipment. Technology exists on levels as simple as hand tools or other basic instruments and as complex as electronics. The changing aspects of high-level technology, in particular, have caused considerable problems for the user, and understanding how to use, or interface with, products, even very simple ones, had not always been so easy to do. "I can use complicated things," the psychologist Donald Norman, originator of the term "user-centered design" (later "human-centered design"), assured the readers of *The Psychology* (later *Design) of Everyday Things* (1988). "I am quite expert at computers, and electronics, and complex laboratory equipment. Why do I have trouble with doors, light switches, and water faucets?" This, he realized, was because designers were often engineers who concentrated on achieving maximum functionality for their products without thinking deeply about whether consumers needed them or how they would learn to use them, and who added multiple features that complicated design rather than simplifying it.

Beginning in the 1980s, Klaus Krippendorff, a communications theorist, and Reinhart Butter, an industrial designer, laid the foundations for a new field of design research that they called "product semantics," which focused on the meaning objects had for users and promoted the approach of human-centered over technology-centered design. This was intended to help designers understand how users perceived their products in order to make design more friendly for them. Product semantics studied visual clues about how objects functioned, their signals for use, and their symbolic aspects. This was a wake-up call to the design world to broaden its approach by studying the psychology of the consumer and opening up to multiple understandings of the context of their designs (see Sidebar 22).

Half a century after the publication of *Design for the Real World*, designers are certainly aware of the kinds of issues that Papanek raised, and now most accept the need to make their products fit a responsible profile, although how that is to be done is not always apparent. This has been a long time in coming for many designers, even high-profile ones such as Philippe Starck. Like other designers during the 1970s and 1980s, he paid relatively little attention to such problems, although by the 1990s he had taken a more responsible approach to design, for example using natural materials and designing for the ease of recycling. In an interview in 2011, spoken with a rhetoric that harked back to that of Victor Papanek, he admitted his failings in the past and claimed that he had defined a new mission of making his design efficient, affordable, environmentally sound, and aware of social needs, what he had already defined as the "future moral market":

Today we see very talented, intelligent designers who use their skills to create useless products, which are developed not to help people but to put money in the pockets of companies, and to take money out of the pocket of a "target consumer." It's a very cynical way to work, and done with greed and no respect. We need to design things that are more ecological, more social.

SIDEBAR 22   Klaus Krippendorff and Reinhart Butter, "Semantics: Meanings and Contexts of Artifacts," 2007

Our approach to design is human-centered, which contrasts with the technology-centered design of engineering and functionalism. Human-centeredness acknowledges the role of humans in actively constructing artifacts—conceptually, linguistically, and materially—being concerned with them, handling them, and putting them to work. It acknowledges the diversity of human conceptions that motivate how things are acquired, exchanged, rendered meaningful, and used. Consequently, when we talk about meanings, we must be clear about whose meanings we are talking of, and allow for the possibility that we may see things differently. A technology-centered approach, by contrast, seeks objective, generalizable, and non-experiential accounts of things . . .

Technology-centered designers can work within a language that addresses their concerns without reference to the concerns of outsiders. Commitments to objectivity; belief in universalist theories of functionalism, economy, and aesthetics; the conviction that particular forms are responsible for particular uses, experiences, and feelings; and the privileging of one's own views over those of less qualified people, makes design relatively easy. It implicates an authority which assures that designs are used as intended, on the one hand, and creates the distinction between knowledgeable designers and merely responsive users in need of instruction and guidance, on the other hand.

In contrast, human-centered designers are committed to designing artifacts for use by others who may experience the same designs quite differently. It follows that human-centered designers cannot universalize their own conceptions of what they see and do. They have to understand how those that come in touch with their design understand it in the context of their own world. Understanding others' understanding requires listening to what they say they experience, and acknowledging their understanding as legitimate, not inferior or mistaken, even when it deviates significantly from one's own. Understanding others' understanding is an understanding of understanding and this recursion is of a qualitatively different kind.

And, yes, we have to produce less.

I have no regrets that, over the years, I've designed what some might deem frivolous items. That was before. I can't alter the past. But I have changed my views as the world has changed.

Since then he has followed through on this vision in many of his projects, among them his Ideas Box for Libraries Without Borders (Figure 10.3). Founded in 2007, this international organization brings communications and cultural and educational resources to the masses of displaced persons housed in refugee camps (later expanded to bring these resources to underserved communities in developed countries also). Starck's Ideas Box, what he calls a "caravan of knowledge," is a tent-covered center of culture easily assembled from portable suitcases packed with computers, tablets, software, televisions, films, books, cameras, games, and craft materials, along with the necessary furniture and a built-in stage. "Dreaming is the foremost essence of the project," he explained. "Dreaming is the first and the last thing that we should give to people who have lost everything. It's like a circus coming into a small village and all of a sudden there are people coming out of nowhere with colorful suitcases, rising up tents, and there is wonder in every suitcase. There are wonders, stories and images. And they come in paper, or

FIGURE 10.3. Philippe Starck, Ideas Box, Multimedia Library in Kit Form, 2011. Made by Libraries Without Borders.

appear on a screen. And we try to make everything transformable because everything must serve multiple purposes."

Self-Reliance

Victor Papanek, in looking to what he saw as the failings of his own industrial society, proposed a return to a self-sufficient way of life, compiling a book in collaboration with the designer James Hennessey called *Nomadic Furniture*, which was published in 1973. They presented ideas for making simple, lightweight, multipurpose objects by hand with basic tools and commonplace materials such as corrugated cardboard, plywood, and recycled tin cans. Many of their examples were drawn from the world of current design, such as a disposable, die-cut and folded-paper child's chair with a polka-dot coating designed by the Englishman Peter Murdoch (born 1940) in 1964 (Figure 10.4). Consumers could buy these simple chairs in flat packs for little money and put them together easily at home, but Papanek and Hennessey suggested that their readers make their own versions of furniture like this drawn from ideas that had already been put into practice. Among the

other objects they presented was the Easy Edges cardboard furniture that Frank Gehry designed in 1971–72. It was stronger and more substantial than Murdoch's designs yet could be easily die-cut into extremely complicated forms. These pieces were made of sheets of cardboard laminated together and stacked on end, what Gehry called "edgeboard," creating a soft surface that he characterized as resembling corduroy (Figure 10.5).

FIGURE 10.4. Peter Murdoch, Chair Thing, 1964. Made by New Merton Board Mills. Polyurethane-coated laminated paper.

FIGURE 10.5. Frank Gehry, Easy Edges Rocking Chair, 1971–72. Made by Jack Brogan. Cardboard.

Grassroots reaction to the impact of big business and governmental policies had already spurred back-to-the-land and do-it-yourself movements in the United States. Participants of all political persuasions took to the countryside, went off the electric grid, farmed the land, and created independent lifestyles that thumbed their noses at the establishment. Many built their communities by adopting the stable, readily assembled, geodesic-dome structure designed by R. Buckminster Fuller, which he first created in 1951 and unveiled to the public in an exhibition at the Milan Triennale in 1954. Among them, the inhabitants of Drop City, a very loosely organized "creative" community founded in Colorado in 1965, took whatever materials were at hand, including sheet metal from automobiles, to make colorful geodesic structures and artistic furnishings for their dwellings (Figure 10.6).

The alternative communities (and eventually also the Global Tools movement) had help from the *Whole Earth Catalog*, which was published in 1968 and subtitled *Access to Tools*. This was the brainchild of the counterculture writer Stewart Brand (born 1938), who edited what was essentially a vast shopping guide with extensive commentary and a conscience, and set the tone for this and what turned out to be a series of successful later editions (Figure 10.7; see also Figure 10.1). The catalog was an invitation for participation, both from experts and from readers, who suggested what "tools" might be added, reviewed them, recounted their own experiences, and contributed their own ideas and philosophies for independent

FIGURE 10.6. Drop City, an experimental, countercultural community based around cheaply constructed geodesic-dome structures, Trinidad, Colorado, 1967.

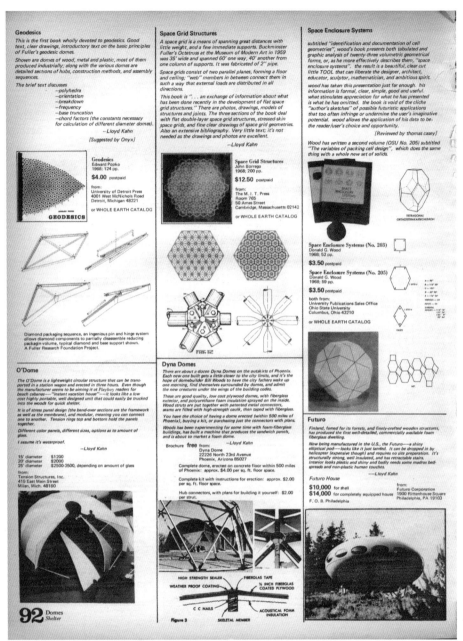

FIGURE 10.7.   Page from *Last Whole Earth Catalog*, 1971.

living. In describing the purpose of the catalogue, Brand established its utopian tone: "We *are* as gods and might as well get used to it. So far, remotely done power and glory—as via government, big business, formal education, church—has succeeded to the point where gross defects obscure actual gain. In response to this dilemma and to these gains a realm of intimate, personal power is developing—power of the individual to conduct his own education, find his own inspiration, shape his own environment, and share his adventure with whoever is interested. Tools that aid this process are sought and promoted by the WHOLE EARTH CATALOG."

Care for the Planet

A challenge to come to terms with what design had done to, and could do for, the well-being of the planet was thrown down on April 22, 1970, with the first celebration of Earth Day. The idea had come from the American Gaylord Nelson (1916–2005), a Democratic senator from Wisconsin, who, deeply troubled by a recent mammoth oil spill in Santa Barbara, California, had called for a "national teach-in on the environment." He based his tactics on those that had been used by activists protesting against the war in Vietnam, and with bipartisan support and an organization promoting nationwide rallies and other teaching events, he drew some twenty million Americans to the streets to demonstrate their concern for the environment (Figure 10.8). Demonstrators marched in rallies in towns and cities but also took it upon themselves to clean up their own spaces as personal actions

of support. The same year, the popular *National Geographic* magazine voiced its concern, challenging its millions of readers throughout the world with an issue entitled *Our Ecological Crisis*. Within a year, the United States Congress had created the Environmental Protection Agency and had passed bills for the protection of endangered species and to clean up the nation's air and water quality. In 1972, the United Nations took action with its Conference on the Human Environment in Stockholm, which established the United Nations Environment Programme, an initiative to encourage and coordinate international environmental activity.

The OPEC oil embargo of 1973 only exacerbated the unease for advocates of Earth Day ideals. With gas shortages looming and the upcoming deadline for meeting new US Clean Air Act standards on automobile emissions, the American automotive industry took stop-gap actions to have their new models comply when

FIGURE 10.8.   First Earth Day, Fifth Avenue, New York, April 22, 1970.

SIDEBAR 23   Richard Buckminster Fuller, *Operating Manual for Spaceship Earth*, 1969

Now we have comprehended and peeled off the layers of petals which disclosed not only that physical energy is conserved but also that it is ever increasingly deposited as a fossil-fuel savings account aboard our Spaceship Earth through photosynthesis and progressive, complex, topsoil fossilization buried ever deeper within Earth's crust by frost, wind, flood, volcanoes, and earthquake upheavals. We have thus discovered also that we can make all of humanity successful through science's world-engulfing industrial evolution provided that we are not so foolish as to continue to exhaust in a split second of astronomical history the orderly energy savings of billions of years' energy conservation aboard our Spaceship Earth . . .

The fossil fuel deposits of our Spaceship Earth correspond to our automobile's storage battery which must be conserved to turn over our main engine's self-starter. Thereafter, our "main engine," the life regenerating processes, must operate exclusively on our vast daily energy income from the powers of wind, tide, water, and the direct Sun radiation energy. The fossil-fuel savings account has been put aboard Spaceship Earth for the exclusive function of getting the new machinery built with which to support life and humanity at ever more effective standards of vital physical energy . . . The daily income energies are excessively adequate for the operation of our main industrial engines and their automated productions. The energy expanded in one minute of a tropical hurricane equals the combined energy of all the U.S.A. and U.S.S.R. nuclear weapons. Only by understanding this scheme may we continue for all time ahead to enjoy and explore universe as we progressively harness evermore of the celestially generated tidal and storm generated wind, water, and electrical power concentrations. We cannot afford to expend our fossil fuels faster than we are "recharging our battery," which means precisely the rate at which fossil fuels are being continually deposited within Earth's spherical crust.

the legislation went into effect in 1975. But the Japanese manufacturer Honda, which had begun to sell passenger cars in the United States in 1970, had taken proactive steps for its Civic model, putting it in the forefront of economical, fuel-efficient design. Instead of simply adding catalytic converters to reduce emissions as other manufacturers were doing, Honda designed a new, nonpolluting engine, which gave unusually high mileage for that era, and which could run on any gas available (during the crisis, shortages occurred frequently for all grades of gasoline). Many Americans turned to the utilitarian Honda for its fuel efficiency and low price and away from style-based models, which helped persuade the American automotive industry to take its own steps toward lowering pollution and reducing the consumption of gasoline.

Further developments to increase the energy efficiency of automobiles have occurred since then, with the introduction of hybrid and electric cars standing out as a positive step toward stemming climate change by reducing the world's dependency on fossil fuels. In 1997 in Japan (and worldwide in 2000), the Japanese automobile manufacturer Toyota released the first commercially viable hybrid car, its Prius model, which is powered by a gasoline engine and an electric-drive system, with the battery being charged by the gasoline engine during cruising, when it is most efficient. Following the push to market hybrid cars, the first successful mid-priced electric cars, the Leaf by the Japanese company Nissan and the Volt by the American manufacturer Chevrolet, were on the market in 2010. The upstart American manufacturer Tesla, under its chairman and CEO Elon Musk (born 1971), introduced its high-end Model S in 2013 after setting up a chain of charging locations so that drivers would have assurance that they would be able to travel far from their home charging stations and have the necessary energy to return (Figure 10.9).

With more significant and visionary ideas than perhaps any other thinker of his time, Buckminster Fuller became the leading spokesperson for the sustainability of the planet and the improvement of the state of its inhabitants. He had convincingly stated the case for the conservation of the natural resources of the planet, particularly its fossil fuel reserves, in his book *Operating Manual for Spaceship Earth*, published in 1969 (see Sidebar 23). This was an urgent call to arms in which he implored planners, architects, and engineers to work for change, for "the realization of the enormous educational task which must be successfully accomplished right now in a hurry in order to convert man's spin-dive toward oblivion into an intellectually mastered power pullout into safe and level flight of physical and metaphysical success, whereafter he may turn his Spaceship Earth's occupancy into a universe exploring advantage."

Environmental programs emerging from Earth Day initiatives eventually led to such community-based activities as recycling and to large-scale sustainable design initiatives such as the European Union's directive on packaging and packaging waste of 1994 and its end-of-life vehicles directive for automobile manufacturers. Launched in 2000, the vehicles directive mandated the recycling of automotive materials and the reuse of parts. This meant that the design of automobiles had to include life-cycle planning, with manufacturers taking back cars at the end of their useful life and following strategies for the disposition of their components for recycling or remanufacture. Once an automobile was returned to the dealer free of charge, the engine was reconditioned and reused, and recycling of the body components undertaken by removing glass, sorting plastics, and separating metal into ferrous and nonferrous components.

Worldwide, programs for consumer recycling took shape but caught on only slowly, seemingly at first the do-good acts of the counterculture, and educational programs had to be developed to encourage it. The German design group BÄR + KNELL, founded in 1992 by Beata Bär (born 1962), Gerhard Bär (born 1959), and Harmut

FIGURE 10.9. Tesla Model S, 2013, at a company charging station.

FIGURE 10.10.
Bär + Knell, Chairs, 1994. Recycled plastic packaging.

Knell (born 1966), worked with the country's national recycling agency to increase environmental awareness. They produced molded furniture from recycled plastic packaging, leaving the products' labels and logos prominently in view as a way to instruct the public that packaging could be a valuable raw material, not just a waste product (Figure 10.10). Other designers and manufacturers looked for ways of preventing the heaps of waste generated by our consumer society from entering landfills, and not only reusing it for such construction activities as resurfacing roadways and sports fields but upcycling it. The production of synthetic fleece from recycled water bottles made of PET (polyethylene terephthalate) plastic for the manufacture of outdoor clothing was an early example of the successful reuse and upcycling of waste materials, with Malden Mills in Lawrence, Massachusetts (now owned by Polartec), announcing in 2015, for example, that they had recycled their billionth PET bottle. Another high-profile upcycling program was shepherded by the Coca-Cola Company in collaboration with Emeco (Electrical Machine and Equipment Company), which was founded in 1944. From its beginnings, Emeco had been producing a welded aluminum chair for the United States Navy that had a reputation for longevity and resistance to rust, water, heat, and the hard use of navy personnel on its submarines. Between 2006 and 2010, Emeco, at the request of Coca-Cola, developed an equally durable chair of the same design that was made out of recycled soda bottles produced in several colors, including the signature Coca-Cola red. This system recycles 111 Coca-Cola bottles for each chair that is manufactured and saved fifteen million bottles from landfills in the first five years of its production (Figure 10.11).

FIGURE 10.11.   Emeco and Coca-Cola, 111 Navy Chair, 2010. Recycled plastic (PET) bottles.

The large, spherical, Tide chandelier was assembled by the English artist and designer Stuart Haygarth (born 1966) from hundreds of translucent plastic objects that he found among the debris that had washed up from the sea over a period of months near his home in England (Figure 10.12). Carefully selecting a variety of objects from the mass he collected, from toys and toothbrushes to eyeglasses, bottles, and tubes of all sorts, Haygarth arranged them into a dense, diverse, glimmering composition. The chandelier can be seen as a cautionary lesson about the dangers of environmental pollution and at the same time, a bid for creative upcycling of a material that we so readily dispose of.

By the end of the twentieth century, upcycling and closed-loop systems had become reasonable goals for manufacturers. In their book *Cradle to Cradle*, published in 2002, the American architect William McDonough (born 1951) and the German chemist Michael Braungart (born 1958) outlined their concept of sustainable, closed systems of manufacture, which they called "cradle-to-cradle" life cycles, replacing the conventional cradle-to-grave system in which products are discarded when their useful lives are finished. This was based on their work with the textile and wall-covering manufacturer DesignTex, for whom they created a textile that was manufactured at a mill in Switzerland with a process that was completely safe for the environment and sustainable, from the materials, dyes, and chemicals to the way water and energy were used during production. McDonough and Braungart envisioned two cycles, the first, natural organic Products of Consumption, which are biodegradable and can be composted after use, and technical Products of Service, such as electronics, which in a closed system can be used and reused and when they are no longer needed, can be remanufactured. The motto they developed for their new method was "waste = food," a positive description of the way resources figure in both cycles. They have continued to work with manufacturers to create sustainable products according to this protocol and have established a certification program for manufacturers who follow it.

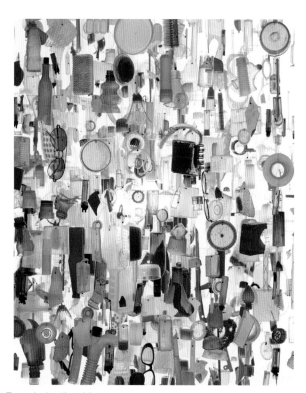

FIGURE 10.12. Stuart Haygarth, Tide Chandelier, 2005. Found plastic objects.

Design for Individuals

For most of the industrial period, the aim of design and manufacturing had been to bring to the market products that everyone could have, identical objects turned out in great numbers by factory methods. How they were made and how efficient they were was not often a concern, although Frederick Winslow Taylor's time-study systems of steelworkers tackled this to a certain degree in the 1890s, and Christine Frederick followed up with her own studies related to housework in the second decade of the twentieth century (see Figure 3.21). But how they were used and the well-being of the user were just not considered. Designing for workplace safety and efficiency was at the core of the development of ergonomic, or human factor, design beginning in the 1930s. Its goal was to accommodate machines and technology to the worker rather than forcing humans to make adjustments for the machine. Ergonomics focused not on individuals but on groups of users, studying a median range of human forms and abilities in order to develop products and environments that were adapted broadly to workers' comfort. Ergonomic products do well with forms that are specific to a task, like the hard, sculptured, orange plastic–handled sewing scissors that Olof Bäckström (1922–1998) designed for the Finnish company Fiskars in 1967 (Figure 10.13). These were geared to the working comfort of a hypothetical median sewer, serving the greater part of the population, but would not easily accommodate a variety of hand sizes or left-handed users (left-handed models were later added) or be useful for those with arthritis or grasping problems.

Henry Dreyfuss had begun to consider the needs and abilities of users in the general population in his early ergonomic designs for Bell Telephone during the 1930s, researching human abilities and bodily disparities in designing their equipment. In his autobiography *Designing for People*, published in 1955, he explained how the spirit of ergonomics was one aspect of his approach: "We begin with men and women and we end with them. We consider the potential user's habits, physical dimensions, and psychological impulses. We also measure their purse, which is what I meant by ending with them, for we must conceive not only a satisfactory design, but also one that incorporates that indefinable appeal to assure purchase."

With "physical dimensions," Dreyfuss was referring to the anthropometric charts of human measurements that he illustrated in the book, introduced with diagrams of an "average" couple, whom he named Joe and Josephine, and their children (Figure 10.14). These charts were based on the available data, much of which came from the American armed forces, where a great deal of ergonomic research had been done during the Second World War, but which were not reliable as a cross-section of measurements of the human (or even American) population. As more data were sourced over the years, this information became more useful, and Dreyfuss's later publication, *Measure of Man: Human Factors in Design* of 1960, included life-size charts of a man and a woman

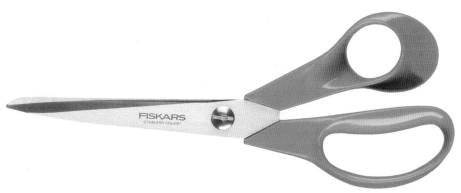

FIGURE 10.13. Olof Bäckström, Sewing Scissors, 1967. Made by Fiskars. Plastic and stainless steel.

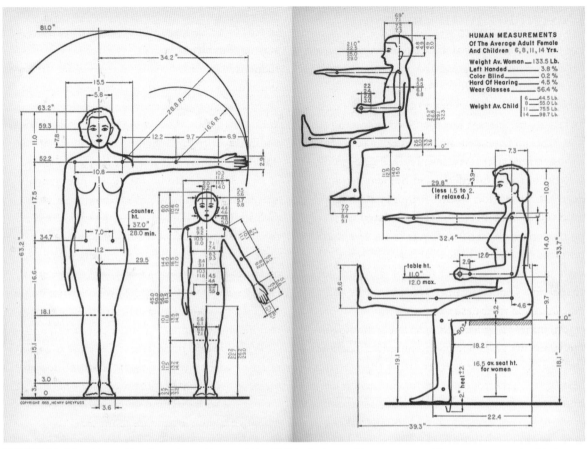

FIGURE 10.14.   Henry Dreyfuss, Josephine and Her Child, diagram of human percentile measurements, from *Designing for People*, 1955.

that provided many more significant statistics. The charts became even more comprehensive in a series called *Human Scale*, the first one published in 1974 by Dreyfuss's design associate Niels Diffrient (1928–2013). The charts that Diffrient included in *Human Scale* went beyond anthropometry, or the study of human measurements and proportions, to include broad guidelines for design while also making an attempt to accommodate the elderly and those with disabilities. These charts, however, had all been based on median measurements of the population that reached from the 97.5th to the 2.5th percentile, thereby excluding those people who were at the outer edges of human measurements, the remaining 2.5th percentile on each side. They excluded those whose measurements were at the extremes and totally omitted anyone who could have been in the range

of what might have then been called "abnormal." Dreyfuss had explained in *The Measure of Man* that "for the designer's purposes, it is not really necessary to work with data on all 100 percentiles. To begin with, the top and bottom few percentiles represent people who are extremely rare."

This was the kind of exclusion that the Americans with Disabilities Act (ADA) overrode in 1990, and after that, design for public accommodation had to encompass the entire population, providing access to physical spaces and educational and communication aids to those with disabilities. The passage of the bill had a major impact on design in the United States, more far-reaching than any other piece of design legislation except for the Patent Act of 1790 (which established the United States patent office). It acknowledged that people with physical or mental disabilities should have the same rights of barrier-free access to buildings, transportation, and telecommunications as other citizens. The fight for these rights had taken many years, following the activist methods of the American civil rights movement, with a forceful participation of Vietnam veterans who had lost limbs or become wheelchair users as an outcome of their tours of duty. This act, and related actions elsewhere, including the adoption of the United Nations Standard Rules for the Equalization of Opportunity for Persons with Disabilities in 1993 and of the Disability Discrimination Act in the United Kingdom in 1995, meant that designers who interacted with the public now had to be aware of inclusivity and that every member of the population was to be considered in their designs.

An initial surge focused on altering the physical landscape with a campaign to remove the barriers that might hinder the right of access, with the most immediate and obvious environmental changes being the addition of ramps to existing buildings that served the public, however difficult that may have been (Figure 10.15). An unintended benefit of the corrective actions was that many of the mandated changes also helped the entire population. Curb cuts, for example, gave those using wheelchairs or other assistive devices an easier approach to sidewalks but also served those with mobility issues among the elderly or those pushing strollers, wheeling suitcases, or making deliveries, benefits that reinforced thinking about universal, or inclusive, design.

The term "universal design" was coined by the American architect, educator, and barrier-free activist Ronald Mace (1942–1998), whose life work was directed to teaching about design for individual needs and to making the environment accessible to all, starting out with an understanding of the vocabulary of disability. "If you could separate barrier-free, universal, and assistive technology distinctly," he wrote in trying to clarify these terms, "they would look like this: assistive technology is devices and equipment we need to be functional in the environment; barrier-free, ADA, and building codes are disability mandates; and *universal design* is design for the built environment and consumer products for a very broad definition of user that encourages attractive, marketable products that are more usable by everyone. The reality, however, is that the three blend and move into each other."

FIGURE 10.15.
After the passage of the Americans with Disability Act in 1990, existing buildings like the Etz Chaim synagogue in Biddeford, Maine, were retrofitted with ramps and other means of barrier-free access.

Barrier-free design is the broad and inclusive requirement of government legislation that mandated physical and mental accessibility, resulting in such aids as handrails and ample space for wheelchairs in public toilets and curb cuts and ramps in public spaces. Assistive devices are in the best case individualized and specific, custom-designed or adapted for each user, like the lightweight aluminum Tiga wheelchair manufactured by the British firm RGK, which is made to measure and offers numerous options for ergonomic seating and backrests, with color and other design choices included as an emotional adjunct for the satisfaction of the user (Figure 10.16). In an effort to make wheelchair users less self-conscious and more confident, the Accessible Icon Project, created by Brian Glenney (born 1974), Sara Hendren (born 1973), and Tim Ferguson Sauder (born 1972), worked to replace the standard but passive accessibility icon in use since the 1960s with one showing the user and wheelchair actively moving through space (Figure 10.17). Introduced between 2009 and 2011 through an activist street campaign in Boston, the icon also brought accessibility issues to wider public notice, giving the image of those with disabilities a more positive spin as active members of society.

FIGURE 10.17.   Accessible Icon Project, Accessible Icon, 2009–11.

FIGURE 10.16.   RGK Wheelchairs, Tiga Daily Wheelchair, 2010s.

Mace, a wheel-chair user himself, created the Center for Universal Design at North Carolina University in 1989, eventually working with a committee of architects, product designers, engineers, and environmental-design researchers to develop the Seven Principles of Universal Design in 1997 (see Sidebar 24). These principles became the standard for designers who wanted to understand inclusivity in design. Universal design recognizes that society is a continuum of individuals who have distinct abilities and needs that should be taken into account when environments and products are created. Society creates barriers that prevent individuals from taking advantage of the plenitude of our world, and it is generally agreed that this can be corrected by design, sometimes even by the simplest means like replacing round door handles, traditionally used in the United States, with conventional lever handles, like the aluminum set designed by the Australian Marc Newson (born 1963), which give users with strength issues greater access to their environment (Figure 10.18). Unlike ergonomic apparatuses, Universal Design requires generalized forms, like the soft, rounded

SIDEBAR 24   Center for Universal Design, Seven Principles of Universal Design, 1997

Principle 1: Equitable Use
The design is useful and marketable to people with diverse abilities.

Principle 2: Flexibility in Use
The design accommodates a wide range of individual preferences and abilities.

Principle 3: Simple and Intuitive Use
Use of design is easy to understand, regardless of the user's experience, knowledge, language skills, or current concentration level.

Principle 4: Perceptible Information
The design communicates necessary information effectively to the user, regardless of ambient conditions or the user's sensory abilities.

Principle 5: Tolerance for Error
The design minimizes hazards and the adverse consequences of accidental or unintended actions.

Principle 6: Low Physical Effort
The design can be used efficiently and comfortably and with a minimum of fatigue.

Principle 7: Size and Space for Approach and Use
Appropriate size and space is provided for approach, reach, manipulation, and use regardless of a user's body size, posture, or mobility.

Santoprene handle of the OXO vegetable peeler (see Figure 0.5), which aim to take everyone, including those with disabilities, into account as potential users.

With disability acts in place and their physical effects taking hold, communication barriers also had to be removed, but few specifics were outlined about how that was to be done. In the area of telecommunications, assistive technologies such as teleprinters, or teletypewriters (TTY), were installed in public spaces for those whose hearing was impaired. In the area of electronics, the introduction of such features as speech recognition software, visual and aural alerts, and typing aids in computers supported accessibility for those with a range of special needs. Many such accessibility features, initially introduced by IBM and Apple, allowed actions essential for computer (and later cellular phone) use by those with different needs to be modified individually. These included altering keyboard, mouse, display, and sound functions and allowing for dictation and visual and aural descriptions of screen images, features that could also be used by those in the general population and were particularly advantageous to graphic and web designers as well. Inclusivity has been enhanced by sensory design, a movement that emphasizes the value of designing for all of the senses, touch, sound, smell, and taste, not just sight, which plays to the strength of individual users and expands the concept of universal design even further, although it was not developed specifically to do so.

FIGURE 10.18.   Marc Newson, Lever Door Handle, 2001. Made by Erreti. Aluminum.

Accessibility and functionality are of course the essential requisites for design for those with special needs, but when a concern for the aesthetic aspects of design is included, it can only raise the self-image and satisfaction of users. In his book *Design Meets Disability* (2009), the British designer and disabilities advocate Graham Pullin (born 1964) stressed the need to incorporate the knowledge of commercial designers and users along with technicians in the design process. "Disability-related design needs designers who are not specialists and will never be, yet bring other skills and sensibilities to the table instead," Graham has said. "Otherwise design for disabled people will remain marginalised—and mediocre, which can be the most offensive thing of all." Among the earliest firms dedicated to creating well-designed products for those with disabilities was Sweden's Ergonomi Design Gruppen, which was established in Bromma in 1979. Maria Benktzon (born 1946), one of the founders of the group, had been directly inspired by Victor Papanek when in 1968 she heard him speak about design for need at a conference in Stockholm. Benktzon and her associate Sven-Eric Juhlin (born 1940) have worked with organizations and corporations supported by the Swedish government, for which such design was a priority, to research ergonomic and functionality issues in order to develop a wide range of specialized products, like their knife and cutting frame from 1974 (Figure 10.19). It was designed to ease the task of slicing bread for those who had difficulty using a traditional knife, replacing it with a knife in the form of a saw, which used a totally different range of motion. They set it in a frame that held the bread in place and gave it an attractive design that would avoid stigmatizing the users of an unconventional product.

Design for those with disabilities became personal for Michael Graves after he contracted a viral infection toward the end of his life and became a wheelchair user himself. He was soon to design thoughtful personal and household products, such as folding walking sticks and bathtub safety rails, that gave dignity to these objects and their users (Figure 10.20). He also became an advisor on hospital buildings and facilities and medical equipment and collaborated with the United States Wounded Warriors program. His prototype houses for disabled veterans included ample space for

FIGURE 10.19.
Ergonomi Design Gruppen, Knife and Cutting Frame, 1974. Made by Gustavsberg. Plastic and stainless steel.

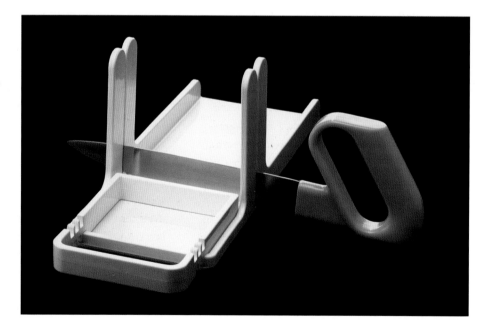

FIGURE 10.20. Michael Graves, Clamp-On Tub Rail, 2007. Made by Drive Medical. Steel and plastic.

FIGURE 10.21. Francesca Lanzavecchia, Neck Brace, 2008. Plastic-coated lace.

wheelchair use and adaptable cabinetry and fixtures for specific needs of the veterans but also provided conventional interior spaces to accommodate the rest of the family.

The Italian designer Francesca Lanzavecchia (born 1983) studied disability design empathetically by listening to the personal stories of those who might use her designs. Her early work with orthotics, artificial supports for the body, and with the needs of the elderly, brought her considerable recognition for the thesis research she did on design for disability. Her series No Country for Old Men includes products such as canes, furniture with built-in mobility aids, and mobile accessories for transporting objects, while her Proaesthetics comprise decorative corrective devices such as neck and arm braces for those with temporary disabling conditions owing to accidents. Her Victorian neck brace uses plastic-coated lace in the form of a collar to support the neck, which becomes a design accessory instead of an obtrusive device (Figure 10.21). Large-scale production of such disability designs is difficult to achieve through industry because of a still narrow vision of the economic possibilities of this niche market.

The well-known Paralympian Aimee Mullins (born 1975), whose lower legs were amputated when she was young and who later raced fiercely on newly developed carbon-fiber legs, has refused to accept the definition of her body as disabled (Figure 10.22). Her record-breaking athletic accomplishments brought her wide notice, and despite her use of prosthetic limbs, she became an actress and a model. In 1998 she appeared in the "Fashion-Able?" issue of the English magazine *Dazed & Confused*, which was guest edited by the fashion designer Alexander McQueen (1969–2010) in order to bring a new status to those with disabilities and to demonstrate that they too could be dressed in style. For a runway show in 1999, McQueen conceived a pair of wooden legs for Mullins that were based on the form of Victorian knee-length boots and ornamented with sculptural grapevines inspired by the fine English wood carving of the seventeenth and eighteenth centuries (Figure 10.23). The legs were made specifically for her by the prosthetist Bob Watts and sculpted by

the wood-carver and gilder Paul Ferguson. Few at
the fashion show realized that these stylish boots
were actually prosthetic legs, and with them Mullins
could show that there is no reason that design for
those with disabilities cannot also be beautiful.

FIGURE 10.22.   Aimee Mullins competing in the
Paralympics at Olympic Stadium, Atlanta, 1996.

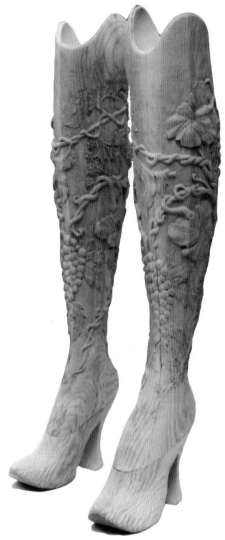

FIGURE 10.23.   Prosthetic legs conceived by Alexander
McQueen for Aimee Mullins, 1999. Made by Bob Watts
and carved by Paul Ferguson. Ash (before staining).

DESIGN AND TECHNOLOGY

since 2000

CHAPTER 11

Design in the Digital Age

By the start of the new millennium, technology had become the prime mover of design and past debates about form and function suddenly seemed antiquated. Function often meant exploiting digital platforms for controlling one's life and one's lifestyle, and expressing the way things functioned was no longer part of the rhetoric of design. Most of the elements that regulated functions were hidden in the digital underpinnings of these devices, which were driven by keyboards, touch screens, and voice activation, and the way these products were configured could be anything designers wanted them to be. Not only was smart technology the mover of remarkable new objects introduced for personal connectivity, but it also encompassed an even greater ubiquity with the microchips that were being embedded in virtually every device that was produced—automobiles, appliances, air-handling systems, lighting, environmental controls, fitness gadgets (see Figure 0.8), even clothing, with sensors introduced into them for sports and medical applications. Design also took a completely new turn with its extension into intangible creations, digital interfaces for the computer, for the web, for social media platforms, for gaming, for apps

(applications, or programs that can be downloaded to digital devices), and for a world of virtual reality.

Once the nail biting over the anticipated dire consequences of the year 2000 digital turnover had subsided (because electronics in the twentieth century had used only the final two digits to designate years, some thought that the early systems would not be able to recognize a four-digit year when the millennium arrived, thereby causing major computer crashes), technology achieved its attraction again. Software tools that had been developed during the last two decades of the twentieth century, computer-aided design (CAD) and computer-aided manufacturing (CAM), became the universal elements of the design process. CAD took over much of the tedium of the mathematics and drafting of design and CAM controlled three-dimensional (3-D) printing, or rapid prototyping, during the design process as well as the machinery used to manufacture the products themselves. The color-mixing Vortexx chandelier designed in 2005 by the Iraqi-born British architect Dame Zaha Hadid (1950–2016) with her partner, the German architect Patrik Schumacher (born 1961), brought soaring aspects of her futuristic

Smart Products and Processes

Apple became the standard bearer for inventive personal electronics technology and innovative, minimalist design. Its iPod, a miniature personal music player completely different from other MP3 (small-format) digital audio devices already on the market, was unveiled late in 2001 and was immediately (if prematurely) acknowledged as the outstanding design of the new century (Figure 11.2). This was a direct descendent of Sony's personal Walkman tape-cassette player from 1979 (see Figure 9.8) but with all the benefits of digital technology, miniaturization, and expanded access to music. The iPod reset the routines of millions of people's lives: it was intimate and irresistible, captivating the listeners' attention and occupying them tightly in a way no other object, even the Walkman, had done before. But it was especially the ease of accessibility of the music, organized on the computer using Apple's new iTunes music store and then synchronized with the iPod to follow preset playlists or to shuffle music by chance, that made listening almost seamless. The total freedom of accessing music anytime, anywhere was captured brilliantly in the dancing-silhouette advertising campaign led by Susan Alinsangan (born 1961) for the TBWA\Chiat\Day agency in 2003. There, cool listeners silhouetted in black against boldly colored grounds danced to music transmitted through the white earbuds of their iPods (Figure 11.3)

In designing its revolutionary product, Apple discarded the expressive playfulness of its recent colorful computer, the translucent iMac (see Figure 9.18), for the cool, pure-white look that the company was then favoring for its other products. The tough polycarbonate case and its gleaming stainless-steel back were conceived by the Apple design team led by Jonathan Ive (with Apple's co-founder Steve Jobs in the background overseeing every aspect of the product as it was

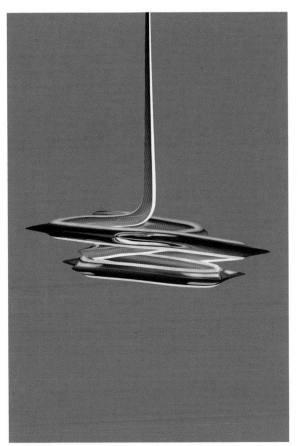

FIGURE 11.1.   Dame Zaha Hadid and Patrik Schumacher, Vortexx Chandelier, 2005. Made by Zumtobel in collaboration with Sawaya & Moroni. Acrylic, fiberglass-reinforced polyester, and LED lights.

architecture into interior fittings through 3-D printing, an object with a large scale and an intricacy that could only have been produced with digital means (Figure 11.1). Its double-helix form, a whirlpool of changing, colored light, incorporates a programmable ribbon of LEDs that evokes the complexity of its endless design. Hadid, who had established her personal aesthetic of dynamic, angular geometries for buildings throughout the world, was also heavily invested in design, bringing her fragmented forms to furniture, metalware, jewelry, fashion, interiors, and lighting such as this.

being designed), who took as their inspiration the minimalist aesthetic of Braun's director of design Dieter Rams and his mantra that "good design is as little design as possible" (see Sidebar 16). A wheel on the front of the device allowed users to scroll quickly through a playlist of some one thousand songs, made possible by the availability of an extra-large storage capacity for its time. The incredibly successful iPod spawned many offshoots at Apple, all even more reduced in size—the iPod touch (2002), iPod mini (2004), iPod shuffle (2005), and iPod nano (2005)—which also became fashion accessories, with some small enough to clip onto one's outfit for listening while running or exercising.

The design of Apple's smart iPhone, introduced six years later, in 2007, followed the same minimalist aesthetic, the device reduced simply to a glass screen and a stainless-steel back that

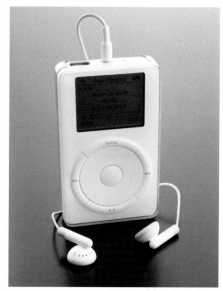

FIGURE 11.2.   Jonathan Ive and Apple, iPod Digital Audio Player, 2001. Made by Apple. Polycarbonate/ABS plastic and stainless steel.

FIGURE 11.3.   Susan Alinsangan, Advertising Campaign for Apple iPod, 2003.

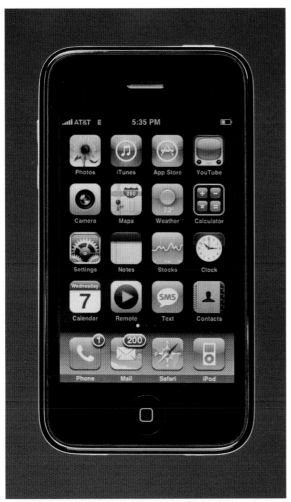

FIGURE 11.4. Jonathan Ive and Apple, iPhone, 2007. Made by Apple. Glass and stainless steel.

In 2011, Ingo Maurer surprisingly added wallpaper to the list of smart products, another of his unusual products that touched on the cutting edge of technology without leaving behind his singular sense of humor. A combination of wall covering and lighting, his design revealed the technology of the design itself by printing the circuits that command the LEDs on the face of wallpaper (Figure 11.5). The rhombic pattern of blue (or red) diodes and irregularly placed white ones created a changeable display, with the circuits controlling the degree of light emitted and the frequency with which the lights could be turned on and off.

Three-dimensional (3-D) printing, in which computers direct machines to form one-off, three-dimensional objects, is the revolutionary manufacturing technique of this century. Although it had been around since the 1980s, the process

rolled over to form a thin rim around the display on the front (Figure 11.4). The iPhone was really a pocket-size computer with an easy-to-operate touch-screen platform that could do many things besides telephone communication. While the iPhone was more all-encompassing than the iPod, the experience of using it seemed less intimate, the consequence of its transformation from a private artifact to a public instrument. Its array of built-in internet-based features and its hundreds of thousands of other information and entertainment applications (apps) that beginning in 2008 could be downloaded through the online Apple App store added apparently limitless possibilities to the device.

FIGURE 11.5. Ingo Maurer, LED Wallpaper, 2012. Made by Architects Paper.

had been prohibitively expensive and was mostly used by large companies for the prototyping (model making) of new products, manufacturing small parts for machinery repair, and creating models and specialized components for architects, designers, and artists. Suddenly in the first years of the millennium, it became more and more economical and the use of this technology grew rapidly. In the most popular three-dimensional printing processes, digital (CAM) files instruct these printers to create objects by extruding melted material (Fused Deposition Modeling; FDM), or by solidifying a liquid resin (stereolithography; SLA) or a polymer powder (selective laser sintering; SLS) as horizontal cross-sections are built up sequentially until the entire form is completed.

Early in the twenty-first century, manufacturers of these machines saw greater potential for the technology and worked with designers to demonstrate that prototyping could also be used to create finished objects, some considerably larger than had ever been done before. In 2004, Materialise, a Belgian manufacturer founded in 1990, joined with the French designer Patrick Jouin (born 1967) to produce furniture by stereolithography, in which an ultraviolet laser, instructed by a CAD file, scans the surface of liquid resin in a tray and hardens it selectively to produce a three-dimensional object layer by layer. When Jouin's Solid C2 chair, with its jungle of vertical supports, was unveiled, it started a new and newsworthy path for manufacturing and became an immediate icon of this new technology (Figure 11.6). The prototyping processes, and the unusual objects with complex, organic forms that were being produced by it, inspired other designers and prototyping firms to explore new methods for commercial manufacturing, although their output was essentially restricted to one-off production.

Front, a Swedish women's collaborative design firm established in Stockholm in 2002, took the immediacy of this technology one step further for its Sketch furniture series. In a much noted "happening," its members freely sketched images

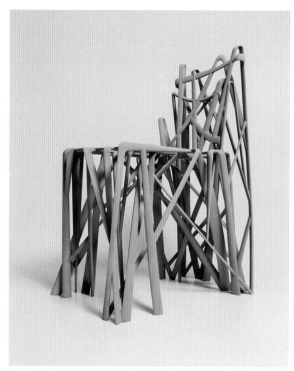

FIGURE 11.6. Patrick Jouin, Solid C2 Chair, 2004. Made by Materialise. Liquid resin.

of furniture in the air with a motion-capture pen (Figure 11.7). A computer caught these images and generated digital files that instructed a stereolithography machine to produce the spontaneous pieces that they had sketched (Figures 11.8, 11.9). Both the pieces by Jouin and those by Front seemed to be born of a new aesthetic of complexity, replacing the simplicity that Le Corbusier had equated with modern form, but by the time that rapid prototyping matured in the commercial world, it had become apparent that complexity was only one aspect of the products that could be produced by these means.

Three-dimensional printing also entered the field of fashion. Much of this activity was centered around creating garments for celebrities and costumes for the stage and cinema. The American design firm Nervous Systems, which was established in 2007 by Jessica Rosenkrantz (born 1983) and Jesse Louis-Rosenberg (born 1986), introduced dedicated software for designing

FIGURE 11.7.   Members of the Front collective drawing furniture forms in the air with a motion-capture pen for its Sketch series, which would then be 3-D printed, 2005.

FIGURE 11.8.   Front, 3-D Printed Sketch Table, 2005. Polyamide.

FIGURE 11.9.   Front, 3-D Printed Sketch Chair, 2005. Polyamide.

and producing computer-generated clothing, but unlike others who made their digital clothing in small sections, their Kinematics folding system could produce a complete, full-size garment. They had invented a process for producing a dress in a folded system, which they were then able to open to its full length after the printing was finished (Figure 11.10). Structured as small interlinking elements, their dresses are flexible and flow freely as they are worn.

While the Bone chair designed by Joris Laarman (born 1979) was not produced by a 3-D printing process, the complex mold used to enable the casting of the Dutch designer's object in one aluminum piece was. The structure of Laarman's chair was created by biomimicry, the modeling of design after natural processes, following the fundamental principles of the growth of bones in which unnecessary material has been eliminated

from their structure through the processes of evolution. Using a software developed for the automobile industry, he analyzed where the stresses would be heaviest on the chair. The program added materials in those areas while removing material where the stresses would be less great and thus was not needed, which allowed for great reduction of the amount of aluminum required (Figure 11.11). The Bone chair then had to be adjusted for the properties of aluminum and a mold made from parts that were digitally printed so that the chair could be cast all at once.

Marcel Wanders, whose bizarre sense of humor led him to seek a source for his design in an unusual area of microscopic nature, used sprays of mucous from the sneezes of five different nasal conditions, sinusitus, pollinosis, and coryza among them, to create the forms of his Airborne Snotty vases (Figure 11.12). The sneezes were caught as digital

FIGURE 11.10.   Nervous System, Kinematics Dress, 2013. Laser-sintered nylon.

FIGURE 11.11.   Joris Laarman, Bone Chair, 2006. Made by Joris Laarman Lab. Aluminum.

FIGURE 11.12. Marcel Wanders, Airborne Snotty Vases: Sinusitus, Pollinosis, and Coryza, 2001. Made by Cappellini. Polyamide.

images with a three-dimensional scanner to form the objects in this series. The computer scans, from which Wanders selected the five formats, were then enlarged and digitally edited to add hollows for the flowers, and translated into physical objects using the selective laser-sintering 3-D printing technique.

Ornament Made Modern

Freed from the existence of design dogmas, many designers have once again been looking to past styles for inspiration. When Philippe Starck introduced his Louis Ghost armchair in 2002, few complained that this transparent, polycarbonate adaptation of a French eighteenth-century precedent transgressed the boundaries of modern design (Figure 11.13). Instead, his creation was seen as a serious reconciliation with the past, not ironic in any way, bringing the richness of historicism into the contemporary mainstream. It clearly demonstrated the continuing value of the past for the present and how simplicity of form can render even historicism modern if objects lack the sculptural and ornamental details of the earlier pieces that inspire from.

Around the turn of the twenty-first century, a number of designers began to revive another type of eighteenth-century ornamental design, notably the French fabrics that became known as *toiles* (a French word for "cloth"), which were printed with romanticized scenes of village life (although some had gritty subjects as well). Among them was the Scottish firm Timorous Beasties, their name taken from a line in the poem "To a Mouse" by the Scotsman Robert Burns (1759–1796). Timorous Beasties, which was founded in 2000 by two textile-design students at the Glasgow School of Art, Alistair McAuly (born 1967) and Paul Simmons (born 1967), took the decorative format of the *toile* fabrics at face value but created subtle subversions of their picturesque rural designs. Instead of showing rustic scenes, their fabrics included vignettes of contemporary urban locales, including Glasgow, London, and New York. In their London *toile*, Timorous Beasties presented uneasy visions of life today, including a robbery at gunpoint in process, and intermingled them with images of the diversity of the city's residents, all placed in park-like settings with some of the city's notable old and new monuments seen in the distance (Figure 11.14).

FIGURE 11.13.
Philippe Starck, Louis
Ghost Chair, 2002.
Made by Kartell.
Polycarbonate.

Reviving ornament could also mean
reintroducing manufacturing techniques that had
been discarded in the past. For his glimmering
Bobbin Lace hanging lamp, the Dutch designer
Neils Van Eijk (born 1970) reinvented the
chandelier in a form that omitted conventional
lightbulbs, combining the traditional technique
of bobbin lace with modern light-transmitting
fiber-optic filaments (Figure 11.15). Bobbin lace,
first seen in Italy and Belgium during the sixteenth
century and revived by Van Eijk in 2001, uses
threads held on bobbins, or spools, as an aid in
creating complex lace patterns by twisting and
knotting. When the fiber-optic threads used for
the lace are knotted, they break, which allows light
to be released from the filaments at hundreds of
unanticipated points and allows the lamp to be
softly illuminated all over.

The Dutch designer Tord Boontje (born 1968)
invites buyers to finish his Garland lights by
arranging a floral metal spray over a lightbulb in
any way they desire, one of the many examples
today of the loosening of designer control
by allowing consumers to complete products
themselves (Figure 11.16). For this series, Boontje,

FIGURE 11.14.   Timorous Beasties, London Toile,
2006. Printed linen.

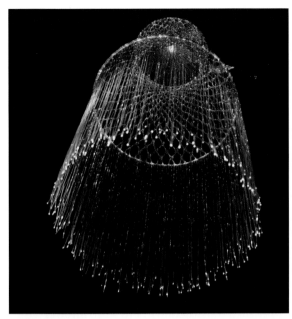

FIGURE 11.15.   Neils Van Eijk, Bobbin Lace Hanging Lamp, 2001. Fiber optic filaments.

whose work combines a romantic interest in nature with modern technology, created an ornamental shade made from a single piece of metal, laser cut into the form of leaves, flowers, and stems, which can easily be removed from the metal sheet and hung over the bulb. Another design that depends on its users is the Algue (seaweed) modular clipping system by the French brothers Ronan Bouroullec (born 1971) and Erwan Bouroullec (born 1976) (Figure 11.17). This is an open-ended product made of modular ABS plastic components that look like plant forms, which are meant to be linked together by the consumer for transparent ornamental screens, room dividers, curtains, or whatever else they might think to do with them.

FIGURE 11.17.   Ronan Bouroullec and Erwan Bouroullec, Algue Modular Clipping System, 2004. Made by Vitra. ABS plastic.

FIGURE 11.16.   Tord Boontje, Garland Light, 2002. Made by Artecnica. Brass.

Conceptual and Critical Design

Recent years have seen an upsurge in design that is driven by ideas, not practicality or sales, although sometimes the outcomes of these new ideas have found their way to the marketplace. Pursuits that fall into the theoretical, that invite unpredictability and the accidental, that are decidedly experimental, that comment on society's foibles, and that use humor to make their point—all are encompassed by the term "conceptual design." This is not new, as we have seen. Radical design involved the polemics of future possibilities for design, while concept cars and houses of the future worked on a more practical level—but the explorations of conceptual design have now expanded widely.

As an ironic initiative and a comment on the then growing fad for user collaboration, the Dutch Droog Design collective in 2001 invited a group of designers to contribute ideas for their new "Do Create series," objects that had to involve consumers in completing their purchases. The Do Hit chair by Marijn Van Der Poll (born 1973), known best from photographs of a man swinging a sledge hammer to transform a large cube of stainless steel into a chair, was one of the tongue-in-cheek results of this quest (Figure 11.18). Among others in the conceptual series was the Do Break vase, created by the designer Frank Tjepkema (born 1970). The undecorated ceramic vase came with instructions for the consumer to ornament its surface with a crackle design by smashing it on the floor (while an interior rubber backing held the broken shards together and kept the vase with its new decoration intact).

The Japanese designer Tokujin Yoshioka (born 1967) has experimented with growing furniture rather than constructing it. His work involves considerable research into materials and processes, and his experiments with science and technology have led to singular solutions such as his Venus Natural Crystal chair (Figure 11.19). He began this project by submerging a thin, mesh-like, polyester

FIGURE 11.18. Man completing Marijn Van Der Poll's Do Hit Chair, 2001. Made by Droog. Stainless steel.

FIGURE 11.19.   Tokujin Yoshioka, Venus Natural Crystal Chair, 2008. Glass crystals.

FIGURE 11.20.   Front, Rat creating wallpaper, 2005.

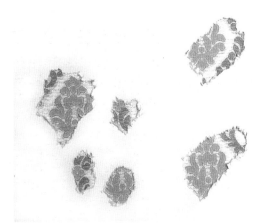

FIGURE 11.21.   Front, Rat wallpaper installed over previous wall covering, 2005. Gnawed paper.

chair form in a mineral-filled liquid and allowed it to grow slowly as crystals precipitated on it and developed its angular silhouette, relying on the creative energy of nature to complete the object. Yoshioka is above all focused on the splendors of nature, and with this and other experimental designs grown from crystals, including chandeliers for the Swarovski crystal glass firm, he aims to bring a new appreciation of its grandeur to the public.

The Front collective also harnessed the forces of nature, animal activity, for their "Design by" series: "Wallpaper, hooks, lamps and other everyday objects designed by rats, dogs, snakes and beetles. We asked animals to help us. Sure, we'll help you out! they answered. Make something nice, we told them. And so they did." Among these nice objects was their Rat wallpaper: a rodent chewed through rolls of unprinted wallpaper in different places, creating an allover pattern of voids. When the wallpaper was hung in a room, the underlying wall covering showed through in these areas and added color to the pattern along with recollections of its earlier decoration (Figures 11.20, 11.21).

Turning to conceptual design as commentary in his perforated polypropylene Rest in Peace chair in

2004, the Austrian-born Parisian designer Robert Stadler (born 1966) expressed his dismay over the widespread distribution of the familiar plastic monobloc (single-piece) chair since it was first manufactured in the 1970s. His was an ironic bid to rid the planet of these ubiquitous chairs, which he considered just too many plastic intrusions (Figure 11.22). "This project arose from a utopian desire to speed up the disappearance of this chair that has invaded the planet—probably one of the most widely produced chairs in history," he wrote. "The shape of the perforations reproduces the damage caused by osteoporosis at various stages. The object becomes a skeleton that might be dug up during an archaeological excavation in the future." For some like Stadler, the monobloc chair is an example of the waywardness of design, but for others throughout the world, it is the happy outcome of an economical material and process that brings cheap, durable furnishings to their homes and workplaces, which stands as an exceptional example of an immensely successful object of everyday aesthetics.

While conceptual design exploits humor and irony, critical design is serious in intent, cutting-edge, and controversial as it critiques issues faced by design today and anticipates those that the future might bring. In attempting to offer possible

FIGURE 11.22. Robert Stadler, Rest in Peace Chair, 2004. Altered polypropylene chair.

FIGURE 11.23. Dunne and Raby, Designs for an Overpopulated Planet: Foragers, 2009.

SIDEBAR 25   Anthony Dunne and Fiona Raby, "Design as Critique," 2013

Critique is not necessarily negative; it can also be a gentle refusal, a turning away from what exists, a longing, wishful thinking, a desire, and even a dream. Critical designs are testimonials to what could be, but at the same time, they offer alternatives that highlight weaknesses within existing normality.

When people encounter the term *critical design* for the first time, they often assume it has something to do with critical theory and the Frankfurt School [a philosophical and sociological movement interpreting Marxist social and economic ideas] or just plain criticism. But it is neither. We are more interested in critical thinking, that is, not taking things for granted, being skeptical, and always questioning what is given. All good design is critical. Designers start by identifying shortcomings in the thing they are redesigning and offer a better

version. Critical design applies this to larger more complex issues. Critical design is critical thought translated into materiality. It is about thinking through design rather than through words and using the language and structure of design to engage people. It is an expression or manifestation of our skeptical fascination with technology, a way of unpicking the different hopes, fears, promises, delusions, and nightmares of technological development and change, especially how scientific discoveries move from the laboratory into everyday life through the marketplace. The subject can vary. On the most basic level it is about questioning underlying assumptions in design itself, on the next level it is directed at the technology industry and its market-driven limitations, and beyond that, general social theory, politics, and ideology.

solutions to such problems, critical-design thinkers work with interdisciplinary advisors from fields such as ethics, philosophy, political science, life sciences, and biology. Critical design "is about thinking through design rather than through words and using the language and structure of design to engage people," according to the team of Anthony Dunne (born 1964) and Fiona Raby (born 1963), who coined the term (see Sidebar 25). It is mostly practiced in schools of design, an academic undertaking that was introduced by Dunne & Raby at the Royal College of Art in London, where they began to teach early in this century. Other design schools have followed their lead, among them the Art Academy Eindhoven in the Netherlands and the New School in New York.

In their Designs for an Overpopulated Planet: Foragers from 2009, for example, Dunne & Raby confronted the issue of what would happen should there not be sufficient food on our planet to feed all its inhabitants. "What if we could extract nutritional value from non-human foods," they

asked, "using a combination of synthetic biology and new devices inspired by digestive systems of other mammals, birds, fish and insects?" They envisioned human digestion being altered to digest foreign substances, the last hope for human nourishment. Basing their work on multidisciplinary research into these issues, they conceived a type of equipment that would help humans forage for the shreds of the non-digestive substances that remained on Earth, and through computer modeling, depicted the way their solutions would be carried out (Figure 11.23). Such fictional narratives, films, and forays into the future that are part of critical design have become controversial, with concern focusing on the misunderstanding of the reality or super-reality of the situations that designers have envisioned as well as their disregard for the real problems faced by the developing world today, which these designers could help to alleviate. Yet critical designers are moving in a direction that others have not yet faced, giving an early warning for the path that design might be called upon to take in the future.

since 2000

CHAPTER 12

Extending Design

Design is being extended today in two widely disparate directions. One major focus of design extends beyond the production of objects, graphics, architecture, and interiors to the application of the design process to organizational structures, a pursuit of innovation that has become known as "design thinking." Design is no longer an exclusive hands-on activity but can also involve collaborations with outsiders from a range of institutions and organizations on conceptual and theoretical levels. In their 2011 preface to the MIT series of publications called "Design Thinking, Design Theory," Ken Friedman and Erik Stolterman described the wider and wider evolution of design into what is now called the "design sciences." "Today," they wrote, "the word *design* means many things. The common factor linking them is service: designers are engaged in a service profession in which the results of their work meet human needs." They attempt to see problems from a client's perspective and find practical solutions through collaborative engagement.

But at the same time, design is working in another direction on a broad grassroots level, bringing nontraditional designer-makers into areas formerly restricted to design and manufacturing professionals. The field is opening up to creative workers from different backgrounds and of all ages to revive a hands-on approach to design in what has become known as the "Maker Movement." With the founding of *Make Magazine* in 2005 and the first Maker Faire event in 2006, the movement has unfolded with a spirit of sharing and open-source collaboration.

Design Thinking

"More and more companies, governments, and institutions are turning towards the field of design for help," the Dutch designer and critic Kees Dorst has explained. "Designers have naturally been dealing with these kinds of complex, networked problems that involve multiple stakeholders for many years. And designers have been trained to come up with creative solutions that satisfy many of the relevant parties with their design solutions. Their 'design thinking' involves the creative exploration of problems and the creation of solutions that somehow overcome the paradoxes in the problem area that would be insurmountable using traditional problem-solving."

This new way of looking at design goes back to the development of human-centered design (or "user experience" [UX] design, a term also coined by Donald Norman) and the recognition that conventional design activities are part of larger systems. The experiences of the major international design firm IDEO, which in the 1990s worked out a new approach to innovation to aid their product planning as they became champions of human-centered design, had a great impact on this. For IDEO, "embracing human-centered design means believing that all problems, even the seemingly intractable ones like poverty, gender equality, and clean water, are solvable. Moreover, it means believing that the people who face those problems every day are the ones who hold the key to their answer. Human-centered design offers problem solvers of any stripe a chance to design with communities, to deeply understand the people they're looking to serve, to dream up scores of ideas, and to create innovative new solutions rooted in people's actual needs." An early, inside look at how their work was done was broadcast to the public on the American television program *Nightline* in 1999, when they successfully took the challenge of redesigning an ordinary shopping cart in five days. The program demonstrated their egalitarian, anti-corporate, somewhat chaotic teamwork process, which combined fieldwork, anthropology, group involvement, and equal respect for all those involved. Teamwork led them to make better decisions than any one of its individuals would have made alone, bringing a more nuanced understanding of problems and leading to more innovative proposals for their products. This method was widely discussed and adopted wholly or in part as a way to encourage innovation by many design firms, and aided by the publication of *Change by Design* by Tim Brown, CEO of IDEO, in 2009, it now has expanded to other areas, applied to the organization of institutions and corporations with the aid of design professionals.

The nonprofit arm of IDEO has followed through by making information about their design method freely available through their online courses and their "toolkit," *The Field Guide to Human-Centered Design* (2015), which can be downloaded by anyone without cost (Figure 12.1). It offers step-by-step instructions for creative design, from "inspiration" (conceptualizing a project, using various research tools) to "ideation" (brainstorming solutions) to "implementation" (testing, funding, and evaluating). This is a totally new look for the field of design, and IDEO, the agency that set much of this new approach going, now defines itself as "a global design company committed to creating positive impact" with a collaborative approach to human-centered design that lists products as only one part of its wide corporate mission. This refashioned role, and the broader possibilities, of

FIGURE 12.1.   IDEO, *The Field Guide to Human-Centered Design: Design Kit*, 2009.

the design profession demanded changes in design education, which in many schools now emphasizes theoretical studies, research, and team endeavors along with traditional workshops.

Design Making

While design thinking has brought design beyond the product and the maker, the Maker Movement has brought craftspeople, designer hopefuls, and amateurs back to the workbench in a major revival of the do-it-yourself movement. Rather than simply using hand tools and traditional materials to create their products, however, many among this new breed of craft workers rely on state-of-the-art equipment driven by smart software and digital files to work on robotics and other sophisticated projects using high-tech materials. A newfound accessibility to state-of-the-art tools of design and production, especially the result of the rapidly decreasing cost of three-dimensional printing during the second decade of the century, has turned areas of design and manufacturing from a professional and industrial activity into one that is open to all, much as the Macintosh personal computer (see Figure 9.9) turned widespread communication into an at-home or small-business activity when desktop printing and publishing became possible in the 1980s. With the rapid introduction of makerspaces, where individuals can avail themselves of such new technologies, design has also become the domain of users, and the intricate types of projects that were restricted to commercial production in the past because of the high cost of tools are now at the fingertips of virtually anyone.

Some design professionals have been supporting the universal accessibility of maker technology with projects created for nonprofessionals. Joris Laarman, for example, introduced a project in 2014 that he called "Makerchairs," free plans and instructions for creating chairs out of small components, which can be downloaded by anyone and printed or milled at local facilities and assembled into full-size objects. "We believe in the symbiosis of handcrafts and technology," he explained. "The Makerchairs fit right into that dream. All of the chairs are composed of digitally fabricated 3D parts that fit together exactly, like a three-dimensional puzzle. By fractioning designs into many small parts, we radically expanded the potential of small consumer 3D printers and CNC [computer numerical controlled] milling machines. Building these pieces out of small parts is essential, given the small building platforms of most affordable machines." He followed this up with his Bits & Parts initiative, a simpler, more affordable version (Figure 12.2), and then a still simpler one with which schools and community groups can teach maker skills to their students by allowing them to construct their own furniture from locally printed components.

The same mentality that wants to make objects often wants to change them, rejecting or reconfiguring products bought in stores or online. Furnishings from the major international retailer IKEA especially have been the source of such product vandalism. Founded in 1943 by Ingvar Kamprad (1926–2018), whose initials and those of the farm and village where he was raised made up the name of his company, IKEA was a mail-order business until 1958 (knock-down designs came only in 1956), when its first store in Sweden opened and eventually expanded throughout the world. Because users are already accustomed to putting flat-pack products together following IKEA's instructions, its relatively cheap items have been customized for years by makers who hack its objects with their own ideas for personalization, with hundreds of their practical projects being illustrated on dedicated websites such as Ikea Hackers (www.ikeahackers.net). To take control of this fad for remanufacturing its products, and to profit from it, IKEA introduced its own version of hacking in 2018. Its Delaktig sofa bed created with the British minimalist designer Tom Dixon

FIGURE 12.2.   Joris Laarman, Bits and Parts Chair, 2014. Resin.

(born 1959) supports add-ons for customization (Figure 12.3). Using Dixon's aluminum sofa frame as its base, a material chosen for its longevity, IKEA and Dixon came up with a range of add-ons for consumers to choose from. Ideas for other add-ons were also gathered from meetings and workshops with design schools across the world and the company has encouraged others to create add-ons as well (Figure 12.4).

Centering this upswing of do-it-yourself activity around maker facilities, whether commercial or nonprofit, popup spaces, or maker faires, has allowed the economy of large numbers to make sophisticated professional software and equipment available: 3-D printing machines, CNC milling machines, laser cutters, equipment for textile production, and many others. Makerspaces often offer training in the use of the equipment and classes for project design, furthering the accessibility of lay designers and students to the means of design and manufacture (Figure 12.5). Entrepreneurs and inventors have also used these spaces to produce prototypes of products that helped them start their own businesses with little expense, often

FIGURE 12.3.   Tom Dixon and Ikea, Delaktig Sofa Bed, 2018. Aluminum and upholstery.

Open Source IKEA

IKEA has designed a platform that allows designers—or anyone, really—to add to or modify its furniture. Here are some elements and variations.

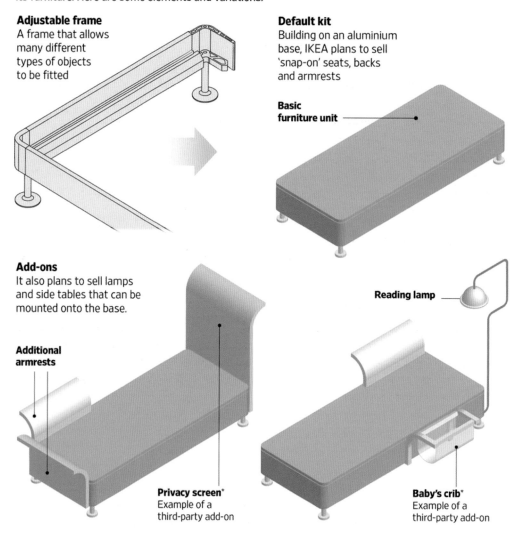

Adjustable frame
A frame that allows many different types of objects to be fitted

Default kit
Building on an aluminium base, IKEA plans to sell 'snap-on' seats, backs and armrests

Basic furniture unit

Add-ons
It also plans to sell lamps and side tables that can be mounted onto the base.

Reading lamp

Additional armrests

Privacy screen*
Example of a third-party add-on

Baby's crib*
Example of a third-party add-on

*Screen and crib were proposed designs from Royal Academy of Art students during an IKEA sponsored workshop
Note: Drawings are approximate and not to scale.   Source: the company

FIGURE 12.4.   Open Source Ikea: Ideas for variations of the Delaktig Sofa Bed, 2018.

SIDEBAR 26   Mark Hatch, "Maker Movement Manifesto," 2013

Make: Making is fundamental to what it means to be human. We must make, create, and express ourselves to feel whole. There is something unique about making physical things. These things are like little pieces of us and seem to embody portions of our souls.

Share: Sharing what you have made and what you know about making with others is the method by which a maker's feeling of wholeness is achieved. You cannot make and not share.

Give: There are few things more selfless and satisfying than giving away something you have made. The act of making puts a small piece of you in the object. Giving that to someone else is like giving someone a small piece of yourself. Such things are often the most cherished items we possess.

Learn: You must learn to make. You must always seek to learn more about your making. You may become a journeyman or master craftsman, but you will still learn, want to learn, and push yourself to learn new techniques, materials, and processes. Building a lifelong learning path ensures a rich and rewarding making life and, importantly, enables one to share.

Tool Up: You must have access to the right tools for the project at hand. Invest in and develop local access to the tools you need to do the making you want to do. The tools of making have never been cheaper, easier to use, or more powerful.

Play: Be playful with what you are making, and you will be surprised, excited, and proud of what you discover.

Participate: Join the Maker Movement and reach out to those around you who are discovering the joy of making. Hold seminars, parties, events, maker days, fairs, expos, classes, and dinners with and for the other makers in your community.

Support: This is a movement, and it requires emotional, intellectual, financial, political, and institutional support. The best hope for improving the world is us, and we are responsible for making a better future.

Change: Embrace the change that will naturally occur as you go through your maker journey. Since making is fundamental to what it means to be human, you will become a more complete version of you as you make.

with the support of crowdsourcing through the web. This energy has materialized from a large, idealistic Maker Movement, with its figurehead the management specialist Mark Hatch, who wrote a feel-good manifesto for it in 2013 (see Sidebar 26). As the CEO of TechShop, founded in 2006, he helped to turn an already established maker concept into a large and lucrative national do-it-yourself phenomenon. But his has been only one of a great many popular efforts launched to provide access to making through such spaces, now often supported by such institutions as schools and universities, which have universalized design and brought it into the hands of a new population of latter-day craftspeople, a throwback to the idealistic world of William Morris.

FIGURE 12.5.   A visitor watches a toy rocket being printed by a Makerbot 3-D printer at a popup makerspace in Virginia, 2017.

For Further Reading

Monographs on individual designers and manufacturers can be found by searching the catalogs of research libraries and the internet.

Art Nouveau: 1890–1914. London: Victoria and Albert Museum, 2000.

Aynsley, Jeremy. *Designing Modern Germany*. London: Reaktion, 2009.

Benton, Charlotte, Tim Benton, and Ghislaine Wood. *Art Deco 1910–1939*. Boston: Bulfinch, 2003.

Buckley, Cheryl. *Designing Modern Britain*. London: Reaktion, 2007.

Burke, Doreen Bolger. *In Pursuit of Beauty: Americans and the Aesthetic Movement*. New York: Metropolitan Museum of Art, 1986.

Cramsie, Patrick. *The Story of Graphic Design: From the Invention of Writing to the Birth of Digital Design*. New York: Abrams, 2010.

Didero, Maria Cristina. *Superdesign: Italian Radical Design 1965–75*. New York: Monacelli, 2017.

Droste, Magdalena. *Bauhaus 1919–1933*. Cologne: Taschen, 1993.

Dunne, Anthony, and Fiona Raby. *Speculative Everything: Design, Fiction, and Social Dreaming*. Cambridge, MA: MIT, 2013.

Fairs, Marcus, *21st Century Design: New Design Icons from Mass Market to Avant-Garde*. Rev. ed. London: Carlton, 2013.

Forest, Dominique. *The Art of Things: Product Design since 1945*. New York: Abbeville, 2015.

Forsey, Jane. *The Aesthetics of Design*. New York: Oxford University Press, 2013.

Gere, Charlotte, and Michael Whiteway. *Nineteenth-Century Design: From Pugin to Mackintosh*. New York: Abrams, 1994.

Guffey, Elizabeth E. *Retro: The Culture of Revival*. London: Reaktion, 2006.

Gura, Judith, and Charles Jencks. *Postmodern Design Complete*. London: Thames & Hudson, 2017.

Hiesinger, Kathryn B., and Felice Fischer. *Japanese Design: A Survey since 1950*. Philadelphia: Philadelphia Museum of Art, 1994.

Hiesinger, Kathryn B., and George H. Marcus. *Landmarks of Twentieth-Century Design: An Illustrated Handbook*. New York: Abbeville, 1993.

Hudson, Jennifer. *Process: 50 Product Designs from Concept to Manufacture*. London: Laurence King, 2008.

Hyde, Rory, et al. *The Future Starts Here*. London: Victoria and Albert Museum, 2018.

Jackson, Lesley. *Contemporary: Architecture and Interiors of the 1950s*. London: Phaidon, 1994.

Jackson, Lesley. *The New Look: Design in the Fifties*. New York: Thames and Hudson, 1991.

Kaplan, Wendy, and Alan Crawford. *The Arts & Crafts Movement in Europe & America: Design for the Modern World*. New York: Thames & Hudson in association with the Los Angeles County Museum of Art, 2004.

Kirkham, Pat. *Women Designers in the USA, 1900–2000: Diversity and Difference*. New York: Bard, 2000.

Kirkham, Pat, and Susan Weber. *History of Design: Decorative Arts and Material Culture, 1400–2000*. New Haven, CT: Yale University Press, 2013.

Marcus, George H. *Design in the Fifties: When Everyone Went Modern*. Munich: Prestel, 1998.

Marcus, George H. *Masters of Modern Design: A Critical Assessment*. New York: Monacelli, 2005.

Marcus, George H. *What Is Design Today?* New York: Abrams, 2002.

Meikle, Jeffrey L. *Design in the USA*. Oxford: Oxford University Press, 2005.

Meikle, Jeffrey L. *Twentieth Century Limited: Industrial Design in America, 1925–1939*. 2nd ed. Philadelphia: Temple University Press, 2001.

Newson, Alex, Eleanor Suggett, and Deyan Sudjic. *Designer Maker User*. London: Phaidon and the Design Museum, 2016.

Norman, Donald A. *The Design of Everyday Things*. Rev. ed. New York: Basic Books, 2013.

Pater, Ruben. *The Politics of Design: A (Not So) Global Design Manual for Visual Communication*. Amsterdam: BIS, 2016.

Petroski, Henry. *The Evolution of Useful Things*. New York: Knopf, 1992.

Pilloton, Emily. *Design Revolution: 100 Products That Empower People*. New York: Metropolis, 2009.

Pullin, Graham, *Design Meets Disability*. Cambridge, MA: MIT, 2009.

Radice, Barbara. *Memphis: Research, Experiences, Results, Failures, and Successes of New Design*. New York: Rizzoli, 1984.

Raizman, David Seth. *History of Modern Design*. 2nd ed. Upper Saddle River, NJ: Pearson Prentice Hall, 2011.

Snodin, Michael, and John Styles. *Design & the Decorative Arts: Britain, 1500–1900*. London: Victoria and Albert Museum, 2001.

Sparke, Penny. *Design in Italy: 1870 to the Present*. New York: Abbeville, 1988.

Sparke, Penny. *An Introduction to Design and Culture: 1900 to the Present*. 2nd ed. London: Routledge, 2004.

Wilk, Christopher. *Modernism: Designing a New World: 1914–1939*. London: Victoria and Albert Museum, 2006.

Wilson, Richard Guy, Dianne H. Pilgrim, and Dickran Tashjian. *The Machine Age in America, 1918–1941*. New York: Abrams, 1986.

Woodham, Jonathan M. *Twentieth Century Design*. Oxford: Oxford University Press, 1997.

Sources for Sidebar Excerpts

Sidebar 1
Adam Smith, "The Division of Labour," in *Inquiry into the Nature and Causes of the Wealth of Nations* [1776], ed. Edwin Cannan, vol. 1, p. 5. London: Methuen, 1904.

Sidebar 2
William Morris, "The Lesser Arts" [1877], in *The Collected Works of William Morris*, vol. 22, pp. 4–5. London: Longmans Green, 1914.

Sidebar 3
Candace Wheeler, "The Philosophy of Beauty Applied to House Interiors," in *Household Art*, pp. 13–14. New York: Harper & Brothers, 1893.

Sidebar 4
Henry van de Velde, "A Chapter on the Design and Construction of Modern Furniture" [1897], in *Form and Function: A Source Book for the History of Architecture and Design 1890–1939*, eds. Tim and Charlotte Benton, pp. 18–19. London: Crosby Lockwood Staples in association with the Open University Press, 1975.

Sidebar 5
Walter Gropius, Program of the Staatliche Bauhaus im Weimar [1919], in Hans M. Wingler, *The Bauhaus: Weimar Dessau Berlin Chicago*, p. 31. Cambridge, MA: MIT, 1969.

Sidebar 6
Peter Behrens, "Art in Technology" [1907], in Tilmann Buddensieg, *Industriekultur: Peter Behrens and the AEG, 1907–1914*, p. 208. Cambridge, MA: MIT, 1984.

Sidebar 7
Hermann Muthesius, Proposals at the Congress of the German Werkbund [1914], in *Documents: A Collection of Source Material on the Modern Movement*, ed. Charlotte Benton, p. 5. Milton Keynes, England: Open University Press, 1975.

Sidebar 8
Le Corbusier, "Eyes Which Do Not See: Automobiles" [1923], in *Towards a New Architecture*, pp. 133–38. New York: Payson & Clarke, 1927.

Sidebar 9
Theo van Doesburg, "The Will to Style" [1922], in *Form and Function: A Source Book for the History of Architecture and Design 1890–1939*, eds. Tim and Charlotte Benton, pp. 93–94. London: Crosby Lockwood Staples in association with the Open University Press, 1975.

Sidebar 10
Walter Gropius, "Bauhaus Dessau—Principles of Bauhaus Production" [1926], in Hans M. Wingler, *The Bauhaus: Weimar Dessau Berlin Chicago*, p. 110. Cambridge, MA: MIT, 1969.

Sidebar 11
Norman Bel Geddes, *Horizons*, pp. 44–45. Boston: Little, Brown, 1932.

Sidebar 12
Raymond Loewy, "The Maya Stage," in *Never Leave Well Enough Alone*, pp. 277–78. New York: Simon and Schuster, 1951.

Sidebar 13
Roland Barthes, "Plastic" [1955], in *Mythologies*, pp. 98–99. New York: Hill and Wang, 1972.

Sidebar 14
Edgar Kaufmann, Jr., "Twelve Precepts of Modern Design," in *What Is Modern Design?*, p. 7. New York: Museum of Modern Art, 1950.

Sidebar 15
Josef Müller-Brockmann, *Grid Systems in Graphic Design*, p. 10. Sulgen, Switzerland: Niggli, 1981.

Sources for Sidebar Excerpts

Sidebar 16

Dieter Rams, Speech at the International Marketing Meeting, 1976, in François Burkhardt and Inez Franksen, eds., *Design: Dieter Rams &*, p. 187. West Berlin: Gerhardt, 1980–81.

Sidebar 17

Achille Castiglioni, Design Survey [1965], in Sergio Polano, *Achille Castiglioni: Complete Works*, p. 448. Milan: Electa, 2001.

Sidebar 18

Emilio Ambasz, introduction, *Italy: The New Domestic Landscape*, pp. 19–20. New York: Museum of Modern Art, 1972.

Sidebar 19

Robert Venturi, "Nonstraightforward Architecture: A Gentle Manifesto," in *Complexity and Contradiction in Architecture*, p. 22. New York: Museum of Modern Art, 1966.

Sidebar 20

Ettore Sottsass, Jr., interview, n.p. Memphis catalogue, Milan, 1982.

Sidebar 21

Gert Selle, "There Is No Kitsch, There Is Only Design!" *Design Issues*, vol. 1, no. 1 (1984), p. 49.

Sidebar 22

Klaus Krippendorff and Reinhart Butter, "Semantics: Meanings and Contexts of Artifacts," in *Product Experience*, H. N. J. Schifferstein and P. Hekkert, eds., p. 354. New York: Elsevier, 2007.

Sidebar 23

R. Buckminster Fuller, *Operating Manual for Spaceship Earth* [1969], pp. 122–24. New York: E. P. Dutton, 1978.

Sidebar 24

Center for Universal Design, Seven Principles of Universal Design, 1977, Version 2.0. Raleigh, NC: North Carolina State University, https://projects.ncsu.edu/design/cud/about_ud/udprinciplestext.htm.

Sidebar 25

Anthony Dunne and Fiona Raby, "Design as Critique," in *Speculative Everything: Design, Fiction, and Social Dreaming*, pp. 34–35. Cambridge, MA: MIT, 2013.

Sidebar 26

Mark Hatch, "Maker Movement Manifesto," in *The Maker Movement Manifesto: Rules for Innovation in the New World of Crafters, Hackers, and Tinkerers*, pp. 1–2. New York: McGraw Hill, 2013.

References for Quotations

Preface

"a pivoted blade . . . peeling stroke" p. 9
U. S. Patent 2,232,940, February 25, 1941.

Chapter 1

"Ornament . . . possess" p. 16
Christopher Dresser, *The Art of Decorative Design*, p. 1.
    London: Day and Son, 1862.

"The excellent . . . almost universal" p. 18
London, International Exhibition, Juror's Reports, 1862, Class
    XXX, p. 5. London: Bell & Daldy, 1862.

"such . . . cannot Err" p. 19
Josiah Wedgwood, Letter to Thomas Bentley, October 7, 1769,
    in Ann Finer and George Savage, eds., *The Selected Letters
    of Josiah Wedgwood*, pp. 82–83. London: Cory, Adams &
    Mackay, 1965.

"A large number . . . are insured" p. 25
Samuel Colt, "On the Application of Machinery . . ." [1851], in
    Charles T. Haven and Frank A. Belden, *A History of the Colt
    Revolver*, p. 319. New York: Bonanza Books, 1940.

"It will ever . . . comforts of life" p. 27
H. W. and A. Arrowsmith, *The House Decorator & Painter's
    Guide*, pp. 111–12. London: Thomas Kelly, 1840.

"From this manufacture . . . characterless age" p. 29
Richard Redgrave, "Supplementary Report on Design," in
    *Exhibition of the Works of Industry of All Nations, 1851:
    Reports of the Juries*, p. 713. London: William Clowes, 1852.

"Gentleman . . . exertions" p. 30
Prince Albert, Speech, 1851, *Journal of the Society of Arts*,
    November 21, 1862, p. 7.

"painted windows . . . this epoch" p. 34–35
In M. F. Hearn, ed., *The Architectural Theory of Viollet-le Duc*,
    p. 287. Cambridge, MA: MIT, 1990.

"The Sculptor . . . can impart" p. 35
Catalogue, Patent Wood Carving Company, 1848, reproduced
    in Rosamond Allwood, "Machine Carving of the 1840s,
    and the Catalogue of the Patent Wood Carving Company,"
    Furniture History, vol. 32 (1996), Figure 4.

The great . . . was erected" p. 36
A. W. N. Pugin, *Contrasts: or, a Parallel between the Noble
    Edifices of the Fourteenth and Fifteenth Centuries, and Similar
    Buildings of the Present Day; Shewing the Present Decay of
    Taste* [1836], p. 1. 2nd ed. London: Charles Dolman, 1841.

"It is impossible . . . the result" p. 36
Richard Redgrave, "Supplementary Report on Design," in
    *Exhibition of the Works of Industry of All Nations, 1851:
    Reports of the Juries*, p. 708. London: William Clowes, 1852.

"There has . . . imitate it" p. 37
Richard Redgrave, "Supplementary Report on Design," in
    *Exhibition of the Works of Industry of All Nations, 1851:
    Reports of the Juries*, p. 710. London: William Clowes, 1852.

"must consist . . . the noblest" p. 37
John Ruskin, *The Seven Lamps of Architecture*, pp. 106–7.
    London: Smith, Elder, 1849.

"absurdities . . . over door" p. 38
A. W. N. Pugin, *The True Principles of Pointed or Christian
    Architecture*, p. 25. London: J. Weale, 1841.

"to obtain . . . outlines" p. 38
Henry Cole, *Fifty Years of Public Work of Sir Henry Cole,
    K.C.B.*, vol. 2, pp. 178–79. London: George Bell, 1884.

"to produce . . . from nature" p. 39
Henry Cole, *Fifty Years of Public Work of Sir Henry Cole,
    K.C.B.*, vol. 2, p. 108. London: George Bell, 1884.

Chapter 2

"We have . . . advantages" p. 42–43
John Ruskin, "The Nature of Gothic," in *The Stones of Venice*,
    vol. 2, p. 165. London: Smith Eden, 1853.

"have nothing . . . beautiful" p. 45
William Morris, "Beauty of Life" [1880], in *The Collected Works
    of William Morris*, vol. 22, p. 76. London: Longmans Green,
    1914.

"The aim . . . the people" p. 47
The Century Guild Hobby Horse, no. 5 (January 1887), n.p.

"Modern civilization . . . recognize this" p. 48
C.R. Ashbee, *Should We Stop Teaching Art*, p. 2. London: B. T. Batsford, 1911.

"deepening conviction . . . civilization" p. 48–49
Frank Lloyd Wright, "The Art and Craft of the Machine" [1901], in *Collected Writings*, ed. Bruce Brooks Pfeiffer, vol. 1, p. 59. New York: Rizzoli, 1992.

"The essence . . . effect much" p. 50
Walter Hamilton, *The Aesthetic Movement in England*, p. vii. 3rd ed. London: Reeves and Turner, 1882.

"No mouldings . . . broken outline" p. 51
E. W. Godwin, "My Chambers and What I Did to Them" [1876], in *Is Mr. Ruskin Living Too Long: Selected Writings of E. W. Godwin*, pp. 195–96. Oxford: White Cockade, 2005.

"The inevitable . . . of gold" p. 53
Elizabeth Williams Perry, "Decorative Pottery of Cincinnati," *Harper's New Monthly Magazine*, 1881, p. 837, in Nancy Owen, *Rookwood and the Industry of Art*, pp. 146–47. Athens, OH: Ohio University Press, 2001.

"an artist's . . . a factory" p. 53
Nancy Owen, *Rookwood and the Industry of Art*, p. 93. Athens, OH: Ohio University Press, 2001.

"The effect . . . with ornament" p. 55
Artistic Houses, vol. 1, pt. 2, p. 113. New York: D. Appleton, 1883.

"rendering . . . supernatural light" p. 57
Siegfried Bing, "Louis C. Tiffany's Coloured Glass Work," in *Artistic America, Tiffany Glass, and Art Nouveau*, p. 211. Cambridge, MA: MIT, 1970.

"The rain . . . is here" p. 59–60
Theophile Gautier, "What the Swallows Say," translated by the Corning Museum of Glass, www.cmog.org/artwork/la-pluie-au-bassin-fait-des-bulles-rain-splashes-basin?search=collection%3A4386f13f90ae4d72d919c57834c21718&page=4.

"We will seek . . . at any cost" p. 62
Josef Hoffmann and Koloman Moser, Working Program, in Werner J. Schweiger, *Wiener Werkstätte: Design in Vienna, 1903–1932*, p. 42. New York: Abbeville, 1984.

Chapter 3

"The idea . . . nothing else" p. 66
Hermann Muthesius, "The Problem of Form in Engineering," in Tim Benton, comp., *Form and Function: A Source Book for the History of Architecture and Design 1890–1939*, p. 66. London: Crosby Lockwood Staples, 1975.

"First of all . . . daring colors" p. 67–68
André Mare, 1912, in Nancy Troy, *Modernism and the Decorative Arts in France,"* p. 72. New Haven, CT: Yale, 1991.

"urge to ornament . . . are ruined" p. 68
Adolf Loos, "Ornament and Crime," [1908], in Arts Council of Great Britain, *The Architecture of Adolf Loos*, pp. 100–103. London: Arts Council of Great Britain, 1985.

"chairs to sit . . . write with" p. 70
Le Corbusier, *Decorative Art of Today*, p. 75. Cambridge, MA: MIT, 1987.

"The present . . . by hand" p. 71
Frank Lloyd Wright, "In the Cause of Architecture" [1908], in *Collected Writings*, ed. Bruce Brooks Pfeiffer, vol. 1, p. 97. New York: Rizzoli, 1992.

"to promote . . . socialistic sense" p. 73
Gustav Stickley, foreword, *The Craftsman*, vol. 1, no. 1 (October 1901), p. i.

"Their constituent . . . its production" p. 76–77
L. Deubner, "German Architecture and Decoration," in *"The Studio" Yearbook of Decorative Art*, pp. 93–94. London: The Studio, 1914.

"By his . . . a canon" p. 80
Henry van de Velde, "Counter-Propositions," Proposals and Discussions at the Congress of the German Werkbund, 1914, in Charlotte Benton, ed., *Documents: A Collection of Source Material on the Modern Movement*, p. 6. Milton Keynes, England: Open University Press, 1975.

"meticulously fixed . . . etc., etc.)" p. 82
Le Corbusier, *Almanach d'architecture moderne*, p. 112. Paris: G. Grès, 1926.

"The beginnings . . . ever complained" p. 84
Christine Frederick, *The New Housekeeping: Efficiency Studies in Home Management*, p. ix. Garden City, NY: Doubleday, 1913.

Chapter 4

"we live . . . purely pictorial" p. 89
Quoted by G. S. Sandilands, *Commercial Art*, vol. 3, no.13 (July 1927), reprinted in Brian Webb and Peyton Skipwith, *E. McKnight Kauffer: Design*, p. 19. Woodbridge, England: Antique Collectors' Club, 2007.

"The first . . . Picasso abstraction" p. 91
Helen Appleton Read, "The Exposition in Paris," *International Studio*, vol. 82 (November 1925), p. 96.

"open to all . . . modern tendencies" p. 92
In Victor Arwas, *Art Deco*, p. 13. New York: Abrams, 1980.

"American manufacturers . . . modern spirit" p. 92
International Exposition of Modern Decorative and Industrial
    Art, Paris, *Report of Commission* (Washington, DC, 1925),
    p. 16.

"socially useful . . . use" p. 93
Christina Lodder, *Russian Constructivism*, p. 135. New Haven,
    CT: Yale, 1983.

"the craziest . . . in glassware" p. 94
In Thomas A. Jiamachello, "Reuben Haley: 20th Century Glass
    Master," http://www.pcgcc.org/articles/people/38-people.

"A thing . . . machined materials" p. 101
In Paul Overy, "Carpentering the Classic: A Very Peculiar
    Practice," *Journal of Design History*, vol. 4, no. 3 (1991), p.
    157.

Chapter 5

"genuine . . . century" p. 103
Nikolaus Pevsner, *Pioneers of Modern Design* [1936], p. 38. 3rd
    ed. Harmondsworth, England: Penguin, 1974.

"expression . . . flaw" p. 104
Lewis Mumford, *Technics and Civilization*, pp. 350–51. New
    York: Harcourt, Brace, 1934.

"The designing . . . as such" p. 104
R. Rowand Anderson, address to the Architectural Section of
    the National Association for the Advancement of Art and
    Its Application to Industry, *The Builder*, November 9, 1889,
    p. 324.

"We affirm . . . orbit" p. 105
Filippo Tommaso Marinetti, "The Founding and Manifesto
    of Futurism" [1909], in *Futurist Manifestos*, ed. Umbro
    Apollonio, p. 21. New York: Viking, 1973.

"Is not . . . human drama?" p. 105
Enrico Prampolini, "The Aesthetic of the Machine and
    Mechanical Introspection in Art," *Broom*, vol. 3, no. 3
    (October 1922), p. 236.

"does not . . . mass production" p. 106
Walter Gropius, "The Theory and Organization of the
    Bauhaus" [1923], in Herbert Bayer, Walter Gropius, and
    Ise Gropius, eds., *Bauhaus: 1919–1928*, p. 27. New York:
    Museum of Modern Art, 1938.

"Dealers . . . handicrafts" p. 108
In Magdalena Droste, *Bauhaus, 1919–1933*, p. 80. Cologne:
    Taschen, 1993.

"we don't embroider cushions here" p. 115
In Charlotte Perriand, *A Life of Creation*, p. 25. New York:
    Monacelli, 2003.

"Why . . . decorative art?" p. 115
Le Corbusier, *The Decorative Art of Today*, p. 24. Cambridge,
    MA: MIT, 1987.

"capable . . . resting" p. 116
French patent no. 672.824, received September 24, 1929.

"utter inhumanity" p. 116
John Gloag, "Wood or Metal?" *The Studio*, vol. 97 (1929), p. 49.

"New aesthetic . . . REVOLUTION" p. 116
Charlotte Perriand, "Wood or Metal?" *The Studio*, vol. 97
    (1929), p. 279.

"is cold . . . the eye" p. 116
John Gloag, "Wood or Metal?" *The Studio*, vol. 97 (1929), p. 49.

"If we . . . geometrically" p. 118
Hugo Häring, "Approaches to Form" [1925], in Christopher
    Wilk, *Modernism: Designing a New World 1914–1939*, p.
    323. London: V & A, 2006.

"Tubular . . . sanatorium" p. 118
Museum of Finnish Architecture, *Alvar Aalto Furniture*, p. 118.
    Cambridge, MA: MIT, 1985.

"Like . . . Arp" p. 120
John McAndrew, foreword, *Architecture and Furniture: Aalto*, p.
    3. New York: Museum of Modern Art, 1938.

Chapter 6

"lipsticks to locomotives" p. 121
Raymond Loewy, *Never Leave Well Enough Alone*, cover. New
    York: Simon and Schuster, 1951.

"consumer engineering . . . merely use" p. 121–122
Earnest Elmo Calkins, "What Consumer Engineering
    Really Is," in Roy Sheldon and Egmont Arens, *Consumer
    Engineering*, pp. 1, 5, 13. New York: Harper and Brothers,
    1932.

"America's triumphs . . . offered today" p. 122
Christine Frederick, *Selling Mrs. Consumer*, p. 245. New York:
    Business Bourse, 1929.

"We want . . . obsolete" p. 122–123
Henry Ford, *My Life and Work*, p. 149. New York: Doubleday,
    Page, 1923.

"Originally . . . men's shoes" p. 126
Norman Bel Geddes, "Streamlining," *Atlantic Monthly*,
    November 1934, p. 553.

"the substitution . . . same time" p. 127
Harold van Doren, "Streamlining," in *Industrial Design: A Practical Guide*, pp. 139. New York: McGraw Hill, 1940.

"the chasm . . . noise" p. 127
Raymond Loewy, *Industrial Design: Raymond Loewy*, p. 10. Woodstock, NY: Overbrook Press, 1979.

"The beauty . . . 'pure pleasures'" p. 128–130
Alfred H. Barr, Jr., foreword, in Philip Johnson, *Machine Art*, n.p. New York: Museum of Modern Art, 1934.

"The process . . . gratifying harmony" p. 130–131
Walter Dorwin Teague, *Design This Day: The Technique of Order in the Machine Age*, pp. 123–24. New York: Harcourt Brace, 1940.

Chapter 7

"extraordinary lustre and soft, smooth surface" p. 144
Edward Kaufmann, Jr., *Prize Designs for Modern Furniture from the International Competition for Low-Cost Furniture*, p. 20. New York: Museum of Modern Art, 1950.

"if you have . . . what they do" p. 144–145
Elizabeth Gordon, "Fine Art for 39¢," *House Beautiful*, vol. 89 (October 1947), p. 131.

"What best . . . chemical-looking ones" p. 145
Roland Barthes, "Plastic" [1955], in *Mythologies*, p. 98. New York: Hill and Wang, 1972.

"compelled . . . that fit" p. 146
George Nelson, "Problems of Design: Modern Decoration," *Interiors*, vol. 109 (November 1949), p. 77.

"eye appeal . . . the first" p. 149
Museum of Modern Art, New York, *Good Design*, inside cover. New York: Museum of Modern Art, 1953.

"to clear up . . . unrestful world" p. 152
Eero Saarinen, in Aline B. Saarinen, ed., *Eero Saarinen on His Work*, p. 66. New Haven, CT: Yale, 1962.

"In the IBM company . . . good business" p. 153
Thomas Watson. Jr., "Good Design is Good Business" [1975], in Michael Bierut et al., eds., *Looking Closer 3: Classic Writings on Graphic Design*, p. 250. New York: Allworth Press, 1999.

"primarily for . . . European automobiles" p. 154
Museum of Modern Art, New York, *10 Automobiles*, pp. 1, 2, 10. New York: Museum of Modern Art, 1953.

"In aesthetics . . . Technological Century" p. 155–157
Reyner Banham, "Vehicles of Desire" [1955], in *A Critic Writes*, p. 6. Berkeley: University of California Press, 1996.

"strive for . . . power of technology" p. 157
In Kathryn B. Hiesinger, ed., *Japanese Design*, p. 48. Philadelphia: Philadelphia Museum of Art, 1994.

"shift from . . . to convenient" p. 161–162
Gio Ponti, 1952, in Andrea Branzi and Michele De Lucchi, eds., *Il design italiano degli anni '50*, p. 296. Milan: IGIS, 1981.

"The school . . . industrial companies" p. 165
Ulm [Hochschule für Gestaltung], no. 1 (October 1958), p. 1.

Chapter 8

"a complex . . . modern experience" p. 168
Robert Venturi, *Complexity and Contradiction in Architecture*, pp. 22–23. New York: Museum of Modern Art, 1966.

"astonishing . . . other materials" p. 169
"The Year in Plastics," *Industrial Design*, vol. 7, no. 9 (September 1960), p. 70.

"for use . . . unpretentious toy" p. 172–173
Ettore Sottsass, Jr., *Abitare* (1969), in Frederick S. Wight Art Gallery, University of California, Los Angeles, *Design Process: Olivetti, 1908–1978*, p. 120. Los Angeles, 1979.

"It is adaptable . . . making love" p. 175
Gatti, Paolini, Teodoro, promotional text, 1969, revised 1981, in Katherine B. Hiesinger and George H. Marcus, *Landmarks of Twentieth-Century Design*, p. 238. New York: Abbeville, 1993.

"Design is . . . market" p. 177
Achille Castiglioni, [1965], in Sergio Polano, *Achille Castiglioni: Complete Works*, p. 453. Milan: Electa, 2001.

"three . . . design" p. 178
Emilio Ambasz, introduction, *Italy: The New Domestic Landscape*, p. 19. New York: Museum of Modern Art, 1972.

"were asked . . . production" p. 178
Emilio Ambasz, ed., Environments, *Italy: The New Domestic Landscape*, p. 137. New York: Museum of Modern Art, 1972.

"necessary to create . . . arrangement" p. 178
Joe Colombo, in Emilio Ambasz, ed., *Italy: The New Domestic Landscape*, p. 172. New York: Museum of Modern Art, 1972.

"the need . . . our society" p. 179
Emilio Ambasz, ed., *Italy: The New Domestic Landscape*, p. 137.
    New York: Museum of Modern Art, 1972.

"a critical . . . symbolical images" p. 179
Superstudio, in Emilio Ambasz, ed., *Italy: The New Domestic
    Landscape*, p. 242. New York: Museum of Modern Art,
    1972.

"the designing . . . paradise" p. 180
Superstudio, in Emilio Ambasz, ed., *Italy: The New Domestic
    Landscape*, p. 251. New York: Museum of Modern Art,
    1972.

"it may occur . . . the planet" p. 180
Ettore Sottsass, Jr., *Design Metaphors*, p. 9. New York: Rizzoli,
    1988.

"wanted to show . . . own dignity" p. 181–182
Alessandro Mendini, Interview, in Aileen Kwun and Bryn
    Smith, *Twenty over Eighty: Conversations on a Lifetime
    of Architecture and Design*, p. 121. New York: Princeton
    Architectural Press, 2016.

"all it admits . . . modern architecture" p. 182
Charles Jencks, *The Language of Post-Modern Architecture*, p. 7.
    New York: Rizzoli, 1977.

"use to . . . time or place" p. 184
Smithsonian Institution, Washington, DC, *Signs of Life:
    Symbols in the American City*, n.p. Washington, DC:
    Renwick Gallery, 1976.

"What I propose . . . Modern movement" p. 185
Robert Venturi, in David B. Brownlee, David G. De Long, and
    Katherine B. Hiesinger, *Out of the Ordinary: Robert Venturi,
    Denise Scott Brown and Associates: Architecture, Urbanism,
    Design*, pp. 201–2. Philadelphia: Philadelphia Museum of
    Art, 2001.

"Everything today . . . important step" p. 188
Michele De Lucchi, Statement [1979], Archivio Michele De
    Lucchi, http://www.archive.amdl.it/.

"Unorganized areas . . . in gestation" p. 189
Ettore Sottsass, Jr., Memphis catalogue, n.p. Milan: Memphis,
    1982.

Chapter 9

"the chance . . . expenditure" p. 193
Alessi Miniatures, promotional description, http://wss01.
    alessi.com/en/products/detail/miniature-miniatures.

"My job . . . experiences" p. 194–195
Philippe Starck Biography, https://www.starck.com/about.

"own style of decoration" p. 199
Shiro Kuramata, in *Shiro Kuramata: 1934–1991*, p. 181.
    Tokyo: Hara Museum of Contemporary Art, 1996.

"about solving . . . emotionally" p. 201
Karim Rashid, Karimanifesto, http://www.karimrashid.com/
    karimanifesto.

"indicated that . . . (Emotionally)" p. 203
Robert Blaich, Interview, 2007, http://www.design-emotion.
    com/2007/04/12/getting-emotional-with-robert-blaich/.

"so integrated . . . producer" p. 205
Alvin Toffler, *The Third Wave*, p. 201. New York: Morrow,
    1980.

"structure . . . design" p. 205
Frank Gehry, interview, *Architectural Record*, 1992, https://
    www.knoll.com/designer/Frank-Gehry.

"tried . . . real bad" p. 208
Stefan Sagmeister, interview, 2016, https://creativepro.com/
    typetalk-the-typographic-expressions-of-stefan-sagmeister/.

Chapter 10

"There are . . . close second" p. 210
Victor Papanek, *Design for the Real World: Human Ecology and
    Social Change*, p. xxi. New York: Pantheon, 1971.

"to empower . . . through education" p. 210
One Laptop Per Child, http://one.laptop.org/about/mission.

"I can use . . . water faucets" p. 211
Donald Norman, preface, *The Design of Everyday Things*
    [1988], p. xviii. Rev. ed. New York: Basic Books, 2013.

"future moral . . . has changed" p. 211–212
Philippe Starck, "French Visionary Stark's Advice to Designers:
    Create Fewer Useless Products," *Wired*, July 19, 2011,
    https://www.wired.com/2011/07/philippe-starck-design/.

"caravan . . . purposes." p. 212–213
Philippe Starck, "Les Ideas Box," https://www.youtube.com/
    watch?v=Q9u7Saczcqw.

"We are . . . WHOLE EARTH CATALOG" p. 215
Stewart Brand, *Whole Earth Catalog*, n.p. 1968.

"national . . . environment" p. 216
Gaylord Nelson, 1970, http://www.nelsonearthday.net/earth-
    day/index.php.

"the realization . . . advantage" p. 218
R. Buckminster Fuller, *Operating Manual for Spaceship Earth* [1969], p. 122. New York: E. P. Dutton, 1978.

"We begin with . . . assure purchase" p. 221
Henry Dreyfuss, *Designing for People*, p. 219. New York: Simon & Schuster, 1955.

"for the designer's . . . extremely rare" p. 222
Henry Dreyfuss, *The Measure of Man: Human Factors in Design*, p. 5. 2nd ed. New York: Whitney Library of Design, 1967.

"If you . . . each other" p. 223
Ronald L. Mace, "A Perpspective on Universal Design, 1998, https://projects.ncsu.edu/design/cud/about_us/usronmacespeech.htm.

"Disability-related . . . thing of all" p. 226
"Graham Pullin—Disability-Related Design," https://www.vandadundee.org/news-and-blog/blog/graham-pullin—disability-related-design.

Chapter 11

"Wallpaper, hooks, . . . so they did" p. 241
Front, Wallpaper by Rat, http://frontdesign.se/wallpaper-rat-project.

"This project . . . future" p. 242
http://www.robertstadler.net/all/limited/Rest-in-Peace/.

"is about . . . engage people" p. 243
Anthony Dunne and Fiona Raby, "Design as Critique" (excerpt), from *Speculative Everything: Design, Fiction, and Social Dreaming*, p. 35. Cambridge, MA: MIT, 2013.

"What if . . . and insects?" p. 243
Dunne &Fiona Raby, http://www.dunneandraby.co.uk/content/projects/510/0.

Chapter 12

"Today. . . human needs" p. 244
Ken Friedman and Erik Stolterman, series foreword, in Mads Nygaard Folkmann, *The Aesthetics of Imagination in Design*, p. ix. Cambridge, MA: MIT, 2013.

"More . . . problem solving" p. 244
Kees Dorst, "Design Intelligence," in Sharon Poggenpohl and Keiichi Sato, *Design Integrations: Research and Collaboration*, pp. 278–79. Chicago: University of Chicago Press, 2009.

"embracing . . . actual needs" p. 245
IDEO.org., *The Field Guide to Human Centered Design*, p. 9. IDEO, 2015.

"a global . . . positive impact" p. 245
"About IDEO," https://www.ideo.com/about.

"We . . . machines" p. 246
Joris Laarman, Maker Chairs, http://www.jorislaarman.com/work/makechairs/.

Image Credits

All reasonable attempts have been made to trace copyright holders of images and to obtain their permission for the use of copyright material. Images without specific credit have been determined to be in the public domain or the publisher has been unable to trace the copyright holder. The publisher apologizes for any errors or omissions in copyright acknowledgment and would be grateful if notified of any corrections that should be incorporated in future reprints or editions of this book.

Preface
0.1 Guy Corbishley/Alamy Live News
0.2 Images courtesy of IDEO
0.3 Author photograph
0.5 Courtesy of Oxo
0.7 Philippe Starck
0.8 © Neil Godwin/T3 Magazine via Getty Images

Chapter 1
1.1 The Metropolitan Museum of Art. Purchase, Friends of European Sculpture and Decorative Arts Gifts and The Charles E. Sampson Memorial Fund, 2006
1.2 Photo by DeAgostini/Getty Images
1.3 Photo by Universal History Archive/UIG via Getty Images
1.4 The Metropolitan Museum of Art, Robert A. Ellison Jr. Collection, Gift of Robert A. Ellison Jr., 2014 - public domain
1.5 © The Trustees of the British Museum
1.6 Division of Work and Industry, National Museum of American History, Smithsonian Institution
1.7 Metropolitan Museum of Art - Gift of John E. Parsons, 1968 - public domain
1.8 © Victoria and Albert Museum, London
1.9 Harris Brisbane Dick Fund, 1925
1.10 Courtesy of the University of Pennsylvania
1.11 Photo by SSPL/Getty Images
1.12 Photo by SSPL/Getty Images
1.13 The Metropolitan Museum of Art. Robert Lehman Collection, 1975
1.14 Courtesy of New York Public Library

1.15 Metropolitan Museum of Art, Purchase, Cynthia Hazen Polsky Gift, 1994 - public domain
1.16 The Metropolitan Museum of Art. Eugène-Emmanuel Viollet-le-Duc (French, Paris 1814–1879 Lausanne), Gift of Louis de Bayser, 2007
1.17 Photo by © Hulton-Deutsch Collection/CORBIS/ Corbis via Getty Images
1.18 The Metropolitan Museum of Art. Owen Jones (British, London 1809–1874 London), Purchase, Rogers Fund, 2003
1.19 © Victoria and Albert Museum, London
1.20 Metropolitan Museum of Art, Purchase, Gift of Irwin Untermyer, by exchange, 2015 - public domain
1.21 Metropolitan Museum of Art - Rogers Fund, 1963- public domain
1.22 Mintons Ltd. (England, Staffordshire, Stoke-on-Trent, founded 1793), Henry Cole (England, 1808-1882) England, 1846 Earthenware Teapot, Purchased with funds provided by Mr. and Mrs. Russell A. McKinnon (M.2001.19.2a-b). Provided by www.lacma.org
1.23 Scan provided by Rawpixel, shared under the Creative Commons licence (CC BY-SA)
1.24 Scan provided by Rawpixel, shared under the Creative Commons licence (CC BY-SA)

Chapter 2
2.1 Author photograph
2.2 V&A Images/Alamy Stock Photo
2.3 © Victoria and Albert Museum, London
2.4 The Modernism Collection, gift of Norwest Bank Minnesota. Minneapolis Institute of Art
2.5 The Frank P. Leslie Collection, Gift of Mr. and Mrs. Frank P. Leslie in memory of Mr. and Mrs. John Leslie. Minneapolis Institute of Art
2.6 Los Angeles County Museum of Art, Gift of Max Palevsky and Jodie Evans (M.91.375.60a-c); Photo © Museum Associates/LACMA
2.7 © Victoria and Albert Museum, London
2.8 © Victoria and Albert Museum, London
2.9 Photo by: Christophel Fine Art/UIG via Getty Images
2.10 Metropolitan Museum of Art - Gift of Robert L. Isaacson, 1988 - public domain

2.11 Metropolitan Museum of Art - Gift of Marcia and William Goodman, 1981 - public domain

2.12 Wheeler, Candace (1827-1923): Tulips Panel, 1883-87. (Maker: for Associated Artists, 1883-1907; Manufacturer: Ground fabric by, Cheney Brothers, 1838-1955). New York, Metropolitan Museum of Art. Silk and metallic cloth appliqued with silk velvet and embroidered with silk and metallic-wrapped cotton threads, 74 x 50 1/2 in. (188.0 cm x 128.3 cm). Gift of family of Mrs. Candace Wheeler, 1928. Acc.n.: 28.34.2 © 2018. Image copyright The Metropolitan Museum of Art/Art Resource/Scala, Florence

2.13 Metropolitan Museum of Art - public domain

2.14 The Metropolitan Museum of Art. Harris Brisbane Dick Fund, 1992

2.15 Designed by Louis Comfort Tiffany (American, New York 1848–1933 New York), Gift of H. O. Havemeyer, 1896. The Metropolitan Museum of Art

2.16 Courtesy of CIVA Brussels

2.17 Velde, Henri van de (1863-1957): Side chair, ca. 1898 - Front. Manufacturer: Societe Van de Velde & Company, Belgium. The design of this chair goes back to van de Velde's 'new style', presented to the public at Bloemenwerf, the home he designed and built for himself in 1895 in the Brussels suburb of Uccles. New York, Metropolitan Museum of Art. Elm, leather, brass. H. 37 5/8 in. (95.6 cm). Gift of Jacqueline Loewe Fowler, 2011 (2011.234).© 2018. Image copyright The Metropolitan Museum of Art/Art Resource/Scala, Florence

2.18 Photo by LL/Roger Viollet/Getty Images

2.19 Alexandre Prévot via Flickr, used under the Creative Commons licence CC BY-SA

2.20 Gift of the 2014 Collectors Committee, with additional funds provided by Kitzia and Richard Goodman, J. Ben Bourgeois and Andrew Rhoda, Viveca Paulin-Ferrell and Will Ferrell, and Olivier and Zoe de Givenchy (M.2014.90), from www.lacma.org

2.21 The National Trust for Scotland, The Hill House

2.22 Hoffmann, Josef (1870-1956): Tea Service, ca. 1910. Designer: Josef Hoffmann. Manufacturer: Wiener Werkstätte. New York, Metropolitan Museum of Art. Silver, amethyst, carnelian, and ebony. Various dimensions. Cynthia Hazen Polsky and Leon B. Polsky Fund, 2000 (2000.278.1-.9).© 2018. Image copyright The Metropolitan Museum of Art/Art Resource/Scala, Florence

2.23 Minneapolis Institute of Art, The Modernism Collection, gift of Norwest Bank Minnesota 98.276.247a,b
Photo: Minneapolis Institute of Art

Chapter 3

3.1 Published with the permission of The Wolfsonian – Florida International University (Miami, Florida)

3.2 Photo by Stock Montage/Getty Images

3.3 The Metropolitan Museum of Art. Purchase, Edward C. Moore Jr. Gift, 1923

3.4 The Metropolitan Museum of Art. André Mare (French, Argentan 1887–1932 Paris), silk and cotton, Purchase, Edward C. Moore Jr. Gift, 1923

3.5 © FLC/ADAGP, Paris and DACS, London 2018

3.6 © FLC/ADAGP, Paris and DACS, London 2018

3.7 Wedgwood, Josiah (1730-1795): Partial Coffee and Tea Service, 1768. New York, Museum of Modern Art (MoMA). Black basalt with glazed interior. 1 (coffee pot and lid): h. 6 5/8 x w. 7 1/4' (h. 16.8 x w. 18.4 cm), diam. 4 1/4' (10.8 cm).2a (teacup): h. 2 1/4' (5.7 cm), diam. 3 1/4' (8.3 cm). Gift of Josiah Wedgwood & Sons, Inc. of America. Acc.n.: 220.1954.2.© 2018. Digital image, The Museum of Modern Art, New York/Scala, Florence

3.8 Wright, Frank Lloyd (1867-1959): Side Chair, 1904. New York, Museum of Modern Art (MoMA). Oak and leather, 35 5/8 x 15 x 18 5/8" (80.5 x 38.1 x 47.3 cm), seat h. 18" (45.7 cm). Gift of the designer. Acc. no.: 202.1947.2. © 2018. Digital image, The Museum of Modern Art, New York/Scala, Florence © ARS, NY and DACS, London 2018

3.9 The Modernism Collection, gift of Norwest Bank Minnesota. Minneapolis Institute of Art

3.10 The Ethel Morrison Van Derlip Fund, Minneapolis Institute of Art

3.12 Metropolitan Museum of Art - Gift of Cyril Farny, in memory of his wife, Phyllis Holt Farny, 1976 - public domain

3.13 Bauhaus-Archiv Berlin. Photo: Gunter Lepkowski.

3.14 © bpk/Kunstbibliothek, SMB/Dietmar Katz

3.15 © DACS 2018

3.16 Photo by ullstein bild/ullstein bild via Getty Images

3.17 Image courtesy of Fedor Roth

3.18 Klingspor Museum Offenbach, Germany

3.19 Photo by © Historical Picture Archive/CORBIS/Corbis via Getty Images

3.20 Schuette-Lihotzky, Margarete (1897-2000): Frankfurt Kitchen from the Ginnheim-Hoehenblick Housing Estate, Frankfurt am Main, Germany, 1926-27 (Ernst May architect). New York, Museum of Modern Art (MoMA). Various materials, 8'9" x 12'10" x 6'10" (266.7 x 391.2 x 208.3 cm). Gift of Joan R. Brewster in memory of her Husband George W.W. Brewster, by exchange and the Architecture and Design Purchase Fund. Acc. n.: 83.2009. © 2018. Digital image, The Museum of Modern Art, New York/Scala, Florence

3.23 Courtesy of Herman Miller, Inc

3.24 Wagenfeld, Wilhelm (1900-1990): Kubus storage container set. Produced by Vereinigte Lausitzer Glaswerke; Germany, 1938. New York, Cooper-Hewitt - Smithsonian Design Museum. Machine-molded and pressed glass. 21 x 27.5 x 26 cm (8 1/4 x 10 13/16 x 10 1/4 in.). Museum purchase from Sir Arthur Bryan and General Acquisitions Endowment Funds, 1990-1-4-1/18© 2018. Cooper-Hewitt, Smithsonian Design Museum/Art Resource, NY/Scala, Florence

Chapter 4

4.1 Picasso, Pablo (1881-1973): Daniel-Henry Kahnweiler, autumn 1910. Chicago (IL), Art Institute of Chicago. Oil on canvas, 39 9/16 x 28 9/16 in. (100.4 x 72.4 cm). Gift of Mrs. Gilbert W. Chapman in memory of Charles B. Goodspeed, 1948.561.© 2018. The Art Institute of Chicago/Art Resource, NY/Scala, Florence © Succession Picasso/DACS, London 2018

4.2 Petr Bonek/Alamy Stock Photo

4.3 Poster, Variant of the Poster: Soaring to Success: The Early Bird, 1918; Edward McKnight Kauffer (American, active England, 1890–1954); England; offset color lithograph on white wove paper; (shrink-wrapped): 76.5 x 38.8 cm (30 1/8 x 15 1/4 in.); Gift of Mrs. E. McKnight Kauffer; 1963-39-1229. © Simon Rendall

4.4 Gray, Eileen (1879-1976): Screen, 1922. New York, Museum of Modern Art (MoMA). Lacquered wood on metal rods, 74 1/8 x 53 1/2' (188.5 x 136 cm). Guimard Fund. Acc. n.: 476.1978.© 2018. Digital image, The Museum of Modern Art, New York/Scala, Florence

4.5 Delaunay Terk, Sonia (1885-1979): Plate 14 from Sonia Delaunay: ses peintures, ses objets, ses tissus simultanés, ses modes. Published by Librairie des Arts Décoratifs. Paris. [1925]. Pochoir and relief process. Sheet: 14 15/16 x 21 7/8 in. (38 x 55.6 cm). The Elisha Whittlesey Collection, The Elisha Whittlesey Fund, 1968 (68.580.1[14]). New York, Metropolitan Museum of Art. © 2018. Image copyright The Metropolitan Museum of Art/Art Resource/Scala, Florence

4.6 Chronicle/Alamy Stock Photo

4.7 Rodchenko, Alexander (1891-1956): Worker's Club U.S.S.R. in the International Exhibition. Paris, 1925. New York, Museum of Modern Art (MoMA). Alfred H. Barr, Jr. Papers, 13.l.E. The Museum of Modern Art Archives. MA303.© 2018. Digital image, The Museum of Modern Art, New York/Scala, Florence © Rodchenko & Stepanova Archive, DACS, RAO 2018

4.9 92.4.121, Collection of the Corning Museum of Glass, Corning, New York

4.10 Photo by DeAgostini/Getty Images

4.11 Archive PL/Alamy Stock Photo

4.12 Malevic, Kasimir (1878-1935): Painterly Realism. Boy with Knapsack - Color Masses in the Fourth Dimension, 1915. New York, Museum of Modern Art (MoMA). Oil on canvas, 28 x 17 1/2' (71.1 x 44.5 cm). Acquisition confirmed in 1999 by agreement with the Estate of Kazimir Malevich and made possible with funds from the Mrs. John Hay Whitney Bequest (by exchange). 816.1935 © 2018. Digital image, The Museum of Modern Art, New York/Scala, Florence

4.13 Photo by Michael Nicholson/Corbis via Getty Images

4.14 Kazimir Malevich (Russian, 1878-1935), State Porcelain Factory (St. Petersburg, Russia), Suprematist Teapot designed 1923, manuf. circa 1930, Porcelain, 6.25 x 9.25 x 4", Collection of the Kamm Teapot Foundation

4.15 Art Collection 3/Alamy Stock Photo

4.16 Pictorial Press Ltd/Alamy Stock Photo

4.17 Photo by Christophel Fine Art/UIG via Getty Images

4.18 Photo by DEA PICTURE LIBRARY/De Agostini/Getty Images

4.19 Rietveld, Gerrit (1888-1964): Red and Blue Chair, c. 1918. New York, Museum of Modern Art (MoMA). Wood, painted, height, 34 1/8'; width, 26'; depth, 26 1/2' (86.5 x 66 x 83.8 cm); Seat height: 13' (33 cm). Gift of Philip Johnson. Acc. no.: 487.1953.© 2018. Digital image, The Museum of Modern Art, New York/Scala, Florence

Chapter 5

5.1 Gift of Clarence McK. Lewis, 1954, from the Metropolitan Museum of Art collection

5.2 Breuer, Marcel (1902-1981): Armchair, 1922. New York, Museum of Modern Art (MoMA). Oak and hand-woven wool, 37 1/4 x 22 x 22 1/2' (94.6 x 55.9 x 57.2 cm), seat h. 17 1/4' (43.8 cm). Phyllis B. Lambert Fund. Acc.n.: 160.1958© 2018. Digital image, The Museum of Modern Art, New York/Scala, Florence

5.3 © DACS 2018

5.4 Courtesy of Hattula Moholy-Nagy

5.5 Brandt, Marianne (1893-1983): Tea Infuser and Strainer, c. 1924. New York, Metropolitan Museum of Art. Silver and ebony, H. 2-7/8 inches (7.3 cm). Marking: Infuser stamped on base with German assay marks: a crescent moon, a crown with cross, and '900.' Infuser also stamped on base with hallmark: '··ZII' [?]. Lid and strainer each stamped with hallmark: 'UZ··' [?].. The Beatrice G. Warren and Leila W. Redstone Fund, 2000. Acc.n.: 2000.63a-c © 2018. Image copyright The Metropolitan Museum of Art/Art Resource/Scala, Florence © DACS 2018

5.6 Jucker, Karl J. (1902-1997) and Wagenfeld, Wilhelm (1900-1990): Table Lamp, 1923-24. New York, Museum of Modern Art (MoMA). Chromed metal and glass, 18 x 8" (45.7 x 20.3 cm) diam.; 5 1/2" (14 cm) diam. at base. Manufactured by Bauhaus Metal Workshop, Germany. Gift of Philip Johnson. Acc. n.: 490.1953.© 2018. Digital image, The Museum of Modern Art, New York/Scala, Florence

5.7 Thonet GmbH

5.8 © Roberto Conte

5.9 Albers, Anni (1899-1994): Design for Wall Hanging, 1926. New York, Digitale Museum of Modern Art (MoMA). Gouache and pencil on paper, 12 1/2 x 8 1/8' (31.8 x 20.6 cm). Gift of the designer. Acc. n.: 401.1951.© 2018. Digital image, The Museum of Modern Art, New York/Scala, Florence © DACS 2018

5.10 Harvard Art Museums/Busch-Reisinger Museum, Gift of Josef Albers, BR49.286.G © The Josef and Anni Albers Foundation/Artists Rights Society (ARS), New York Photo: Imaging Department © President and Fellows of Harvard College © The Josef and Anni Albers Foundation/DACS 2018

5.11 Photo by Buyenlarge/Getty Images

5.12 Courtesy of the University of Pennsylvania

5.13 Arcaid Images/Alamy Stock Photo

5.14 © David Židlický

5.15 Peter Horree/Alamy Stock Photo

5.17 Arp, Jean (Arp, Hans 1888-1966): Torso, Navel, Mustache-Flower. 1930. New York, Metropolitan Museum of Art. Oil on wood relief, 31 1/2 x 39 3/8 x 1 1/2 in. (80 x 100 x 3.8 cm). The Muriel Kallis Steinberg Newman Collection, Gift of Muriel Kallis Newman, 2006 (2006.32.1).© 2018. Image copyright The Metropolitan Museum of Art/Art Resource/Scala, Florence © DACS 2018

5.18 Photo: Maija Holma, Alvar Aalto Museum

5.19 Aalto, Alvar (1898-1976): Paimio Lounge Chair, 1931-33. New York, Museum of Modern Art (MoMA). Laminated birch, molded plywood, lacquered, height, 26'; width, 23 3/4; depth, 34 7/8' (66 x 60.5 x 88.5 cm); Manufacturer: Huonekalu-ja Rakennustyötehdas Oy, Turku, Finland. Gift of Edgar Kaufmann, Jr. 710.1943.1© 2018. Digital image, The Museum of Modern Art, New York/Scala, Florence

5.20 Aalto, Alvar (1898-1976): '31' Armchair, 1931-32. New York, Metropolitan Museum of Art. Laminated and painted birch plywood and bentwood. H. 25-3/4, W. 23-1/2, D. 30-1/2 in. (65.4 x 59.7 x 77.5 cm.) 16 lb. (7.3 kg). Purchase, Mr. and Mrs. Robert Meltzer Gift, 1984 (1984.223).© 2018. Image copyright The Metropolitan Museum of Art/Art Resource/Scala, Florence

5.21 Mathsson, Bruno (1907-1988): Eva Side Chair T101, 1941. New York, Museum of Modern Art (MoMA). Molded laminated beech wood and hemp webbing, 31 1/2 x 19 1/4 x 28 3/8' (80 x 48.9 x 72.1 cm), seat h. 15 7/8' (40.3 cm). Purchase. Acc.n.: 831.1942© 2018. Digital image, The Museum of Modern Art, New York/Scala, Florence

Chapter 6

6.1 Photo by Bettmann/Getty Images

6.2 Photo by S005/Gamma-Rapho via Getty Images

6.3 Based on Principle of Streamlining, from Norman Bel Geddes, Horizons, 1932

6.4 Photo by Frank Scherschel/The LIFE Premium Collection/Getty Images

6.5 Photo by Swim Ink 2, LLC/CORBIS/Corbis via Getty Images

6.6 Photo by Indianapolis Museum of Art/Getty Images

6.7 INTERFOTO/Alamy Stock Photo

6.9 ********: Installation view of the exhibition 'Machine Art' (MoMA 1934). New York, Museum of Modern Art (MoMA). Photo by Wurts Brothers; IN34.2© 2018. Digital image, The Museum of Modern Art, New York/Scala, Florence

6.10 ********: The Metropolitan Museum of Art, Special Exhibition: Thirteenth Annual Exhibition of Contemporary American Industrial Art, November 6, 1934 - January 6, 1935. View: Industrial Designer's Office, designers: Raymond Loewy and Lee Simonson. New York, Metropolitan Museum of Art. Black and white photograph.© 2018. Image copyright The Metropolitan Museum of Art/Art Resource/Scala, Florence

6.11 Teague, Walter Dorwin, Jr. (1910-2004): Baby Brownie Camera and Packaging, ca. 1934. Designed by Walter Dorwin Teague (American, 1883-1960). Manufactured by Eastman Kodak Company (Rochester, New York). New York, Cooper-Hewitt - Smithsonian Design Museum. Molded Bakelite, metal, glass, H x W x D: 8 x 8.5 x 7.3 cm (3 1/8 x 3 3/8 x 2 7/8 in.). Gift of George R. Kravis II. 2014-25-4-a,b. Photo: Matt Flynn © Smithsonian Institution.© 2018. Cooper-Hewitt, Smithsonian Design Museum/Art Resource, NY/Scala, Florence

6.12 Published with the permission of The Wolfsonian – Florida International University (Miami, Florida). Television, RCA Victor TRK 12, 1939 The Wolfsonian–Florida International University, Miami Beach, Florida Purchase, Visionaries Acquisition Fund 2012.6.1 Photo: Lynton Gardiner

6.13 Wright, Russel (1904-1976): American Modern Dinnerware, 1937. Manufacturer: Produttore:

Steubenville Pottery (East Liverpool, Ohio). New York, Metropolitan Museum of Art. John C. Waddell Collection, Gift of John C. Waddell, 2002 © 2018. Image copyright The Metropolitan Museum of Art/Art Resource/Scala, Florence

6.14 Photo by Carol M. Highsmith/Buyenlarge/Getty Images

6.15 Photo by Marka/UIG via Getty Images

6.16 Photo by Science & Society Picture Library/SSPL/Getty Images

6.17 © TfL from the London Transport Museum collection http://www.ltmuseum.co.uk/

6.18 Matter, Herbert (1907-1984): Fur shone Autofahrten die Schweiz, 1935. New York, Museum of Modern Art (MoMA). Gravure 39 3/4 x 25 1/8' Gift of Bernard Davis 170.1950© 2018. Digital image, The Museum of Modern Art, New York/Scala, Florence

6.19 Photo by Universal History Archive/UIG via Getty Images

6.20 Photo by Library of Congress/Corbis/VCG via Getty Images

6.21 Photo by Library of Congress/Corbis/VCG via Getty Images

Chapter 7

7.1 Photo by Fotosearch/Getty Images

7.2 © Victoria and Albert Museum, London

7.3 Photo by Keystone-France/Gamma-Keystone via Getty Image

7.4 Courtesy of the University of Pennsylvania

7.5 Courtesy of Herman Miller, Inc

7.6 Photo by David Cooper/Toronto Star via Getty Images

7.7 Tupper, Earl S. (1907-1983): Covered Canisters, 1945. New York, Museum of Modern Art (MoMA). .1 (overall): h. 5 1/8' (13cm), diam. 7 3/8' (18.7 cm).1a (container): h. 4 7/8' (12.4 cm), diam. 6 7/8' (17.5 cm).1b (lid): h. 1/4' (0.6 cm), diam. 7 3/8' (18.7 cm).2 (overall): h. 4 3/4' (12.1 cm), diam. 6 3/8' (16.2 cm). Acc.n.: 172.1948.1-2 © 2018. Digital image, The Museum of Modern Art, New York/Scala, Florence

7.8 Schlumbohm, Peter (1896-1962): Chemex Coffee Maker, 1941. New York, Museum of Modern Art (MoMA). Pyrex glass, wood, and leather. 9 1/2 X 6 1/8 (24.2 X 15.5 cm). Gift of Lewis and Conger, Inc. Acc. num. 51.1943. © 2018. Digital image, The Museum of Modern Art, New York/Scala, Florence

7.11 Courtesy of the University of Pennsylvania

7.12 Courtesy of Herman Miller, Inc

7.13 Photographs in the Carol M. Highsmith Archive, Library of Congress, Prints and Photographs Division

7.14 Image courtesy of Knoll, Inc.

7.15 Noyes, Eliot (1910-1977): Selectric I Typewriter, 1961. Manufactured by International Business Machines Corp. (IBM), Armonk, New York, USA. New York, Cooper-Hewitt – Smithsonian Design Museum. Aluminum, steel, molded plastic. Gift of George R. Kravis II, 2014-25-1. Photo: Matt Flynn © Smithsonian Institution.© 2018. Cooper-Hewitt, Smithsonian Design Museum/Art Resource, NY/Scala, Florence

7.16 Photograph © Brent C. Brolin

7.17 ********: Studebaker Starliner Coupe, from the curatorial files, 'Eight Automobiles' exhibition, MoMA, NY, August 28, 1951 through November 11, 1951. New York, Museum of Modern Art (MoMA). Curatorial Exhibition Files, #488. The Museum of Modern Art Archives, New York. Acc. n.: MA749.© 2018. Digital image, The Museum of Modern Art, New York/Scala, Florence

7.18 Neil Baylis/Alamy Stock Photo

7.20 INTERFOTO/Alamy Stock Photo

7.21 INTERFOTO/Alamy Stock Photo

7.22 Geffrye Museum/Alamy Stock Photo

7.23 Science Museum, London. Gift of Dr. Helen Dick Megaw and used under the Creative Commons Zero licence, courtesy of Bettina Kirkham

7.24 Plate courtesy of Martin Barden

7.25 Le Corbusier (Jeanneret, Charles-Edouard 1887-1965), Perriand, Charlotte (1903-1999) and ATBAT: Kitchen from the Unité d'Habitation, Marseille, France, c. 1952. New York, Museum of Modern Art (MoMA). Various materials, 88 x 105 1/2 x 72" (223.5 x 268 x 182.9 cm). Fabricator: Charles Barberis Menuiseries modernes, Corsica. Gift of Andrea Woodner. Acc. n.: 1112.2011.© 2018. Digital image, The Museum of Modern Art, New York/Scala, Florence

7.26 Ponti, Gio (1891-1979): Design, Italy twentieth century. Superleggera chair, 1957. Production Cassina Spa. © 2018. DeAgostini Picture Library/Scala, Florence

7.27 Photo by SSPL/Getty Images

7.28 Wegner, Hans (1914-2007): Armchair, 1949. New York, Museum of Modern Art (MoMA). Oak and cane 30 x 24 5/8 x 21 1/4' (76.2 x 62.5 x 54 cm), seat h. 17' (43.2 cm). Gift of Georg Jensen, Inc. Acc.n.: 486.1953© 2018. Digital image, The Museum of Modern Art, New York/Scala, Florence

7.29 © Victoria and Albert Museum, London

7.30 Mueller-Brockmann, Josef (b. 1914): Musica Viva, 1957. New York, Museum of Modern Art (MoMA). Photolithograph 35 1/2 x 50 1/4' (90.1 x 127.6 cm). Gift of the artist. Acc.n.: 58.1960© 2018. Digital image, The Museum of Modern Art, New York/Scala, Florence © DACS 2018

7.31 INTERFOTO/Alamy Stock Photo

7.32 Photo by Indianapolis Museum of Art/Getty Images

Chapter 8

8.1 Aarnio, Eero (b. 1932): Pastilli Rocking Chair, 1968. Designed by Eero Aarnio (Finnish, b. 1932). Manufactured by Asko Oy (Lahti, Finland). New York, Cooper-Hewitt - Smithsonian Design Museum. Molded fiberglass-reinforced polyester. H x diam.: 52 x 92 cm (20 1/2 x 36 1/4 in.). Gift of The Lake St. Louis Historical Society; 2001-31-2. Photo © Smithsonian Institution.© 2018. Cooper-Hewitt, Smithsonian Design Museum/Art Resource, NY/Scala, Florence

8.2 V&A Images/Alamy Stock Photo

8.3 © Vitra

8.5 Pesce, Gaetano (b. 1939): Up 5 Lounge Chair with Up 6 Ottoman, 1969. New York, Museum of Modern Art (MoMA). Polyurethane foam covered in stretch fabric, .a (chair): 40 x 43 1/2 x 45" (101.6 x 110.5 x 114.3 cm) .b (ottoman): diam. 22 1/2" (57.2 cm). Gift of the manufacturer. Acc. no.: 124.1992.a-b.© 2018. Digital image, The Museum of Modern Art, New York/Scala, Florence

8.6 "Bulb" (Ingo Maurer 1966), photo: Tom Vack. © Ingo Maurer GmbH, Munich

8.7 Casati, Cesare (b. 1936): 'Pillola' Lamps, 1968. New York, Museum of Modern Art (MoMA). ABS polymer and acrylic, each 21 3/4 high x 5 1/8' diameter (55.2 x 13 cm). Celeste Bartos Purchase Fund. 1422.2000.1-5 © 2018. Digital image, The Museum of Modern Art, New York/Scala, Florence

8.8 Ronnie McMillan/Alamy Stock Photo

8.9 Zanuso, Marco (1916-2001); Sapper, Richard (b. 1932): Grillo Folding Telephone, 1965. New York, Museum of Modern Art (MoMA). ABS plastic, 2 3/4 x 6 1/2 x 3 1/4" (7 x 16.5 x 8.3 cm). Manufactured by Società Italiana Telecomunicazioni Siemens, Milan, Italy. Gift of the manufacturer. Acc. n.: 1238.1968.1-5.© 2018. Digital image, The Museum of Modern Art, New York/Scala, Florence

8.10 Colombo, Cesare Joe (1930-1971). A Tube Chair. Designed by Joe Cesare Colombo (1930-1971), 1969, for Flexiform Prima. Polyurethane, vinyl, chromed metal. 61cm wide. Christie's Images Limited. polyurethane, vinyl, chromed metal 61cm wide© 2018. Christie's Images, London/Scala, Florence

8.11 Courtesy of Zanotta SpA

8.12 Moscoso, Victor (b. 1936): Young Bloods, 1967. New York, Museum of Modern Art (MoMA). Offset lithograph 20 1/4 x 14' (51.5 x 35.5 cm). Peter Stone Poster Fund. Acc. no.: 490.1987.© 2018. Digital image, The Museum of Modern Art, New York/Scala, Florence

8.13 Photo by Eric Préau/Sygma via Getty Images

8.14 Castiglioni, Achille (1918-2002): 'Toio' Floor Lamps, 1962 (Flos S.p.A., Brescia, Italy). New York, Museum of Modern Art (MoMA). Steel and nickel-plated brass. 7'1 X 7 3/4 X 8 1/4 (215.9 X 19.7 X 21cm). Gift of the manufacturer. Acc. num. 459.1970© 2018. Digital image, The Museum of Modern Art, New York/Scala, Florence

8.15 Sapper, Richard (b. 1932): 'Tizio' Table Lamp, 1972 (manufactured by Artemide). New York, Museum of Modern Art (MoMA). Black metal, 44' (111.8 cm) maximum height, 4 1/2' (11.4 cm) diameter. Gift of the manufacturer. Acc. n.: 198.1973.© 2018. Digital image, The Museum of Modern Art, New York/Scala, Florence

8.16 © Ignazia Favata/Studio Joe Colombo

8.17 ********: 'Superstudio, A Journey from A to B, 1969, pencil on photomontage'. Illustration from 'The New Domestic Landscape' catalogue of MoMA exhibition, 1972 (photographer: Aldo Ballo). New York, Museum of Modern Art (MoMA). The Museum of Modern Art Library, ref. no.: 300062429_0251.© 2018. Digital image, The Museum of Modern Art, New York/Scala, Florence

8.18 © Alessandro Mendini

8.19 © Stephen Shore. Courtesy 303 Gallery, New York

8.20 Eclectic House Series, 1977. Design sketches by Robert Venturi based on the decorated shed

8.21 The Architectural Archives, University of Pennsylvania by the gift of Robert Venturi and Denise Scott Brown

8.22 The Architectural Archives, University of Pennsylvania by the gift of Robert Venturi and Denise Scott Brown

8.23 The Architectural Archives, University of Pennsylvania by the gift of Robert Venturi and Denise Scott Brown

8.24 dpa picture alliance archive/Alamy Stock Photo

8.25 Alessi, S.p.A., Crusinallo, Italy

8.26 © Alessandro Mendini

8.27 Courtesy of A. Mendini

8.28 Photograph by Giorgio Molnari © Michele De Lucchi Archive

8.29 Photograph by Giorgio Molnari © Michele De Lucchi Archive

8.30 Photo by SSPL/Getty Images

8.32 © ADAGP, Paris and DACS, London 2018/© Victoria and Albert Museum, London

8.33 © Michele De Lucchi archive

Chapter 9

9.1 Alessi, S.p.A., Crusinallo, Italy

9.2 Photo courtesy Michael Graves Architecture & Design

9.3 Alessi, S.p.A., Crusinallo, Italy

9.4 Photo by Hiroko Masuike/Getty Images

9.5 Philippe Starck

Acknowledgments

Support for my work has come from various quarters. My mentor and former colleague at the Philadelphia Museum of Art, Kathryn B. Hiesinger, Curator of European Decorative Arts after 1700, first encouraged me to write about design and to collaborate with her on several books, including *Landmarks of Twentieth-Century Design* (1993). Many of the ideas about modern design presented here were developed at the University of Pennsylvania, where two decades ago I was invited to join the adjunct faculty in the department of the history of art. Others have generously shared their insights about architecture and design over the years, especially William Whitaker, curator and collections manager of the architectural archives at Penn.

My debt to Louise Baird-Smith, senior commissioning editor – design and photography, at Bloomsbury, is measureless, as she followed my writing closely and worked assiduously to bring an abundance of distinctive imagery to this book.

Index